True Crime Library
A Forum Press Book
by the Paperback Division of
Forum Design,
PO Box 158, London SE20 7QA

An Imprint of True Crime Library
© 2001 John Sanders
All rights reserved

Printed and bound in Great Britain by
Cox & Wyman, Reading, Berkshire

ISBN 1 874358 37 0

AUTHOR'S NOTE

I was introduced to George Hoyles, Rotor Chairman of Spalding, Lincolnshire Magistrates' Court, and Chairman of a Board of Prison Visitors, and his wife Tina, in Southern France. Over an excellent lunch during which we discussed the Tony Martin case at great length, they invited my wife and I to stay at their Lincolnshire farm, on the border with Norfolk, while I researched this book. I owe a debt of gratitude to them for that delightfully spontaneous invitation, their generous hospitality, and the diligence with which they pointed me in all the right directions.

I would also like to thank Tony Martin's friend Malcolm Starr, the businessman who launched the Support Martin Campaign. He gave me much helpful advice on this case, throughout which, incidentally, he has shown on behalf of his beleaguered friend a sense of loyalty and devotion I have seldom seen equalled.

CONTENTS

PREFACE

If you have forgotten all the facts you will probably quickly remember the case in outline. Tony Martin, a Norfolk farmer, living alone, had been burgled or was the victim of theft on ten different occasions. In the face of what he considered was total police inaction, he decided to arm himself and protect his property against further attacks. Even so, two burglars each with long criminal records broke into his home yet again and woke him up. As they plundered his ground floor, he came down the stairs in a state of terror and fired his shotgun into the darkness, wounding one and killing the other, a 16-year-old habitual criminal. Martin was subsequently charged with murder and sentenced to life imprisonment.

The verdict and the sentence created uproar among homeowners, especially among the vulnerable living alone in rural Britain. It created too a pathetic defence of the law by police, lawyers and politicians. The principal focus of concern in Middle England was of course the idea in people's minds that they might so easily have been in Martin's position, and that Martin had taken some positive action to deal with something they all instinctively dreaded and which the police and other law-enforcement agencies do little or nothing about – burglary.

Like millions of others, I followed the case avidly. Like millions of others, I did not believe that Tony Martin would be charged with murder; like millions of others I did not believe that a British jury would find him guilty of that extreme charge; like millions of others I could not believe he would be sent to prison for life. Yet all these things happened.

Let me say from the outset that this account of the Tony Martin case will be a partisan one. Like Tony Martin I live in rural England and at the present time I have been burgled three times, which I am told is about average for a home in Britain today. In all three cases the police did not catch the burglars, nor did they show much interest in so doing. In all three cases not one single item of the stolen property – most of it dearly collected personal treasures – was recovered and, I was reliably, almost cheerfully, advised by all the police officers investigating all the cases, probably none of it ever would be. Their chief interest in fact was to make sure that for insurance purposes I listed everything that was euphemistically described as "missing."

In all three cases, pent-up with that impotent fury that only the victim of burglary knows, I said with icy calm to the bored detectives who turned up many hours after the crimes to ask routine questions, "Next time I'll blow their heads off."

Just like Tony Martin said.

There is nothing unusual in my experience – the same story could be told over and over again by hundreds of thousands of people across the length and breadth of Britain. Burglary, a crime that inspires fear and fury in the hearts of homeowners, is simply not rated highly in law-enforcement circles, unless, that is, it turns into something else, like rape or wounding or murder.

In that case, of course, the police will act like a police force should. The problem for the homeowner confronting burglars is, can he or she wait to see if they are going to be raped or wounded or murdered before something is done?

The argument used by the Home Office, which rates racism as a much more important "crime" than burglary, is that as so few burglars resort to violence during the commission of their crimes, burglary is overwhelmingly a crime against property rather than people, and is in consequence suitably "downgraded."

This is a defence that satisfies no one alone in their home

at night. The argument that it is only the homeowner's perception that he or she is in danger, has no credibility when you are suddenly woken at night, you hear a noise downstairs, and you are aware that someone has broken into your home. You are terrified about what will happen next, and there is little point then in someone telling you that statistically what is most likely to happen is that you are only going to get robbed.

Hundreds of thousands of Britons will tell personal stories like mine. In my first experience of burglary I arrived home 24 hours after the crime to survey the debris of 24 valuable Victorian oil paintings ripped from their frames in the night and a house which had been trashed.

"You won't get your paintings back, sir," the investigating officer told me with assured confidence. "They're almost certainly on the Continent by now. I'll give you the crime number for insurance company purposes."

A different view of it was expressed to me next day by another officer at the local police station. He advised me to look at a certain shop in a certain village 30 miles away, and if the paintings weren't there, to look around the antique shops in the same village.

That afternoon I drove to the village, wondering why on earth I was being sent to a place where the police thought my stolen property might be, and why the police were not doing that bit of research themselves. When I got to the village the "certain shop" turned out to be a junk shop, a downmarket version of a dime and nickel store. The owner clearly would have passed out with fright at the sight of a stolen Victorian oil painting. There were no antique shops in the village. I drove back the 30 miles to my home fuming at the police, for their indifference, their inactivity, and for passing misleading information.

My second burglary occurred when I lived in a London suburb. Coming home from an evening at the theatre I found the house had been turned into a tip. Selected items of Victorian furniture and a few paintings had been stolen. Two detectives arrived next day. One of them walked up the garden and returned with a coat button. Holding it up to the light he said, "One of the villains lost this when he escaped out the back. It will be useful evidence."

"That button is mine," I told him.

The burglar was never caught and the stolen property was never recovered.

Twice in the same London suburb I had reason to call the police over other incidents. The first was when I saw two youths attacking cars in the apartment block's open-air car park. I was able to tell the police phone centre the direction the youths were heading and give the numbers of the cars that were being robbed. The police did not attend, nor did they follow the youths. They told me this next day when I rang to find out what happened, and apologised for their inactivity, saying that it took one hour for the phone centre to pass on the message, because the telephonists were so busy.

The second occasion happened when a thief entered my new second-floor flat in broad daylight while my wife went out shopping for ten minutes, and stole all her jewellery. This is not burglary, which happens only during the hour of darkness – it is called housebreaking and is viewed as a lesser crime. The thief in this case must have had keys to the apartment building front door as well as to my flat. Since the apartment building was finished only a month previously, that would suggest that someone who was involved in its building was responsible. A policewoman turned up next day, had a chat, gave me the customary form, and no further investigations were made.

My third burglary happened again while I was away. I was summoned back after a postman had told a neighbour that there was a smashed window at the front of the house, and the key-holders had gone in to investigate.

Again the house had been turned into a tip in a panicky search for money and jewellery. Curiously, there were three points of entry into three different rooms via three different windows – an obvious indication that the burglars knew that the alarm system was based on opening doors, and that there were no infra-red beams. Further, the furniture had been moved in such a way as to indicate that the burglars also knew there were no electronic mats positioned in strategic places, as used to be customary with door operated systems. Significantly, we had had the mats removed by the burglar alarm company only a week previously.

This might have indicated to anyone with a head on their shoulders that a person within the burglar alarm company we were using at that time could possibly have tipped-off the burglars, because our alarm system was an unusual one and because no doors had been opened inside the house.

Before we could report all these clues to the police we had first to persuade them to come to the house. Two days after I phoned to ask if the incident officer could come and see me and tell me what he thought had happened, since I was now back in the country, I received a call from another police department. This was from a lady who asked me if I would like to be counselled.

"Counselled for what?"

"For trauma following your break-in."

"For God's sake, I don't want counselling, I want someone here to investigate the crime. Can't you get things in some sort of logical order?"

In fact, a whole week passed before a detective finally turned up, and only after threats to contact the Chief Constable. The detective pointed out that my house was on the edge of two police districts – exactly nine miles from each of the two nearest police headquarters, which meant they had to come a long way. He said nothing while I explained the possible connection with the burglar alarm company – no doubt he had seen it all before and knew that burglar alarm companies could no more be trusted than burglars. He made a list of the stolen property. Later, when I phoned the police about it, another detective said, "I should think that the kind of property you have had stolen will be at Bermondsey market very early on Friday morning. It might be worth you making a trip there."

"Oh, really?" I said. "As a mater of fact I was given that kind of information once before when I was burgled. If you feel so confident about the missing property whereabouts, why don't you call Bermondsey police and ask them to go and look for it?"

There was no reply.

That night a neighbour phoned. He told me that he had been so suspicious about a car that was parked near our house in our lonely road on the night of the burglary, that he had taken its description and registration number. Again triumphantly, I passed this on to the police.

They never contacted the burglar alarm company and if they checked out the suspicious car number I was told nothing about it. We never heard from them again.

The police will often tell victims of burglary, and victims of other crimes too, that they do not have the resources to police as they would like to. This was one of the excuses given by the Chief Constable of Norfolk, Ken Williams, for his men's inattention to the horrific crime problems being confronted by Tony Martin and all the other folk in rural Norfolk. How the police deploy their existing resources is something that is rarely investigated but I would suggest they could be more skilfully deployed in my county for the following reason.

A week after my third burglary a neighbour, an old age pensioner, who had just returned from abroad after a long absence, was driving into the next village. The speed limitation signs were completely obliterated by foliage. Rounding a bend he was stopped by three policemen, two of whom emerged from concealed cover. Surprised, he asked them what was wrong. "You were driving at 41 m.p.h. in a thirty-mile limit," he was told. When, subsequently in court, he pointed out that the signs were unreadable, the police prosecutor hurriedly looked up the Road Traffic Act and produced the clause which says that in such cases if there are street lamps two hundred yards apart the area must be deemed by motorists to be in the thirty-mile limit. My friend, who had been driving for 45 years with a clean licence, was fined seventy pounds.

Three policemen, two in hiding, springing out on a pensioner, invoking legal semantics to ensure a conviction ... Was it any wonder that there were no resources to catch my burglars?

The truth is probably that even without policemen hiding behind hedges to catch speeding pensioners, there are no adequate resources to protect householders from burglars, and there will not be any in the long foreseeable future. Politicians do not care to give much thought to this kind of insidious crime, the police will always be stretched, and the courts appear to sentence burglars as if they are the unfortunate victims of social deprivation rather than dangerous criminals. Studying the Tony Martin case I came to the conclusion that there can be only one solution to this problem – the law must back homeowners in the use of very considerable force to deter these evil men. And if, as is most likely, they then give up this kind of crime as a bad job, millions of people in Britain will be able to sleep without fear for the first time in their lives.

Such a view may upset the liberal intelligence, those who have never been burgled, who do not live in isolated places, and who do not have anything worth stealing. But millions of homeowners will confirm that it is a price worth paying.

One more break-in was noteworthy in the area where I live. It happened at a neighbour's house, a hundred yards from mine, at 11 a.m. on a summer's day several years ago. When the victim's burglar alarm system sounded off, I called the police. Nothing happened. I called them again. Again nothing happened. When almost an hour had gone by I called them a third time. Well, something did sort of happen then.

It was a police car, and it was first seen by my wife, returning from shopping. She followed it down the road. It whizzed past the burglarised house and its clanging alarm bell, and the knot of helpless neighbours standing in the road. One of the car's two uniformed occupants was studying a map, and both were clearly seen to be laughing. They returned about fifteen minutes later, and were somewhat sheepish when one or two people began to remonstrate with them about missing the vandalised house.

"We didn't know where we were," the one with the map said helplessly. "We were lost."

Over an hour had passed since my first call to the police. Rare porcelain worth £5,000 had been stolen from the house. The property was never recovered and the thieves were never caught.

In May the following year, 1997, Tony Blair's New Labour Party swept to an overwhelming General Election victory. A vital part of its campaign was based on a promise to be, "Tough on crime, tough on the causes of crime." There seemed to be a sudden awareness that government exists above all – as political theorists going back to Plato know – to make sure that citizens are safe in the streets and in their homes.

The Tony Martin case is part of what happened next.

1

DEATH AT BLEAK HOUSE

It had been an ordinary sort of Friday for farmer Tony Martin. He had eaten a light lunch with a friend, worked in his apple orchards, and dined early with his mother at her home in Elm, a few miles from his farmhouse. During the family dinner his mother was to say later that he was "happy and joking," until the conversation came round again to his fear of burglars.

Martin's farmhouse had been attacked ten times in as many years – the last occasion only three months previously, when he lost valuable furniture and a bureau filled with family mementoes. As the intruders left, in their insouciance they scattered family photographs along the drive. Martin had told the police then that he was certain that the burglars would come back, but they took no notice.

"My life has become one long worry," he told his mother.

Hilary Martin nodded sympathetically. She was aware that his fears were shared by most of his neighbours scattered across rural Norfolk, for almost everyone the Martins knew had been victims of burglary. They were people living under siege. They felt vulnerable, and they had all lost faith in the police to protect them.

Martin pushed back his chair and rose from the table. "I'd better go now," he said. "You never know what's going on back at home." He always liked to be home before dark.

He had been burgled more times than he could remember while he was away from his home.

It was 9 p.m. when he kissed his mother goodbye, got into his Nissan Bluebird car and drove the few miles back to his farmhouse in Emneth Hungate. He went upstairs to his bedroom and without bothering to undress or even to take off his boots, lay down on the bed. Within a few minutes he was asleep – within a few more minutes he was awake again.

He woke drowsily in the darkness. Somewhere out there on the road beyond the foliage and the track that crossed his fields a car engine was turning over softly. He turned his head to listen. Cars were rare enough on the road at night. This one had stopped, and that was rarer still.

It was a quarter to ten.

Martin, a bachelor, lived alone in his isolated, verdure-covered farmhouse, appropriately named Bleak House. It is half a mile from the nearest neighbour and buried inside one of the thick coppices that punctuate the flat landscape – a coppice that is halfway between a sliver of a forest and a mass of undergrowth. Two of his three rottweilers were locked in the shed down beyond the front of the house. The third, Bruno, was roaming the grounds.

He listened intently. The noise of the car engine had disappeared. Nothing now penetrated the soundless night. He turned his head on the pillow, reassured. Then came a sharp noise, curious, indecipherable in the darkness, but clearly audible through the open bedroom door.

He thought, it's Bruno. Somehow he must have got into the house.

He raised his head from the pillow. Another sound, this time the distinct rattle of breaking glass, not once but twice, followed by a soft, continuous scraping noise from somewhere downstairs. He felt his blood begin to pound in his head as realisation flooded into his sleep-filled mind. This wasn't Bruno. It was burglars. They had come back again.

He could hear them distinctly now, prising a window –

the only downstairs window he had not protected with iron bars. There was more than one – he could hear them whispering to each other.

Martin, 54 years old and in poor health, sat up in bed in the darkness, stiff and shaking. "I was petrified," he was to say later. "The whole thing was like a horror movie."

He did not have to dress, for such was his fear of burglars now and his determination not to be overpowered that he always slept in his working clothes. But he was frightened. His mind raced over previous break-ins, recalling the farmer who was killed by burglars at a neighbouring farm, the contempt these violent, dangerous men had for homeowners. Perhaps they intended to kill him, too. It crossed his mind that within the next few minutes he might have to fight for his life...

The idea of moving from the bedroom terrified him, for he was experiencing what it was like to be rooted to the spot by fear. Shaking uncontrollably, he swung his booted feet on to the floor. He could hear the burglars moving around downstairs now, whispering quietly, methodically picking up and setting down objects, the occasional chink as one of his antiques was dropped into a bag. He went to the open bedroom door and crept through the adjacent bathroom, listening anxiously, unable to see but only to hear in the darkness.

From the top of the staircase he was aware of the burglars' shadows, revealed in their own torch beams. He stood there, quaking, agonising, wondering what to do next. Almost certainly they would come up the stairs and find him there. Bewildered, terrified, he went back through the bathroom to the bedroom and took his gun from under the bed. He walked quietly to a dresser, where he kept the cartridges in a bag. Fumbling in the dark, his hands trembling, he loaded the shotgun, unable in his fright and confusion to count the number of cartridges.

Even from his bedroom he could now distinctly hear the burglars in the hall downstairs, their arrogant, unhurried movements. Ten minutes had passed since they prised open the window and climbed into Bleak House – that estimate was later to be made by one of the burglars himself.

Martin moved towards the bedroom door again, slowly crossed the bathroom to the stairs and began to descend. His hand on the gun was shaking violently, he was in a state of absolute terror. He could hear them quite clearly now. They were frighteningly close. He could see pinpoints of light from their torches sweeping up and down his furniture.

He moved down another stair – it creaked, and he sensed at once that they had heard him. There was a startled oath in the darkness as one of their torch beams swung round into his face, blinding him. In a state of stark fear Martin fired from the hip, instinctively, below the beam of light.

In his panic he advanced down the stairs, firing again and again, squeezing the trigger. In a frenzy to escape, one of the burglars ripped out the entire frame of a window – Martin heard the wood splintering as they hurled themselves through the gap it left. For what seemed like an eternity the terrible sound of the exploding cartridges echoed in the darkness around Bleak House like rolling thunder.

It was an echo that was to sweep across Britain, across the world, lighting the blue touch paper of helpless fury and despair that fills the minds of homeowners everywhere at the sight or sound, or mention even, of burglars.

For outside, one of the intruders lay dying in the undergrowth. Tony Martin, who had defended his home, his property, and perhaps his life, was now branded a murderer.

★   ★   ★

Martin's strangely dilapidated farmhouse is in the Norfolk Fens, an area of East Anglia which has no parallel anywhere in England.

Ordinarily two aspects of the English landscape are best known to residents and visitors – soft, undulating pastoral and smoky grey towns bustling with industry and commerce. The Fens are neither of these. They are a long stretch of England which are described by Graham Swift in his award-winning novel *Waterland*, as "a landscape which of all landscapes most approximates to Nothing."

The Fens, traversing the three counties of Norfolk, Cambridgeshire and Lincolnshire, are flat, wet and windy. Features of the English landscape which we take for granted, like railway lines and rural buses, hardly exist in Fenland. Lincolnshire, for example, has no motorways and fewer dual carriageways than any county in England. Cars with old number plates trundle along on single track roads through strangely named hamlets, like Tydd Four Gotes, which means that this is the place where four drains (go-outs) meet up to flow into the tide at the mouth of The Wash.

The Fens, despite approximating to Nothing, have produced at least two celebrated Englishmen. Hereward the Wake fought his desperate campaign of resistance against the Norman invaders from his marshy Fenland base at Ely, and Oliver Cromwell, our Chief of Men, was born in Huntingdon. In more recent years Fenland became a lodestone and a settling place for groups of people whose traditions were once nomadic, travelling like 19th century journeymen to wherever there was seasonal work, and then moving on. In some reports of the Tony Martin case these people were wrongly said to be Gypsies. The three burglars in the Bleak House break-in on the night of August 20, 1999, were descended – at least in part – from people of Romany origin, but they came from a community which includes a wide variety of people, and is so ill-defined that we must first make an attempt at deciding who they really were.

Genuine Romany Gypsies, always spelt in the case of Romanies with a capital G, are highly moral, highly principled people who as a race – they are established in law as an ethnic minority – would look with disapproval on participation in the events that happened at Bleak House on that August night. Romany Gypsies began a journey from India to Britain and other Western European countries in the fifteenth century. Their language, Romany, is derived from ancient Sanskrit – many Romany words are similar to Punjabi ones from North East India. Until early in the twentieth century most Romany Gypsies lived separately from the rest of society. Intermarriage with the rest of the population, however, meant that although some of the traditional Romany communities still survive, other communties including many people of mixed race exist within them.

These "travelling" people with Romany origins but mixed blood are generally referred to either as gypsies, with a small g, or travellers. Some are also sometimes called didicois, alternatively spelt diddicoys or even didakais, but travellers regard this slang word and its slang abbreviation, "diddies," as derogatory terms. Didicoi literally means "half-breed" in the Romany language.

The activities of gypsies, like the activities of anyone else wanting to live a nomadic life in Britain, were severely curtailed by legislation in the second half of the twentieth century – even under the new Human Rights Act it is legal to travel but not necessarily to stop anywhere unless the site is legal or the landowner has given consent. As a result, most Romany Gypsies have settled in houses or on private sites. Among those who have intermarried there is no neat divide; there is, rather, a sort of Indian-style caste system within gipsy circles, for defining the various types of gypsies is now as difficult as defining how Anglo-Saxon an Englishman might be.

Through intermarriage some travellers have learned some of the Romany language, which many use among themselves to a greater or lesser extent. While it will be no part of the purpose of this book to defend the activities of thieves and burglars, it is an interesting marginal note that the Romany language contains a word *chore*, which means identically to steal, to take, or to obtain – in other words, it puts no value judgement on that word, as we do on its three separate meanings in English. *Chore* has been adopted by some travellers as part of their lexicon of morality. Taken together with the fact known to criminologists that many burglars have very little idea of the distress and fear they cause their victims, it may give some people food for thought.

Over the years travellers were identified as much as anything by their lifestyle – they travelled from job to job season by season, although today they are mostly settled. At Newark, in Notts, where the three burglars in the Tony Martin case lived, there are also Irish travellers. The travellers living at Wisbech, in Cambridgeshire, the nearest large town to Tony Martin's village of Emneth Hungate, generally have more Romany blood than those at Newark, but paradoxically Fred Barras, the burglar who died in the Bleak House shooting, was part of the Romany Gypsy community of Newark.

Thirty to forty years ago travellers (including many Romany Gypsies) used to descend in thousands on The Fens to pick up seasonal jobs on the farms, like vegetable digging and fruit picking. A number of them still do, and work well and happily for fruit-growers they may have known all their lives. They were enthusiastically welcomed by the farmers, since they provided the only seasonal labour force and without them the fruit would rot on the ground. An especially favoured destination was Wisbech, a town of 19,000 people, which describes itself as the capital of The Fens. Wisbech was once prized for its strawberries and soft fruit – a jam factory processed the harvest and its jam made from Wisbech soft fruit graced most of the tea-tables in England. The travellers were paid in tokens, receiving a token for each punnett of picked fruit they took to the farm manager and exchanging the accumulated tokens at the end of the day for their value in cash.

Then times became hard. The fruit farmers could no longer make a profit against competition from foreign imports and many of them sold up. So instead of making money, some of the travellers, who either stayed in the area or returned to it, jobless and hungry, began to make trouble. Local residents became anxious at the onset of the wave of petty crime that followed and the local council decided in its wisdom to house the travellers on its council estates. Much the same thing happened in other parts of rural Britain where the mobile work force settled. The travellers were now no longer travelling and the estates where they were housed were becoming the headquarters of petty crime. Thirty years ago the people of Wisbech loved them, today many people there live in fear and detestation of them.

It was at March, a few miles south of Wisbech, and just a few miles down the road from Emneth Hungate, that Tony Martin was born in 1944. His father Walter was a wealthy fruit farmer who married Hilary Mitcham, one of five sisters, also from a farming family. Tony and his elder brother Robin were privately educated, but Tony turned out not to be academically inclined. He attended a prep school, Glebe House, Hunstanton, where he won a prize for sports. At that time Glebe, a Victorian building, had 90 boys. Today it accepts both boys and girls, and has a section for young children below prep school age. George Hoyles, Rotor Chairman of the Spalding, Lincs, Bench, who was at Glebe House at the same time, remembers Martin only as a "self-effacing" boy. From there Martin went to a private school, Copethorpe Park in Oxfordshire, where he played rugby with former Manchester United chairman Martin Edwards, and where he was the school's most distinguished sportsman of his year.

Turning his back on the academic success that eluded him, Martin left school at 17 and began to travel. He worked on farms in Australia and served as a steward on cruise liners in the Indo-Pacific Ocean. In New Zealand he jumped ship and was arrested as an illegal immigrant without papers. This caused one newspaper muck-raking through his background at the time of the Bleak House shootings to report that he then "had his first taste of prison."

Since one misleading inference of this report was that

the brief spell of incarceration in New Zealand might have been one of many more "tastes of prison," it is proper to point out that, first, Martin was never in prison again until he was arrested the day after the Bleak House shootings, and secondly, it is customary in most civilised nations, even in enlightened Britain, to put illegal immigrants in jail. He also had a brief spell of employment on Scottish oil rigs before the death of his grandfather brought him back to the Emneth area, where he ran a pig farm on his parents' property.

Martin seemed set for an aimless, drifting life again when in 1979, at the age of 35, he inherited an imposing property of his own. Bleak House, at Emneth, and its farmland, had been in the Martin family for many years, most recently the property of his Uncle Arthur and Aunt Gladys, who had willed it to him. For Hilary Martin the house held happy memories of days with family and friends. "We used to have lovely parties there," she recalled. For Tony Martin it was a special prize, for Robin was to inherit his parents' property. Now both sons were to become landowning farmers.

The main entrance to the house lies off the Outwell road and is reached down a seventy-yard long track. Martin was initially uncertain about the place. Although at first glance it is the sort of property that would prompt anyone seeking isolation to jump over the roof with delight, it is aptly named. Bleak House is extremely bleak.

But Martin was seeking isolation. He was a sensitive man – he liked hobbies such as model-making, he was fond of animals, of watching Nature at its work, of beautiful things like antiques, and he liked farming. He transported to his new home his antique collection, silver, furniture and objets d'art, worth £100,000 in the nineteen-eighties – a fact which became known to neighbourhood thieves – and settled down there to enjoy his farm and his permanent state of bachelorhood.

First of all he moved into the cottage, which was part of his inheritance, down the track from Bleak House. "I liked it more," he said. "I let the ivy grow over it. My dogs sleep on the bed in it and it is untidy. I know my garden looks a mess and rundown but it's a wild garden. If it wasn't overgrown then it wouldn't be wild. That is how I like it. It's not how most people choose to live, but it's my home and life."

When later he moved into the main house he had grand plans for the red-brick Victorian property. But the acreage soon proved insufficient to make the farm an outstanding commercial success, and somewhat in desperation he used all his spare cash to buy more land, leaving the farmhouse to fall into a state of disrepair.

Fed by the lush peat soil of The Fens, unchecked creepers and ivy wrapped themselves around the red brickwork until hardly a brick showed. The untended garden began to close in on the house to such an extent that only those who were aware of it knew there was a house at all behind the verdure. Inside the house Martin started projects and left them half finished. The result was that doors were left hanging off, windows were rotten, the floor was strewn with rubble and rubbish, and plaster was peeling from unpainted walls.

Over the years that followed Bleak House reached a state of dilapidation that most people of Martin's background would describe as almost uninhabitable. Apparently increasingly oblivious to his material comforts, he continued to buy more of the neighbouring land until he had a valuable 350 acres, with arable crops and an orchard of low trees growing apples, pears and plums. A local farmer's estimate is that the value of the house and its acreage at the time of the Bleak House shootings was around £750,000

In another touch of eccentricity the owner of this grim and foreboding place customarily went out into his fields to work, or into the village to shop, wearing only navy blue clothes – a habit which was frequently remarked by those who knew him.

Martin is a folksy sort of man, given to homespun philosophy. After his arrest and when he was awaiting trial he gave an interview that rambled over acres of ground where nothing profound was likely to germinate. He said: "This situation is surreal to me and to my mother and my friends. If we had discussed years ago what the future holds you would never have thought to discuss the situation I'm in today."

He wept as he recalled his childhood. "I don't know why but I always go back to childhood. That's what I'm doing now. I think childhood was great. I'd like to have stayed there. They were happy days.

"I had Victorian grandparents. They lived in a Victorian house. My grandfather used to wear a trilby and a shirt with a detachable collar and studs, and he had a fob watch. They were truly Victorian people. The house was full of clocks, all going tick-tock, tick-tock.

"I like being on my own. I can't go into why – it's very long and complicated. But I'm much happier on my own. I've got a nice garden, nice trees, a bit bleak in the winter. But it's wonderful when you get the full mantle. I like the garden to be natural – it's wonderful like that. And the wild life appreciates it. I tried to create a rain forest, with creepers and that sort of thing, but I haven't got green fingers. I'm not even a particularly good farmer."

On his travels as a young man: "A lot of people are afraid of what's on the other side of the horizon, but it was great for me. Your taste buds, your sense of smell, especially with the different smells you get in different countries, it's all absolutely unbelievable. You couldn't put a price on it."

On modern life: "I like the past. For me, the future, all this plastic, it's just a different way of living. People I know in their eighties feel they were born about right. But who's to know? We all go through our own time warp, don't we?"

And on local burglaries: "There was one guy down the road who got to the point where he didn't know what he was coming home to. He used to go first through the back of the house and in the end the people doing it decided it was easier to go through the front of his house and they smashed his front door down. These people always seem to come around about evening. When I come home late at night it's always there – is someone going to come out of the trees after you? They start by taking batteries off cars, and then you think, what's next?"

When he socialised, Martin enjoyed talking about antiques and gardening. He liked reading books about Sir Winston Churchill, one of his heroes. He was also an occasional visitor to National Trust properties.

He seldom drank, but he was well known among the people of Emneth who thought of him as a private man and a bit of a one-off. Those who had known him for a long time noticed the gradual change that a string of burglaries over a decade was having on him. They remembered that after one break-in he said, "If I caught the bastards, I would shoot them." Many other Fenland people were just as angry and they thought the same way, but they rarely said so, and never publicly. So in that land of tied tongues he was dubbed Madman Martin, and that, as much as anything else, was because he spoke out.

But opinions about his outspokenness among those who knew him in the Fen villages near Emneth were divided. Some believed the "weird" farmer to be harmless; others, who had heard him leading off about burglars were not quite so sure. Once he had liked the travellers, now that they were settled he thought they were "nothing more than light-fingered pykies" and "bastards" – the sort of descriptions which are commonly used about thieves by their exasperated victims but which were nonetheless to be held against him later.

"Hitler was right about gypsies," he was once heard to say. He talked of putting them all in the middle of a field, surrounding it with barbed wire and machine-gunning them – a view which was trumpeted around later in the court where he was tried for the Bleak House murder as well as in the media. When he said it he meant that he was fed up to the teeth with traveller thieves – and who might not be after so many attacks on their home?

Although some local villagers had decided that Martin

was obsessive and a bit of a recluse, none of them had had to put up with quite as much harassment as he had, none had suffered nearly so much, nor lost so much property at the hands of burglars. Had they done so they might have thought differently, for in the face of the sort of law-enforcement ineptitude that was to be revealed in rural Norfolk, those of us who have suffered two or three burglaries have to grin and bear it. We may find the burden much harder to bear, and our tongues consequently much looser, after the tenth time.

His first bad experience with travellers began twelve years earlier, when he employed some of them on his farm during the apple-picking season and found them picking more than just the apples. As he became increasingly subjected to petty crime, so he got to dislike the people he had once welcomed. Why an employer should be given the epithet "Madman" by his acquaintances in modern Britain because among other things he objects to his employees thieving from him remains one of the many enigmas wrapped up inside the conundrum of this case.

The locals did not call the travellers diddies, as Martin did – they called them travellers. But in the minds of most of them the word had only one meaning – it served for a mixture of drop-outs and drifters whose life-style made many Fenland folk wary, watchful, and even afraid for the safety of themselves and their families when it came too close to home. They believed that generally speaking travellers were a nuisance in the countryside; that they were people who did nothing to enhance the land and frequently desecrated it, and that as communities they harboured a disproportionate number of thieves and drug-users. The sadness of this kind of thinking is that inevitably the good are damned with the bad, but that is the way it became in The Fens. It was Martin's continuous experience of the unpleasant side of the travellers' nature, rather than a misplaced sense of romanticism that more remote town-dwellers might have about people who choose to eschew the traditional boundaries to life, that was the spark to the tinder of his fury.

Unprotected, isolated, alone, over the years he began to live in increasing fear, and the more fearful he became for his personal safety in late twentieth century Britain the more it began to change the kind of man he was. Like his friends in Emneth and Wisbech, his mother Mrs. Hilary Martin, noticed the change.

"He told me he felt afraid," she said. "He tried not to leave the house. He did not like the way the police no longer had any interest in guarding the community like they did in the past. He was very uptight, particularly in the last year because of the number of break-ins he had suffered. He was fed up with having his farm tools and so on stolen. He got to the point of saying that if you can't get protection from the police you've got to protect yourself and your own home."

The fact that Martin allowed his home to deteriorate has been much scoffed at. His was, however, not a mode of living unknown to a considerable number of unmarried men. Probably the single most civilising influence in men's lives is a woman, and there was no woman in Tony Martin's life. He had had only a few short-lived romantic relationships. One woman he did trust, though, was Helen Lilley – it was to her hotel in the centre of Wisbech that he went after the shootings on the night of August 20, 1999.

Although guns were always around the house when he was a boy, and cartridges were kept in pots and drawers and every other place, his mother remembers that young Tony did not take to shooting like his father and brother Robin.

She said: "He was very popular when he was a youngster, with lots of good friends. Unfortunately, he didn't settle down and marry, and that was rather disappointing. He never really liked shooting. He didn't like the idea of killing. He didn't like animals to be killed. When he got his own place, which is now a bit of a mess, admittedly, he wanted it to be a bird sanctuary.

"I know he didn't live in a way which was normal. He

had rather grandiose ideas for the house. He wanted to make something rather super of it. But he got bored and also he ran out of money."

The pacific view of Martin was reinforced by Terry Howard, 58, one of his closest friends for the past 30 years, who said that the farmer hated anyone shooting animals, even foxes.

But everyone knew he owned a gun, because everyone owned one. He had used it in 1993 in an incident in his apple orchard when he found a man he described as an unpleasant character stealing his apples. The man threatened and tried to run over Martin's dogs, and in order to protect the animals Martin went into his house, fetched the gun and shot at a tyre on the intruder's vehicle. He then called the police, which the other party did not want, and insisted on them taking a statement. He was obliged to surrender his gun, but he was later offered the opportunity to reclaim his licence.

He had been in gun trouble before the incident in the orchard. There is a story that when he was about 20 he had fallen in love with a girl named Annie who was in love with someone else. He is supposed to have climbed a tree opposite the house where Annie and her boyfriend were living, with a gun in his hand. The incident, it is said, ended painfully for Martin when he fell out of the tree.

In 1976, three years before he moved into Bleak House, he was alleged to have gone to a friend's house in some distress and brandished a First World War revolver. A shot was fired and a pigeon killed. In December, 1987, he became involved in a violent argument with his brother Robin at Robin's house over the division of some property they jointly owned. Martin is said to have got very upset and used a shotgun to smash windows in Robin's home.

We do not know the facts of that incident but they cannot have anything like the relevance to the character of Tony Martin that has been attributed to them. He would scarcely be the first man in Britain who has quarrelled with a brother. In any event, the only side of that story that has been told is the side against Tony Martin, and it has no value in evidence against him unless we know what brought it about. That Robin Martin subsequently moved to Spain was unconnected with the incident.

After his shotgun certificate was revoked, Martin went out and acquired locally a pump-action five chamber Winchester shotgun, a type of weapon which is illegal in Britain today. For those who are unfamiliar with guns, a pump-action is similar to a revolver, where a number of cartridges are inserted into a chamber. The gunman has to eject each cartridge but he can maintain continuous fire until the last round is spent; a pump-action shotgun is therefore capable of doing much more damage than the double-barrel version.

Martin told friends his gun was for frightening away wood pigeons from his rape crop, but few of them doubted that he acquired it for his own security – something about which he was becoming obsessive.

One reason why Martin was such an untidy man was because in the last few years maintaining Bleak House was becoming physically too much for him.

In 1997, when he had been the victim of robberies for years, he began to feel particularly vulnerable after an accident on his racing bike. He developed a deep vein thrombosis in one leg and another in a lung, and during the recuperation process came close to death. Although he recovered, his health and general fitness began to deteriorate, exacerbating his feelings of vulnerability. This was a far cry from his splendidly athletic youth, from the dashing young man who drove around Norfolk in a Lotus Elan and caused many a female head to turn admiringly.

"I used to be a strong man, but all that left me feeling considerably weaker," he said. "I was also unsure about how much physical work I could do and how far I could push myself." Inevitably, he added, Bleak House fell into a greater state of disrepair and as that happened Martin wondered about his ability to cope with the thieves and burglars who were making his life a misery.

His friend Terry Howard said Martin became very lonely in middle age. "He would never admit to that, but I think he was. He would turn up at all times, a stone would rattle at my window at 7.30 a.m. and he would say, 'Are you going to let me in for a cup of coffee?'"

Howard said his friend was "weird" and at times could be "hard work." He said, "I would not call him a rebel, but he's always been his own man. At times it could make him a pain in the arse."

Malcolm Quince, neighbourhood watch representative for Emneth Hungate, expressing horror over the shooting of the burglars, was unequivocal about Martin. He said: "He is a loony. He's got funny ideas. He doesn't like cara-van people – or gypsies and diddies as he calls them. He's never been married and I reckon he's just a strange boy."

Richard Portham, of Wisbech, who was a good deal closer to Martin than Malcolm Quince, had a quite differ-ent view of him. Mr. and Mrs. Portham were always quite happy to leave their three young sons, one of whom has Down's Syndrome, with Martin. Another couple who Martin regularly visited also had three sons, one of whom is autistic, and they too were content to leave the "loony" Tony Martin with their boys.

"If Tony was so loony, I would not have been happy for him to visit my wife while I was at work," Mr. Portham said. "Indeed, on the day of the shooting he had lunch with her and our boys. We know that after the incident he went to see his friend the owner of the Marmion House Hotel. Some recluse!"

Mr. Portman also thought that to get a more accurate picture of the kind of man Tony Martin is, his team of defence lawyers should have interviewed both Mrs. Portman and Helen Lilley the hotel owner. "None of them was interviewed, which contrasted sharply with the police, who left no stone unturned in the community to complete their prosecution," he said.

Martin once confessed that he never really liked Bleak House. "The state my house is kept in has been used to make out that I am some kind of oddity," he said. "But the truth is I would not have built a house with red brick and would never have had Welsh slates on the roof. As soon as I moved in I began pulling the place apart, changing the staircase around. But I never finished it."

In another rambling interview, this time with his local newspaper, the *Eastern Daily Press*, which emphasised the essential simplicity of the man he is, he said: "People say I'm anti-establishment. They said it was travellers who burgled my house, that I didn't like travellers, so I shot them.

"But why does a man who is very interested in life with a terrific amount of freedom put himself in this situation? Why does anyone feel I want to spoil my own life? You see, it all goes completely against my background. I have more worldly experience than most people my age.

"Admittedly I haven't mixed as much as I used to. But what people haven't really understood is that I started going out before I was 16. I used to go to nice parties with evening dress and to pubs.

"There was a young English lady I met when I was 25 or 26 that I fell in love with. But unfortunately the relationship ended."

When Tony Martin was 25 or 26, thirty years ago, guns were not so much a part of the culture of rural Norfolk as they are today. Then farmers used them every day for hunting, now they use them not only for hunting but for protection as well. One woman living in an isolated home told me, "I wouldn't hesitate to use it, nor would most of the rest of us."

She was very typical of her community. In England's sleepy Fenland an air of paranoia, of fear of the intruder, gradually built up as successive governments raucously trumpeted their feeble "tough on crime" campaigns.

That fear is more than palpable as you walk round the villages of Emneth and Emneth Hungate. Signs on lamp-posts and fences warn that "guard dogs are loose," "this is a homewatch area," that "this is private property," and that "scrap dealers are not welcome."

By August, 1999, rural Norfolk had become Fortress England, the citizen's last defence against rampant, unchecked criminality.

2

A NEST OF BURGLARS

Although Brendan Fearon, 30, lived in Middle England, he embodied none of the classic attributes applied to Middle Englanders: those strong, silent, long suffering types encompassing conservatism with a small c, the spinal column of a race built on two thousand years of colourful history.

A tall, dark, slim, swarthy traveller, he was, rather, honed out of the new liberalism that swept over Britain in the last half of the twentieth century. Like many other reflections of that new liberalism he had been allowed to become a frightening menace to Middle England. He was a consummate thief and burglar, a man who by the spring of 1999 had appeared before the courts 35 times for a variety of offences which also included assault, for which he had spent long periods of his life behind bars. He owed it to the new liberalism that at the time of the Bleak House burglary he was a free man, for in some well developed societies he would long ago have been put away until he was no longer a danger to society.

Fearon first heard about Bleak House, the target for the burglary that was to propel him into newspaper headlines, early in July, 1999. He was in a pub in his home town of Newark, in Nottinghamshire, listening to a conversation among fellow criminals when the subject of the rich loot to be had at the farm came up.

It was, he heard, a collection of buildings, which

included a derelict cottage in the grounds of the farm, and the main house itself, where "nobody had lived for a hundred years." One of the buildings, opined one thief, housed a collection of valuable antiques and was good for "smalls" – burglar-speak for easy to carry antique silverware. It was isolated, remote, and presented the easiest pickings for miles around. All this was enough to lighten and brighten the eyes of Brendan Fearon. He decided to "take a pop at it," as he put it.

Darren Bark, 34, another traveller, and a thief and burglar with a string of convictions and custodial sentences – he had 52 court appearances to his name – who was also, somewhat peculiarly, a free man, had likewise heard of the Bleak House farm complex. His informant was a member of a gang that had carried out the successful burglary there only two months previously, in May, and had left behind a good deal of property worth stealing.

Intrigued, Bark paid £100 to a Wisbech man to show him where the remote farm was located. He was told that the story that no one had lived there for a hundred years was untrue; in fact, the informant said, "a fucking old nutter lives there alone."

Fearon and Bark were friends – they had struck up an acquaintance when they met in prison five years earlier. As each knew of the other's interest in the projected burglary of the farm, they pooled their information. It was then that Bark discovered something he didn't much like – that the farm was guarded by three rottweilers. His initial enthusiasm for the project began to wane. He would drive the getaway car, he said, but he would not get himself into any situation where he might have to tangle with rottweilers.

Fearon, who did not share Bark's fear of dogs, remained undeterred. But he now needed a new helpmate. His choice fell on 16-year-old Fred Barras, who, age for age, could more than match the list of criminal convictions of both Fearon and Bark – he already had 28 court appearances on his record. Precisely when Barras joined the burglary team remains a mystery, as, to some extent, does its planning. Some accounts have presented it as an opportunistic crime planned on the spur of the moment, whereas the alternative account, that it was a carefully premeditated if not brilliantly planned robbery, is more likely the case.

August, 1999, the month in which he was to die, was a busy month for Barras. On the third he was brought to the magistrates' court in Newark on a charge of stealing garden furniture, a well-known target for traveller thieves. What happened next suggests that few things are more urgent in Britain than a review of the laws relating to juvenile offenders.

Barras was bailed to appear again at the court on August 10. He failed to surrender to his bail and was arrested. He was brought back to court on August 19 and the court decided, in view of his age, to pass him on to the Youth Court for sentence. Pending that, he was again released on bail, subject to a condition of residence. Next day he set off to burgle Bleak House.

The condition of residence was imposed because the magistrates came to the conclusion that without it he would leave the area and once more fail to surrender to bail. Referring to Barras's last appearance in court on August 19, Graham Hooper, clerk to the justices, told me: "It appears that no further representations were made regarding the risk of the commission of further offences." One conclusion that can be drawn from that is that someone, somewhere within the law enforcement system, let down young Barras as well as the law-abiding public.

Fearon, who knew all of Barras's circumstances, was afterwards to claim that he decided at the very last moment to take the teenager along on the burglary expedition for a ride, "to keep him out of trouble." But friends of Barras in Newark were later to tell a slightly different story. They claimed that twenty-four hours before the burglary Barras was talking about "going on my first big job."

Almost certainly there is an element of truth in both accounts. Probably Fearon's decision to take Barras with him was made some hours before they set out, although it is difficult to understand the logic of taking a young criminal on a burglary job just to keep him out of trouble. If Fearon's decision had been made the day before, which is equally probable, the friends of Barras were equally right. In any event, they were not to know as they listened to Barras's boast that his first big job was to be his last.

Fred Barras pulled his hair down in a wild fringe and his wide mouth was usually set in an engaging smile. This gave him the cheeky, likeable image of a high-spirited teenager. The reality was somewhat different.

His recorded life of crime began just after his thirteenth birthday. By the time he died three years later of Tony Martin's gunshot wound in the back, his 29 offences included two charges of assaulting police officers, theft, common assault, forgery, handling stolen goods, drunkenness, driving offences and obtaining property by deception.

When he died the bail bond ordering him to appear in court at a future date for his latest offence was stuffed in his back pocket. Almost certainly he didn't understand what it meant. Probably he couldn't even read it, because he was only semi-literate.

Barras came from a dysfunctional family of travellers. He never knew his father, a scrap metal dealer, also called Fred, who met his mother, Ellen, in a Wakefield pub when they were both 15. They were married at 18 and lived in a caravan park before moving to a council house in Wakefield.

Their ten-year tempestuous union produced six children, five girls and, last of all Fred, junior. Shortly after his birth, Mrs. Barras went with the children to her mother's home in Newark "for medical treatment" and never returned. The next time Mr. Barras was to see his son was at his funeral, 16 years later.

After a short stay at her mother's home, Ellen Barras and her family moved to a succession of council houses until settling within a strong travelling community at

Hawtonville, a raw, rough, post-war council estate in Newark. The Nottinghamshire town is a magnet for Britain's travelling population; the Hawtonville estate is one of those sad, sick ghettos where the terminally deprived and underprivileged are left to exist. Caravans are parked in many of the front yards and gardens are littered with car parts, scrap metal and children's toys. The estate is a nucleus of drugs and crime, the first fuelling the second.

"Almost all crime in Newark is drug related," I was told by a council official. Barras was already on drugs. Traces of cannabis and amphetamine were found in his blood after he died.

Barras was expelled from Sconce Hills School, Newark, for the first time when he was 12. He was taken back but by the time he was 13 he was expelled again. He was ordered to attend special classes, but rarely turned up. Instead, he took up with a gang of older youths who had hundreds of offences to their names. At 15 he was sentenced to two months in a young offenders' institution.

When he was released he worked briefly on a market stall and in a fast food restaurant. Now and again he did odd labouring jobs. When he wasn't working he spent a lot of his time in the company of a gang of active teenage burglars who had been his associates for at least two years.

Occasionally he would stay with Karl Wright, 19, one of his closest friends, who lived on the estate, for the weekend; at other times he would stay at home and spend entire days in front of the television. Three months before he died he broke his leg lopping trees, but smashed off the plaster cast himself because he wanted to go swimming. As a result, at the time of the Bleak House burglary he was still not able to walk perfectly on the injured leg, still less run away.

He had several casual girlfriends on the estate and was being pursued by the teenage mother of two children. In the month before he died he had a two-week fling with a 27-year-old divorcee, introducing her to drugs.

Karl Wright, Barras's friend on the Hawtonville estate, said, "Everyone here gets into mischief. Most lads here have a criminal record, but just for stupid things. In all the estate, there's only one or two that's not got into trouble."

Ellen Barras seemed to think that her son first "got into trouble" at the age of 12 – a year earlier than the official record. This particular piece of trouble was stealing from a shop. After that, she said, he seemed to be in and out of trouble all the time. She added fiercely, in the way that mothers do when they are searching for something on the upside, "But he would never steal from his family." She agreed that by the time he was 14 he was stealing regularly. "But just daft things, like lawnmowers," she said. "Nowt too bad." Nowt too bad, that is, unless the lawnmower is yours.

In 1998 Barras spent eight weeks in youth custody for car theft. That sentence, when politicians in that same year were stridently proclaiming that they were getting tough on crime and the causes of crime, is in itself incredible. What, one wonders, were those eight weeks supposed to do for him, for the community?

In 1998 too, Mrs. Barras conceded, the police were regular callers to her end-of-terrace home. "They used to say, 'Mrs. Barras, he's back in again. We've got Fred in the cells. Will you come down?' But they liked him." It was all such nice, friendly stuff, this business of getting tough on crime and criminals.

Life in the Barras household on the Hawtonville estate was never easy, though. A month before Fred Barras died, the Barras family had to move out of their home of 10 years after one of Mrs. Barras's sons-in-law flew into a jealous rage and tried to demolish the front wall of the house by repeatedly ramming it with a pick-up truck. No one on the Hawtonville estate pays for the damage they cause to public property, in the way other people have to. The bill for this expensive tantrum, like the bill for all the other damage caused by residents, was picked up by the taxpayers.

During the year before he died Barras had got into the habit of going out on Friday nights with Karl Wright, when Mr. Wright returned from his job in London. On Friday, August 20, though, he broke the habit. Instead, around 6.30 p.m. that evening he sat down in the kitchen of his mother's council house home and ate the chicken and chips she had bought for his tea from the local fish and chip shop.

Pushing back the empty plate he told her, "I'm going out to meet some friends." He surreptitiously slipped a small bag containing a pair of rubber gloves and a screwdriver into one of his pockets. Incongruously, in view of the fact that he was about to embark on his "first big job," he stuffed his bail bond into another pocket and set off from the house on foot to the rendezvous where he was to meet Brendan Fearon and Darren Bark on what was to be his last journey on Earth.

Fred Barras's first big job was scheduled for just twenty-four hours after he had walked free on bail from his last crime.

Half an hour later, Darren Bark left his mother's Newark home in a white Ford Granada and drove to a neighbouring house where Fearon lived with his parents. When Bark drove up, Fearon's father, Joe Fearon, 65, a retired hospital porter, asked him where they were going. Bark replied, "We're going out."

Joe Fearon said, "You're not going pinching, are you?" Bark, according to Mr. Fearon replied, "No, Mr. Fearon. I'll never do a thing like that. I've learned my lesson now. Nothing like that."

Mr. Fearon then said, "Don't you get Brendan into trouble, now. He's been all right these last two and a half years."

"Nothing like that, Mr. Fearon," Bark said again as they drove off. In the boot was Fearon's contribution to the fitting-out department: gloves, a torch, and three holdalls for the property they planned to steal from Bleak House. At exactly 7.30 they arrived at a parade of shops on the

Hawtonville estate, where Barras was waiting for them. The teenager jumped into the back seat of the Granada. He drank two cans of lager on the journey and upset Bark because he talked non-stop for most of the time.

* * *

Bleak House, at Emneth Hungate, was seventy miles away; so it was just about dark when they arrived. The journey was notable for one extraordinary incident. Not far outside Newark they were stopped by police making a routine check. A constable poked his head through the driving window and asked where they were heading.

"We're going for a night out to meet some friends for a drink," Bark replied. He was asked to show his driving documents, his licence and insurance. He had none on him, so he was given a form requesting him to produce the documents for inspection at Newark police station within five days.

For a "routine check" this must have been the mother of all routine checks. Other drivers who have been subjected to the same sort of checks must often have wondered what they might be about and what they lead to. They may now have some idea from that routine check the police made that evening outside Newark. All three occupants of the car were known criminals of long standing, all three were well known to the police in Newark. In the car boot, which was not inspected, were the obvious tools of their forthcoming burglary. Barras did not look a day older than his sixteen years – some say he looked a good deal younger – and was therefore transparently obviously two years below the age of drinking. None of these mind-boggling clues were acted upon – the car with its contents of known criminals was waved on its way with a bureaucratic form for the driver to produce his driving licence at the police station at some time convenient to him. Speeding safely on towards Emneth, Barras, Fearon and Bark must have hugely enjoyed the joke.

Thus the three men who should never have been allowed to leave Newark, arrived at Emneth Hungate at about 9.30

p.m. Fearon and Barras got out, leaving Bark, the getaway driver, with the Granada parked in a lane out of sight of the farm.

As we have already seen, and as was his habit, Tony Martin was home early that night. After the last burglary, in May, Martin told the police operator, one Mrs. Wood, who took down the facts advanced in the manner of hundreds of thousands of other angry victims of this kind of violation, that such was the undeterred insolence of the burglars that they might come back and collect the pieces of furniture they had abandoned at his back door.

"And if they do, I'll blow their heads away," he threatened.

It is worth considering this remark on two counts. Leaving aside for a moment the inherent fear and anxiety that most burglary victims have for their own safety, they usually react in one of two ways. They either cynically shrug their shoulders and decide to take the insurance company for a ride, thus getting back in monetary terms much more than the value of what they have lost, or they genuinely rue the violation of their property, the loss of their valuables, and they feel an overwhelming sense of impotence, of powerlessness to do anything about it, like a man who is punched in the face while he is tied to a tree.

This second group of people are those who are most likely to say within hours of having to report to the police, to list their losses, to go angrily through the tedious business of form-filling, to answer questions from bored detectives who they know have no likelihood whatever of catching the thieves, in a strained, polite and protracted conversation which both sides know will lead nowhere,

"If they come back, I'll blow their heads away."

In this case Martin, in the first stages of seething with anger, was making his first phone call to the first police contact who, as is sometimes the case these days, was not even in the police, which many people might think was further cause for anger. Then Mrs. Wood must have noted what he said, or allowed it to be recorded, and the conversation was passed on apparently to real policemen.

Most detectives would have nodded sympathetically. They might even have felt sufficiently sorry for the victim – who they were having to routinely interrogate long after the burglars had got clear away – to think that if the burglars' heads were blown away they would like to turn a blind eye to it and go off and deal with someone doing thirty-five miles an hour in a thirty-mile limit. For most detectives are human, and most are aware that in Britain today their job of dealing with vicious men is made absurdly difficult by the new liberal attitude of judiciary and legislature – an attitude that considers the "rights" of criminals as more important than the rights of their victims.

But that night in May, 1999, when Martin reported the latest burglary at this home and made that remark to Mrs. Wood there was very little sympathy for him. In fact, remarks like that were to be searched out and used against him in court by the police nearly a year later. The mere fact that they were noted, stored up and used in that way against an innocent victim of burglary would suggest that here was a case where the rights of the perpetrators of the crime were being considered above those of the victim. Here, too, perhaps, is a lesson for all victims of burglary: don't say what you would like to do to those who have smashed their way into your home, for fear that it might later be used in evidence against you.

In all this Martin might have been justified in thinking in hindsight that the police, knowing they were unable to catch the burglars, might have said to themselves that they would nail something against the victim, so that someone, in this case Martin himself, could stand in the dock. If that seems highly surreal and improbable, think about it. Have you never read of a case before this where the victim of a crime has found himself accused and charged, while the perpetrator went free?

In case your answer is no, let's do a quick round of checks. A month before the Bleak House murder, bus driver Mark Coleman, of Liverpool, was approaching a bus stop in the city's Belle Vale area, with four pensioners aboard, when a gang of thugs began throwing things at his bus. The things included bricks, stones, bottles, even a traffic cone. The bus windscreen was smashed, and the elderly passengers, who were in considerable danger, were terrified.

As the youths began to taunt Mr. Coleman he stopped his bus and, anxious to protect his alarmed passengers from further danger, he caught one of the thugs, an 11-year-old boy, holding him by the shoulder to detain him. He was forced to let the youth go when the boy's aunt arrived and attacked him, so he called the police on his mobile phone.

When no officers turned up after he had phoned three times, he went to the police station to report the incident, but the police told him there was nothing they could do. Four days later officers knocked on the door of Mr. Coleman's home and arrested him.

He was charged with assaulting the 11-year-old boy he had detained at the bus stop and faced the prospect of a jail sentence. He was then left agonising about that prospect for three months – the time it took the Crown Prosecution Service to decide to drop the case.

"The whole thing was a nightmare," he said. "I was just doing my job and trying to be a good citizen, but it was me who ended up being punished. I had the spectre of a court case hanging over me for three months because I tried to do the right thing. It's a sad thing to say, but trying to help in this sort of situation is simply not worth the hassle.

"I did not punch the boy or use any force on him. I just laid my hand on his shoulder and told him to stay put. He did not struggle. Then his aunt attacked me, so I let go and drove away as they began to throw more stones. I drove down the road to wait for the police, who never arrived, so I drove to the station to give them a statement.

"Four days later I was arrested in front of my wife and two young sons. I was questioned for seven hours and charged with assault on the say-so of these people.

"Jack Straw [the Home Secretary] urges us not to live in a walk-on-by society, but his laws and his police force make it impossible to make a stand. I was treated like a common criminal for trying to stop these mindless thugs getting away with wanton vandalism."

No action was taken by the police against the young thugs. And after the incident Mr. Coleman's boss said, "We are telling all our drivers not to confront anyone, or else there is a chance they could be arrested."

Liverpool Police, who questioned the innocent man for a full working day, then diligently filled in all the paperwork and sent it off with their criminal charge against him while allowing the malefactors to go scot free, might have sensibly chosen to hang their heads in shame and to keep silent about this outrageous piece of police work. Instead they decided to indulge in some police-speak: "We thoroughly investigate all allegations and take appropriate action where necessary."

An isolated incident of faulty justice? Let's see. A few days before Mr. Coleman was released from his three-month period of agonising, a 37-year-old Rochdale business manager stood in the dock at Manchester Crown Court.

The manager's 12-year-old son, the court was told, had gone off the rails after his mother and father were divorced when the boy was six years old. The boy had broken into his grandmother's house with a gang of thugs, stolen £400, vandalised cars, bullied classmates, stolen from a taxi and been expelled from two schools. He was effectively a thief, a violent and vicious child and, if not speedily checked, was a suitable candidate for a life of permanent crime against society.

A considerable number of people would have said at this stage that to prevent this young hooligan from going the way of Fred Barras, or joining a gang to attack buses carrying elderly passengers, he needed a good hiding. That's what his mother thought too. She called her divorced husband and asked him to come round and do just that because she was "at her wits' end."

The father, who was described as a concerned and caring father, a no-nonsense, down-to-earth man, and a respectable member of the community, was later to say that when he arrived at the boy's house, "I wanted to talk to my boy about this stolen money, but he couldn't give a monkey's. At first it was quite peaceable, but he became cocky. I slapped him a few times and he was upset." Then he took the boy's trousers down when he refused to and smacked him repeatedly on the backside.

After the boy went to school next day his mother received a phone call from the social services, and then a visit from the police. The young hooligan – he was 12, remember – told the police that he wanted to press charges against his father. Afterwards the boy went off to hospital on foot and was "treated for severe bruising." The treatment for severe bruising is to apply cream to the affected part in order to reduce the discomfort.

Standing in the dock, the father pleaded guilty to causing actual bodily harm to his son (since the bruising legally constituted "actual bodily harm" he had no alternative but to plead guilty) and was sent to prison for six months. The judge, Adrian Smith, then delivered a lecture which might have been construed as a warning to us all how we must on no account deal with violent, vicious young thieves.

"Every child has a right to be protected by the courts, even from their fathers," he said. "This was in no sense a case of chastisement. This was a violent attack caused by your complete loss of self control. It was the sort of violent assault that can have a serious impact on a young person. Had a neighbour done this to your son you would have been furious.

"You set a most appalling example to him about how to resolve problems within the family. I am afraid a message has to be sent out to the public that people who beat children in this way will face immediate custody."

How, one is left wondering, was this in no sense a case

of chastisement? For how else was the cocky young thug to be restrained? Was it not the sort of "assault" that was specifically designed to have a serious impact upon him? What on earth had the neighbour got to do with it? The father was doing his duty as a father, no one said anything about a neighbour being involved until the judge threw that in. And how can a good hiding possibly be an "appalling example" of solving a family's problems in dealing with a nasty, vicious and dangerous child who is demonstrating complete indifference to his parents' concern about his already well-developed criminal behaviour? Surely if both parents of a young hooligan decide that his behaviour is so dangerous that he needs a good hiding, what is the purpose of it if it does not hurt him really hard? If it hurts him really hard, it must perforce leave a temporary mark, like bruising, where it will be remembered. Punishment, of course, is meant to hurt and to be remembered, there is no point at all in it if it is not. It is, one must assume, the reason why we send people to prison.

The absurdity of the case was further underlined when the wretched boy declared, "I was really upset when I heard my dad had been sent to prison. He was only trying to show me what was right. I hope he will talk to me when he comes out of jail."

A few months after that a 56-year-old Welsh headmistress was confronted by a 10-year-old boy who verbally and physically abused her. Told that he could not go swimming, the child flew into a temper, kicked her, head-butted her and became impossibly aggressive. To bring him to his senses the headmistress slapped him. She was charged with assault, given a three-month suspended prison sentence and ordered to pay £2,500 costs.

The stipendiary magistrate told her: "You failed completely the child, the school, your honourable profession and the community." The magistrates' court verdict was later quashed on appeal.

There are those who say that the sort of judgement that condemned the headmistress is quite right. There are others who shake their heads in disbelief. They believe that this is the way that future Fred Barrases are made and set at large to terrify peaceful people. They believe that in the past fifty years the pressure of liberal cant has turned wrong into right and right into wrong. They believe that Orwell would have loved every minute of it. They may be the majority, but a silent one.

The liberal consensus on crime essentially holds two positions. One is that there is no crime crisis and everyone has got the threat out of proportion. In absolute terms this may be true, but relative to times past, the risk of being a victim is actually very high.

In 40 years – the period stipulated by Tory leader William Hague for damage done by "liberal thinking" on crime – crime has exploded. In 1958 the police recorded 669,000 crimes, by 1992 this was up above five million. In the mid-Nineties crime numbers began to fall again to about 4.4 million. They went up again towards the end of the decade.

Crime has been going up gradually since the Thirties. By 1950, albeit with a larger population, it had reached 500,000. Crime really started to take off in the early Sixties. By 1970 there were 1.6 million recorded crimes. By 1980 there were 2.5 million. The number peaked in 1993 at 5.2 million offences. This represented one offence per ten people – double the rate in 1979.

The liberal thinkers were given a distinct advantage as a result of the recession of the early Eighties, which linked rising crime to high unemployment and left many ministers feeling they were to blame. Michael Howard, the Home Secretary, did not think he was to blame, however, and confronted the liberal orthodoxy. The years he was in office were the only period since the last war when crime numbers and rates began to fall.

Mr. Howard decided that incarceration was a fitting punishment for criminals, so that by the end of his tenure at the Home Office in 1997, the chance of being sent to prison for an indictable offence was 22 per cent – the highest for 40 years and double what it was in 1990.

During exactly the same period, crime, and acquisitive crime in particular, fell for the first time since the Second World War. Whether the two were linked is arguable. But liberals have found it hard to come to terms with the possibility of a causal relationship between the decline in convictions and the increase in crime.

The crime explosion of the late Nineties has many arguable causes. But one point stands out like a lighthouse on the rocks: the chances of a criminal getting away with it are greater than ever.

Michael Howard was vilified by the liberals for his tough policies, yet after three years in government his successor, Jack Straw, seemed to think it was probably the only way forward, and included in a tougher sentencing regime "three strikes and you're out" for burglars. The problem, of course was catching them in the first place; realists would say that catching them three times under current police methods is star-gazing.

Labour has been presiding over a sharp increase in crime since eschewing Michael Howard's discovery that criminals cannot re-offend while in prison. According to the Home Office, crime in soft-touch country areas has risen by 33 per cent in 10 years. In towns and cities the rise is only 4 per cent. But it is believed that up to 75 per cent of crime goes unreported because victims feel that nothing will be done.

The second position held by the liberal consensus on crime is that if there is a problem, sending people to prison is the wrong way to deal with it. The liberal approach has been to attack those who believe that incarceration might be a fitting punishment for criminals and a means of taking them off the streets. This approach has always found tacit support from the Treasury, for the cost of prison places is high. The taxpayer still pays indirectly, in the form of higher insurance premiums for his property thus made available to an increased number of burglars.

Liberal thinking on crime is not just confined to the

police and the judiciary. Its beliefs are all pervasive in contemporary Britain. A 49-year-old Scottish teacher teacher and father of three took his eight-year-old daughter to the dentist after she had suffered toothache for several days. When the child got to the waiting room she refused to go in and flew into a tantrum, whereupon the father smacked her bottom.

What happened next was another tragic reflection of the state of British society. The dental staff called the police and the father, arrested on Christmas Eve, 1998, was banned from living with his family for two weeks.

He was then charged with assaulting his daughter and brought before the Hamilton Sheriff Court in Scotland in May, 1999, five months after the incident, and found guilty. He received no punishment but his conviction was formally recorded. Nearly a year later he was called before a committee of the General Teaching Council in Edinburgh to answer the allegation that he had been "infamous in a professional respect." He denied this absurd charge; nevertheless this extraordinary kangaroo court decided he must be struck off the teaching list because he was unfit to teach. North Lanarkshire Council, his employers, was left with no alternative but to sack him because he could no longer work.

More gobbledegook followed from an unnamed spokesperson for the Scottish Secondary Teachers' Association, who opined: "Teachers do face double jeopardy. Matters which for other members of the public would be private, unfortunately cannot be for teachers. The General Teaching Council is charged with the duty of maintaining the standards of the profession and has heard the evidence in this case, so I cannot question their decision."

So the idea that people who are innocent are punished and that wrongdoers are not might have gone through Tony Martin's head as he left the police station that May day in 1999 leaving behind his pathetic list of valuable stolen property. Next day police officers went to Bleak

House to take more details of the burglary. They found Martin still seething. Remarkably, instead of brushing aside his angry comments, they wrote them down. They wrote that this innocent victim was "vitriolic about criminals, especially gypsies."

These notes too were stored up, and nearly a year later they too were produced in court to use as evidence to help brand Martin a murderer.

* * *

During the three months after the May, 1999, burglary of Bleak House, Martin, worn out by these constant and violent attacks on his private life and in despair at the law's inertia, decided the time had arrived for him to protect himself, since no one else was going to.

He began by turning his home into a virtual fortress. He removed several steps from the staircase, creating a nasty booby-trap for any unwanted intruder. He built look-out posts in elevated positions in his grounds and installed iron bars over all but one of the downstairs windows. Certain that he would soon be attacked yet again, he took to sleeping in his clothes so as to be in readiness to defend himself against nocturnal aggressors. He kept a sawn-off shotgun hidden in his garage, and the pump-action shotgun under his bed.

If all this seems like over-reaction, it is worth recalling yet again that Bleak House was very isolated, very vulnerable, and that it had repeatedly been attacked. It was about to be attacked for the eleventh time by three young men with appalling criminal records who were contemptuously dismissing its owner as "a fucking old nutter." The police could neither protect this lonely homeowner – this they freely admitted before and after the shootings – nor prevent the three violent criminals continuing to endanger his life, and the lives of any other homeowners they might pick upon. This was the wretched, lawless state of affairs in Norfolk in the last few months of the twentieth century.

And as a result, armed, barred, partly protected by booby-traps, asleep in his clothes, it was perforce the state of being that Tony Martin was reduced to on the night of Friday, August 20, 1999.

It was, some unsympathetic observers have claimed, a state brought upon himself by his own desire for revenge. Martin's view is different, and given all the facts seems much more valid. He had several times made it clear that it was brought on simply by naked fear.

And he was subsequently to make it equally clear that, as he lay in bed that night in the darkness listening to the burglars, he was "petrified." As is the case with a man rooted to the spot by fear, he did not want to get up from the bed, but he told himself he had to, because if he did not they might come at him in the dark. We know that the burglars either thought the house was uninhabited or that the owner was an idiot. If they came into Martin's bedroom and were surprised by the sight of him, shaking with fear, the easiest way to avoid future recognition would be to kill him.

No one should be dismissive of that suggestion. Many hardened criminals kill those who they know could identify them when caught *in flagrante delicto*. As an example, in the 1980s three men intent on theft broke into a house in Staffordshire which they knew was full of antiques. Convinced the place was unoccupied, they were astonished when two women, who had gone there that day to make an inventory of the contents, appeared from upstairs. To avoid recognition, the three men murdered both women after raping them.

In July, 2000, a 74-year-old woman was beaten to death at her Dorset home in a block of sheltered flats, in a suspected botched burglary. In London in 1997 a burglar beat a 79-year-old pensioner to death, was sentenced to life, and then freed by the Appeal Court on a technicality which did not alter the fact that he was the murderer. When the Crown Prosecution Service sought re-instatement of the conviction they missed by one day the deadline to take the case to appeal.

These examples do not by any means constitute an

exhaustive list – they are simply illustrative and are drawn at random from crime files on aggressive burglaries that have occurred among the 1.5 million burglaries in Britain every year. They demonstrate that so long as burglars kill, anyone confronting a burglar in the dark must have the right to strike first and ask questions afterwards.

Tony Martin was a man who had knocked around the world, and who claimed that whatever other people might think of his life-style he had more experience of worldly matters than many other people. He would have been aware of the evil that drives men to break into and plunder other peoples' homes, of how vicious they can be when cornered. He would have been aware of all this when, after that frightening ten minutes alone in the darkness of his bedroom, he took his gun – and we shall show presently that the taking up of that gun was an act of self-defence – and proceeded down the stairs to receive the full beam of a startled burglar's torch in his eyes, blinding him.

Then the firing began. Fearon was hit in both legs by a total of 196 pellets, 11 of which remain in his body to this day. Barras was hit in the leg; probably turning in terror and surprise, he was then hit in the back. He was alleged to have cried out, "He's got me! Please, don't! Mum!" The pair turned and fled, Fearon in such a state of alarm that he ripped a window from its frame, and leapt into the undergrowth in the front garden.

Barras dragged himself through the gap left by the shattered window frame. He was bleeding heavily from the pellet wound in his back two inches in diameter, and he was possibly crying out for his mother. He collapsed in the undergrowth less than five metres from that front window and within two minutes of the shooting his young life ebbed away. His "first big job" had become his last.

The last word he may have uttered was "Mum!" It was ironic that in the fleeting death cry of this burglarising child, who, with his long list of previous convictions was so badly served by the British justice system, was a last agonising thought for his mother.

As the gunsmoke cleared Tony Martin felt his way gingerly down his stairs and left Bleak House by the front door. He got into his car, still carrying the shotgun but without any ammunition, and drove round his farm with the headlights on, looking for burglars. He had no idea that he had hit two of them, less still that one of them was already dead a few yards away in the undergrowth.

Finding no one, at just after 10 p.m. he hammered on the front door of the bungalow of his nearest neighbour, Paul Leet and his wife Jacqui, about half a mile away. Paul Leet appeared at the door and quickly assessed his caller.

"He appeared to be totally calm," he recalled. "He said, 'You will never guess what's happened. I found these people in my house. There were three of them. [The error was Martin's. Darren Bark never entered the house]. I shot at them and they dropped their rucksacks and ran. I don't know whether I have hit them.'"

"You'd better call the police, Tony," Paul Leet replied. But afterwards he was to say that he didn't believe his neighbour's story because "he's a bit eccentric."

It was almost an hour later that Mrs. Jacqui Leet yelled to her husband, who was taking a bath, to tell him that there was a man staggering up the drive. Unbeknown to her, this was Brendan Fearon, who had negotiated the half mile from Bleak House to the Leets' bungalow bleeding from his pellet wounds.

Mrs. Leet said: "He dragged himself to the window and knocked. I could see his legs were ripped apart."

Paul Leet, wrapped in a towel, called to the man from the bathroom window demanding to know what he wanted. Fearon, with large patches of blood seeping through his black tracksuit trousers, called back, "I've been shot. Could you give me a drink of water?"

Mrs. Leet dialled 999. It was now 10.55 p.m. The conversation that followed went like this:

Mrs. Leet: "There's someone outside and they're screaming they're hurt. We daren't go out."

Response: "Right."

Mrs. Leet: "I think he's been shot. You need to come quickly."

"Been shot?"

"Yes."

"What makes you think he's been shot?"

"Because he's shouting he's been shot. Earlier Tony Martin came round and said three blokes had attempted to break into his house and he fired a shot and that's all I know."

The reaction of the policeman who answered the Leets' call provides another interesting aspect of the Bleak House murder. Solicitous for their safety and anxious to protect their lives from someone he assumed might be dangerous, he said, "Don't go outside until we arrive."

Here was a man who had been shot, and was bleeding heavily, pleading for water on the Leets' driveway. The Leets were confused about his identity, because Paul Leet disbelieved Martin's story. Why did the policeman counsel them not to go outside to the man's aid? The only answer can be that he knew that the area was much burgled, that the man was probably a burglar, that the residents were angry about the lack of police protection, and that someone may have fired at him because he was endangering lives. All these assumptions by the policeman, quickly made and rolled into one, beg the obvious question – if the police were aware of all this, why was such an obviously dangerous man allowed to be at large?

Still calling from a window, Paul Leet directed the caller to a tap outside the kitchen window. Then he saw Fearon collapse.

"Conscience got the better of me and I decided to go out to him," he said. "When I got to him I'd never seen anything like it. His thigh was hanging down over his knee to his ankle. There was a big hole in his leg. He wanted a blanket. He kept saying he was cold." Mr. Leet had taken an overcoat with him and he covered the bleeding man with it to keep him warm.

Meanwhile, after Tony Martin left the Leets' bungalow

he drove to his mother's home, Redmoor, in Elm, where he told her what had happened.

"I was horrified," she said afterwards. "When he asked me to look after the gun for him I said, 'Well, you can leave it with me. I'll look after it for the time being.' I didn't let the police know about it straightaway because I thought if no one's involved and they've gone away, they weren't going to report it."

Martin left the gun in a lavatory at Redmoor and from there drove to the Marmion House Hotel in Wisbech, Cambridgeshire, to be with the hotel's owner, Helen Lilley.

"Something bad has happened at the farm, and the police will be here soon," he told her. He gave her some money to cover an unpaid debt and asked her to look after his dogs. The conversation, like the one with Paul Leet, suggests again that Martin had no idea he had hit one of the intruders. Neither he nor the police were to know until the next day that he had killed Barras. He went to the hotel kitchen to make a cup of tea before going to sleep on the sofa in the lounge.

At nine minutes past six on the morning of Saturday August 21 police came to the hotel to arrest him. They were fully armed; interestingly, they had already arrested Fearon on burglary charges but for that arrest they were not armed. Martin was charged only with the wounding of Fearon – the body of Barras, lying in the undergrowth outside the back door at Bleak House, had still not been found.

This was not the fault of the police, but the fault of Fearon. In an attempt to protect his accomplice he insisted after his arrest that he was alone that night. He may not have realised that the teenager was already dead, he may have thought that Barras had got away, although he was the witness who recounted the last words uttered by Barras in the darkness, and one is left wondering what he made of them.

Darren Bark was also under arrest and in custody. He

had driven off when he realised that the burglary had gone awry. Concerned later for the fate of his two criminal accomplices he returned to the scene in the early hours and was arrested near Bleak House at five minutes to five in the morning on suspicion of burglary when he asked one question too many to police at the scene of crime. Like Fearon, he told the police nothing about the involvement of Fred Barras.

At 6.52 a.m. police carried out an initial search of Martin's farm. A more comprehensive search was planned for 10 a.m., but the presence of Martin's three growling rottweilers, which were released into the grounds by the farmer after the burglary, kept the search party at bay.

After a local farmer had rounded up the animals, the search started and at 2.40 p.m., 17 hours after the shooting, the body of Barras was found in the undergrowth by a civilian helper. For the first time the police realised that they were not just dealing with the wounding of one burglar, but the fatal shooting of another. Martin was told of the discovery and to the charge of wounding Fearon was added the charge of murdering Barras.

A post-mortem quickly established that Barras bled to death from wounds to the back and legs caused by the shotgun injuries. A senior detective commented, "He would have died within minutes and it is at least reassuring for us to know that he didn't die as a result of the delay in finding him."

Martin's arrest sent waves of anger through his family and friends. The family protested that he had been driven to the brink of a nervous breakdown by repeated break-ins at his home.

His mother said, "This is the most terrible thing to hear. It would break my heart if he were jailed for murder. It would kill him if he were imprisoned, he is such a free spirit. I just can't believe that such a terrible thing could happen to him.

"The only thing giving me courage is that people are supporting him so well. The phone has been ringing off the hook with offers of help and support."

In Emneth, where one in three of the village houses have been broken into, support was almost universal for Martin. People now began to speak up. Most villagers said that despite his slight eccentricity he was a fundamentally decent man.

The overwhelmingly majority view was that he deserved praise as a man who had at last drawn the line in a local fight against crime. Villagers were aware that this view was likely to be challenged and that it was hardly the ideal solution to community crime, but they claimed that in the last decade they had been the target of thieves too often to consider the moral implications.

Mike White, a parish councillor, said he would press for a campaign in support of Martin. "They don't want to be locking him up," he said.

At the Gaultree Inn, where regulars gathered to pledge their support, a customer said, "If someone is trespassing on your property you should defend it. You'll find no one here who is sympathetic to the people who got shot."

That was not entirely true. One villager thought that for a burglar to lose his life for his crime was taking things a little too far – but it was indicative of the mood of Emneth that the villager declined to be identified.

Carole Mayfield, 51, one of Martin's nearest neighbours, said she had spoken to him by telephone where he was being held in custody and she would sacrifice four or five days to gather in the wheat harvest at his farm. The job had to be done urgently. She asked, "What would you do if it was your friend?" Farmers in other counties, some as far away as Hampshire and Dorset, phoned to offer the Emneth community their support.

The bandwagon to save Tony Martin from a miscarriage of justice had started to roll.

3

A TRAVELLERS' FUNERAL, AND AN ANGRY PROTEST

The length of time it took the police to elicit from Fearon and Bark that there was a third burglar, and that he was nowhere to be seen, and the further delay in finding his body, meant that that they were unable to call on Mrs. Ellen Barras until the Saturday evening following the Friday night burglary. Although she had not seen her 16-year-old son for 24 hours, she was preparing to leave for a night out in Skegness when the policeman's knock was heard at the door. The officer told her that her son was dead.

Mrs. Barras was taken to Norfolk to identify the teenager's body. Afterwards she said, "I don't think I will ever be happy again."

She was to be given her say, because it has become a rule of the proliferating modern media that bereaved mothers are always allowed their space.

"He was just a happy lad, always laughing, always popular and happy," she told reporters at her council house. Standing beside the mantelpiece where a picture of her grinning son – not a picture from the family album, but a police mugshot – held pride of place, she said, "He made me happy. He cared about me all the time. He was a lovable rogue. Everyone loved him."

Everyone loved him. Even the police. Well, perhaps not

all the police.

There were the two officers he was accused of assaulting in 1998, when he was only 15. They didn't love him, did they? "He was a villain," said one officer, employing a euphemism much in use these days for violent criminals. "He wasn't the worst, but he caused a lot of grief."

Back to Mrs. Barras. "Fred wasn't evil," she said. "He just got in with the wrong people. They were always petty crimes, nothing big. I had only one son and I loved him for all the world. We all tried to stop him thieving but he would take no notice. I never gave up on him, though." That view was supported by Tony Joynes, Barras's uncle. "She did everything a single mother could possibly do for him," he said.

In an unfortunate joint statement with her estranged husband which left little doubt that it was written for them, Mrs. Barras added, "As Fred's family we cannot condone and do not condone his actions. We are aware that he had failings and would have expected him to be dealt with and punished in the criminal justice system. He was not given that chance."

One possible inference of that complaint is that Barras was a criminal who was deprived of justice. But in what way was Barras deprived from being punished in the criminal justice system? He had already been "punished" so many times within that system for theft and burglary, and yet here he was roaming free to re-offend. The intention may have been to say that for preference his parents would have liked him to have been tried by a court rather than shot by one of his exasperated victims. This prompts the question: what would the courts in Newark or Norfolk have done with this multi-recidivist had he not been shot, but merely caught by the police? The question is rhetorical, because we know that he would have been set free to terrorise Tony Martin and his neighbours after a few more months on bail or in custody. With that kind of prospect in view, wouldn't all burglars prefer to be punished within such a justice system? Wouldn't they all complain if they were not given the chance of re-offending as quickly as possible?

The funeral of young Barras was inevitably an emotional affair. The youngster in death was unrecognisable from what he had been in life. One headline writer described him as "a rough diamond", a phrase which did not appear anywhere in the story under it. This sort of reaction happens because at such a funeral one mourns not the death of a hardened young thug but the death of a teenage boy, the promise of life's brightness wasted. We do not call to account those responsible for such waste, those who are not under arrest. At a funeral the brusque confrontation with mortality, the sudden awareness of absolute annihilation, gives rise to unguarded moments in which for a brief time we all see ourselves as equals, and treat each other as such, before the spectre of our common destiny. But the fact that you have to die and journey to another world from which no one returns before you are forgiven should not distort our view of reality in this one.

Four hundred and fifty people assembled at St. Mary Magdalene Church in Newark, enough to bring the centre of the town to a standstill. The family travelled in a fleet of seven limousines followed by nearly 100 cars and lorries carrying dozens of wreaths and bouquets. Outside the church 12 teenagers held a single red rose as a mark of respect to their dead friend. The atmosphere, remarked one young observer, was "scary."

A note on one wreath from one of Barras's sisters, said, "You were a brother in a million. A brother who made us laugh and a brother we will miss. Our love will always last." Barras's former girlfriend was among the mourners. She said, "Fred was always funny and smiled all the time."

The Rev. Richard Harlow-Trigg, who conducted the service, said, "Fred's life was cut short in circumstances that have been rehearsed too many times in newspapers and on TV. Everyone here knows he should not have been where he was. But he did not deserve to die like he did."

Mr. Harlow-Trigg evidently suspected the intentions of

some of his congregation for, calling on people not to seek revenge, he said, "Not surprisingly, there is anger and recrimination, as well as sadness and mourning. We are not here to judge Fred, nor are we here to judge anyone else involved in this tragedy." Parts of his monologue, though, must have caused some questions to be asked about his briefing.

"Fred was like so many other 16-year-olds," he opined. "He was a popular lad, happy-go-lucky and always game for a laugh. He was full of life."

And, yes, you have heard it before: "Fred was a lovable rogue," he added.

This should have been an occasion for sadness and grief, underlined by the police, who read a statement on behalf of the family declaring that friends and family were deeply upset by the untimely death of young Fred Barras. "They ask that they be left alone to bury Fred with dignity and to mourn privately. They are waiting for the facts to be established and for justice to prevail."

But was it? For incredibly, even while this solemn statement was being read, the police were well aware that someone acquainted with the friends and family had put out a contract to kill Tony Martin.

Around Emneth, whose only other dubious claim to renown is that it was once the home of a relative of Ronald Ferguson, father of Sarah, Duchess of York, there was no letting up in their angry mood over the arrest of Tony Martin. On Wednesday September 8, days after Martin's arrest, more than 300 villagers packed into a meeting at Emneth Village Hall to voice their discontent.

The meeting, called by the parish council to discuss rural policing, quickly became furious and even ugly. Superintendent Steve Thacker, West Norfolk police divisional commander, was jeered and shouted at when he tried to answer questions. And Harry Humphrey, a member of Norfolk Police Authority, had to abandon his speech as he tried to explain budget shortfalls, because he too was shouted down. These were rural people in rural England, driven to the edge of their patience by negligent policing.

The signs were ominous from the outset, with a visible police presence in the car park and a bevy of reporters and cameramen jostling with the crowd. Inside the hall feelings were running high even before the meeting began.

The Rev. Rachel Larkinson, who took the chair, asked everyone to remember there had been a death, and it was a "tragedy." From the body of the hall a farmer shouted, "Let us never describe the death of a criminal as a tragedy." He was cheered to the rafters.

Supt. Thacker was grilled by a number of people who related horror stories of when they were burgled. At times he looked visibly shaken when told what his officers had reportedly said to victims, agreeing that such remarks were sometimes "inappropriate."

One woman told the meeting how she came home and found a burglar in her home. "The first thing I went for was a knife," she said. "If I had caught him I would have gone for him with it, because it would have been me or him." She said that after dialling 999 the police took half an hour to arrive.

She was then asked if she wanted to press charges. "I was told that if there were any repercussions, the police would not be able to support me."

Another man said he had been burgled on four occasions in the last eight years. "I apprehended someone on my land at 3 a.m. and it took the police so long to get there that I had to let the bugger go."

Supt. Thacker said an average response time was 15 minutes but obviously some locations took longer to reach. He added that there had been a seven-fold increase in the cost of rural crime during the past decade.

The poor response times and the feeling that it was not worth reporting crime came across strongly at the meeting. Wisbech businessman Malcolm Starr, a friend of Tony Martin who was to become a key player in the farmer's support group, said Supt. Thacker had been "living in a cave for five years or more." He told the police officer:

"Your negative attitude makes us negative about you and that is why there is nothing constructive or positive to say to you."

The beleaguered superintendent continued to tilt at windmills, urging people to report crime. He said amid jeers: "I'm imploring you to report crime. My officers like to nick villains. That's what we do best."

Another man said that although residents had made their homes as secure as possible, they needed police back-up. "You are not visible enough," he told Supt. Thacker. "I accept it may be a question of resources but can we be assured that they are being focused correctly?"

The superintendent replied that he had 120 front-line officers to patrol an area, which included Emneth and Emneth Hungate, covering 550 square miles and they had to work four shifts.

Insufficient policing may have been one of the principal reasons why recorded crime in Emneth Hungate – and Martin and many of his neighbours have said that they had stopped recording crime with the police because it was a waste of time – was surprisingly high. In 1998 there were 180 recorded crimes in Emneth (population 220), and in 1999 there were 199. The rate was almost double that of nearby Downham Market.

Among those present on the platform were Gillian Shephard, Tory MP for South-West Norfolk, who lives 20 miles from Bleak House. She said that judging by letters she had received, what had happened [the arrest of Tony Martin] had touched a nerve in rural communities every-where. "I hear crime victims say they have not bothered reporting an incident as the police are over-stretched and the court system lets them down."

She said the principal question on everyone's mind was should they take the law into their own hands. "We know that the answer to that question must be no, for that way lies Kosovo and Corsica. But people will be tempted to do so unless they feel they can report crime without being intimidated, that the legal system is fair and the police have sufficient resources to make them feel safe in their own homes."

She thought the best way forward was to campaign for the government to put more police funding into rural areas and she and fellow area MPs would be doing this.

Afterwards, the more sober view of the meeting was that not many people wanted the teenage burglar dead, but few were mourning his passing.

Stewart Mayfield, a neighbour of Martin's, said, "I have every sympathy with Tony. The talk in the villages is that something like this was bound to happen. You can go to virtually every house down this road and people will tell you they have had something stolen. If the police can't protect your property, what are you supposed to do – just let people take it?"

The Martin case was to provide a litany of unfortunate remarks made by people in positions of authority. It should be used as a case study for officials who have to make public comments, ideally it should be used as the lesson on when to keep your mouth shut. We shall presently hear the curious comment of the judge when passing a life sentence on Tony Martin, "This should be a dire warning to all other burglars"; the spokesman for the Barras family, "Fred was deprived of the chance of being dealt with in the criminal justice system"; and the vicar at Barras's funeral, "Fred was a lovable rogue." Now we come to Norfolk Police.

Acting Assistant Chief Constable Peter Fraser made the first official police response after the arrest. He said: "Large areas of the county are rural and this brings with it certain policing challenges." This was to be the first of several unsatisfactory police responses which were eventually to trigger almost as much criticism of Norfolk's senior policemen as their inadequate policing policy.

Mr. Fraser's statement was followed by another from Ken Williams, Chief Constable of Norfolk. He had heard the judge say that complaints aired during the trial by Norfolk farmers about the high crime rate and lack of police action to deter burglars in Martin's locality should be brought to his – the Chief Constable's – attention.

In a statement issued following the complaints of the Norfolk farmers that the police were indifferent to crime in rural West Norfolk, Mr. Williams said, "In an ideal world I would have all the resources I need. However, we police in the real world and have to make do with what we have."

This was very fair and very honest, even if it was also very unsatisfactory. What the Chief Constable was saying was that he did not have the tools to do his job as well as he would like it to be done. If that was the view of the Chief Constable, the job of policing Norfolk was not being done in the way any of us would have liked it to be done – in other words, it wasn't being done properly. As soon as policing anywhere is not being done properly, the stage is set for any number of criminals to terrorise any number of law-abiding people, and a state of anarchy begins to prevail.

At a Farm Watch meeting many months before the shootings, Tony Martin had put it slightly differently from the Chief Constable, but the purport of what he said amounts to the same thing. He said, "Out there [in the Norfolk countryside] you are on your own and you are the law. The police are a waste of time."

Martin's view was straight to the point, a heartfelt echo of most burglarised people's sentiments; the Chief Constable's statement was tinsel-wrapped official stuff, but both were saying that policing in Norfolk was inadequate. We may therefore assume that the Chief Constable agreed that Martin sensibly chose to defend himself against attacks which the police could not prevent, such as fortifying his house, keeping three rottweilers, and so on, although of course that does not mean that he agreed with the final action itself. It is worth bearing this in mind, because the way Martin fortified his house was in part responsible for his being labelled by the media as "eccentric."

After the shooting the feeling that a man should be able

to protect himself in his own home reverberated around the country. Cheques poured into the Tony Martin defence fund – they came from pensioners, farmers, land workers.

Martin was interviewed on a BBC programme. He said, "We are supposed to live in a civilised society. It's not the way I've been treated. People are not aware of what it's like in the countryside. Criminals prevail. It can't be right."

His first appearance in the committal proceedings was before the magistrates at King's Lynn on Tuesday, August 24. The hearing was brief, although friends and supporters determinedly turned up to listen. He was remanded in custody until the following Wednesday, September 1. As he was sent back to Norwich Prison forensic scientists continued their inch by inch search of his farm for any additional material for the prosecution's case. Some of his friends and neighbours asked the police if they could have access to his farmland to harvest his fruit crop on his behalf during his absence; permission was given after the request had been given consideration.

On September 1, because of police fears that the farmer's supporters could clash with friends of Barras, a bail application was switched at the last minute from King's Lynn to Norwich Magistrates' Court. This was to be an augury for a series of intimidatory events that were to dog Martin's quest for justice for months to come, casting a long shadow of doubt over the entire trial process. Norwich magistrates refused to grant bail – by this time he had spent 12 days in custody. Friends now set a six-figure sum as their target for the legal fighting fund.

The following week, Tuesday, September 7, he was freed by Judge David Mellor from Norwich Prison on conditional bail, the conditions being that he should say where he was living while awaiting trial, and that his address should not be in Norfolk. After the hearing he was whisked away to a secret safe house, where he would undoubtedly have remained until his trial had there not been a singular occurrence.

Only 48 hours after the granting of that conditional bail, Martin went back before the judge in chambers at Norwich Crown Court. He asked that the condition whereby he must declare his address should be varied. We do not officially know why because such applications to a judge are held in camera. But the reason is obvious: the secret address where he had been living, which was known to only three or four people and which is thought to have been 100 miles away from Bleak House, had become more widely known, and he had received threats.

Martin was sufficiently alarmed that day, September 9, to ask for quick action. The judge in chambers decided to review his earlier decision and sent Martin back to prison "for his own protection" while checks were made on an alternative address for him. So here was an untried man who was considered to be harmless to the community released on bail by a judge, and yet within two days being sent back to prison because it was the only safe place where the State could keep him.

Safe from whom? Who and where were the people making threats, and why were they not in custody? Threats against Martin had undoubtedly been received by the police by this time, but they would not confirm whether he had been threatened in the two days during his release, or whether he had been put in danger in any way. No one was arrested for issuing threats. Martin, the victim of the threats, was sent back to a cell while another secret address was found for him.

After Christmas he was interviewed by the *Eastern Daily Press*. He said, "I didn't know a boy had died and that I had taken a life until the police informed me on Saturday. [The day after the murder]. I was taken to King's Lynn police station thinking, 'I can't really believe this is happening.'

"I thought a murder was something you planned, went down the road, and is something you did somewhere else, certainly not your own home.

"Finding myself locked in the cells was like being in a dark hole.

"I felt I should be depressed and could feel a depression coming on but for some unknown reason I never went into it. I have had depressions in my life before, but the only person who can get you out of it is yourself. Whether it was all these letters of support from people, I don't know.

"When you are charged with murder you have a policeman assigned to you for each shift. In other cases it is one for every six prisoners.

"One guy came along and said: 'There are a lot of people who want to see you.' He then said that they couldn't cope and the station wasn't designed for this. I felt like saying: 'Why are you telling me this?'" It seemed to be so barmy.

"Did they think I was going to go out there and say: 'Now look here.'

"I was told not to talk to anyone in jail because they thought I would be attacked, but it wasn't like that. After I had been refused bail I was sent to Norwich Prison and the inmates there were very friendly.

"They were running around saying to me: 'There's your combine on the TV.' I was amazed at the interest in my situation. It even made news in America.

"The most worrying thing is that there are only losers in this case. To win will not mean a change of law and certainly will not make me feel like I've won anything.

"But to lose will mean every criminal looking at the verdict and laughing. They will sit outside people's houses and say: 'We are going to do your house over. You know what may happen to you if you try to stop us.'

Martin described how he filled in his time at the safe house while awaiting trial. He said: "Life in a safe house can be very lonely. I'm free to roam but I don't go very far. I just go out and go pruning trees, do something, somewhere. I get plenty of exercise gardening. Samuel Johnson said drinking port and [eating] hearty meals should be followed by vigorous gardening. It led to heart attacks but they'd think it was a great way to go.

"I keep myself occupied. I get nice paintings out of magazines and get them blown up and put them in my room. I have got a picture of the Battle of Trafalgar.

"The past months I have had to make a totally different life for myself, travel everywhere by bicycle and eat in restaurants. I have been to London a number of times. I like going to Harrods because they have so many things from around the world."

On a visit to Harrods before Christmas he saw a 3ft tall Teddy Bear in the store and thought, 'I'll have that.' But he didn't know the postcode of his safe house and the store would not despatch it without the complete address. When he went back to Harrods again after Christmas the Teddy Bear was still there – 'or one like it.' This time he bought the bear and took it with him under his arm.

"It was funny because people paid no attention while I was on the bus. It was only when I got to Hammersmith and I was in the queue that people made comments to me, saying, 'Excuse me, bear,' and things like that."

Martin told the *Eastern Daily Press* that he made up his mind to take the giant Teddy Bear to court with him. He was true to his word.

But this easy-going, uncomplicated man who cut pictures out of magazines and bought a Teddy Bear for himself was saddened when, about a fortnight before he was due to appear at Norwich Crown Court, he went to see his three rottweiler dogs, Otto, Daniel and Bruno, which were being kept in kennels at public expense. "I almost cried when I saw them," he said.

When Christmas came and went and the new millennium began, Brendan Fearon had other things on his mind which were far removed from Teddy Bears. He had spent weeks in hospital after surgeons repaired the terrible injuries to his legs and groin. When he came out of hospital he was arrested and charged with conspiracy to burgle. He then made a statement to detectives detailing his part in the burglary.

"I got the torch out from under my jumper and got my gloves on after Darren dropped us off. We went along the gravel to look for this house. We was going to rob it. I could hear noises and I didn't know what the noise was. I was just about to kick it [a dog] and it got vicious. Fred shouted, 'There's another one,' and he's holding my shoulder.

"We went back against the wall. I heard a smash. I looked behind and I saw a window. Fred must have smashed it with his elbow. There was another pane of glass there. I punched that through. I couldn't see nothing even with me torch. There was a lot of dust all over the place, cans, bottles, bricks, wood. I was feeling about for a window or a door. Then I heard Fred shout, 'He's got me!' I saw a flash and I heard a noise. My leg felt numb. I saw an old man standing on the stairway. I just went mad and ended up looking for some way to get out. My arm went through a window. I just ripped it out. I thought Fred was behind me. I even thought when I was in the field I heard him shout."

After the botched burglary Fearon, who has a ring in his ear and occasionally wears glasses, confessed to being haunted by what happened to Barras. He could not forget the 16-year-old's dying words, "He's got me. I'm sorry. Please don't!" And the last despairing cry of the boy inside the burglar, "Mum!" Long after the shootings he was receiving psychiatric help to treat his conviction that he had let down his teenage accomplice.

Fearon said, "I still wake up at night in a cold sweat as that moment comes back to me. I am still getting terrible nightmares. Martin pulled the trigger, but I took Fred there and I blame myself."

His mother, Mrs. Glenis Fearon, said in a TV interview, "What can you do when they're out there? You tell them the right thing to do, but when they're out there you can't do anything about it."

In January, 2000, still limping badly and supporting himself on a stick, Fearon listened impassively as he was sentenced to three years imprisonment for his part in the Bleak House burglary.

The other member of the team, Darren Bark, the get-away driver, was brought before magistrates, set free on bail, and promptly skipped it. He disappeared for several weeks before he eventually gave himself up to the police. His girlfriend became pregnant while they were in hiding. He was given 30 months imprisonment.

Both Bark and Fearon were initially placed in Norwich Prison, but after reports of disagreement between them, Fearon was transferred to Weyland Griston Prison, Thetford, Norfolk.

* * *

Meanwhile, Norfolk Police, bemused by the fierceness of local reaction to Martin's arrest, and evidently badly bruised by the public meeting at Emneth Parish Hall, did not help themselves when in reply to Martin's accusation that he despaired of any help from the police after his years as a burglary victim, they allowed one of their spokesmen to be reported as saying that they were not even sure that all the incidents took place.

The reader is left to imagine whether this is a case of a man claiming that his property had been attacked ten times when it wasn't really being attacked at all, or – and this is a view that those among us with experience of being burglary victims might consider to be more accurate – whether the police bothered to recall each incident.

This alternative suggestion is not as far-fetched as it may sound. Emneth has policing difficulties because of its situation on the borders of Norfolk and Cambridgeshire. Aware of this problem, it has been specially targeted by thieves in the travelling community, a fact well known to Norfolk Police. Many people living in a no man's land equidistant from two rural police headquarters suffer from the same lack of attention. Consequently figures produced by NFU Mutual, the farmers' insurance company, show Norfolk as having the highest incidence of rural crime, particularly burglaries and the theft of tractors and trailers, in Britain. Most people living in rural parts of the county keep dogs, positioning their kennels menacingly at the front of their houses.

Raking through the knicker drawer of Martin's background, some journalists discovered that he had as an uncle by marriage one Sir Andrew Fountaine, Bart, a founder of the National Front. Sir Andrew lives at Narford Hall, near Swaffham, Norfolk, where he has organised regular summer camps, prompting the Home Office on one occasion to refuse entry permission to a number of continental fascists.

Most reporters treated this tenuous link between Martin and the fascist leader with the unimportance it clearly deserved, but not so *The Times's* correspondent Tim Jones, who described Martin as a racist and hinted darkly, "He may have inherited his uncle's views."

Indeed, the diligence employed by the press surfing for signs of wickedness in this very ordinary sort of bachelor, is nowhere better demonstrated than in *The Times* report. Upon the sins of the uncles, it seems, are visited the sins of the nephews. Tim Jones's comment must have been mildly disturbing to Home Secretary Jack Straw (who was watching the Martin case closely), for Mr. Straw's teenage son and his brother had both recently been in court on police charges. If we are to be tarnished with the same brush through consanguinity as our relatives, then Martin is indeed tainted with the National Front through his uncle, and it therefore follows that Jack Straw's family associations would make him the least fit man for government office in Westminster. Then there is the Prime Minister himself, whose teenage son was arrested for being drunk...

More interestingly, Sir Andrew Fountaine has warned, "Within a generation, the Norfolkman, his culture, purpose and ethnic succession will be biologically extinguished."

He is not alone in Norfolk in his views. Many people in The Fens nurture a deep-seated hatred for the travelling community. A number of pubs have put up signs "Members Only." The meaning is clear, so too is the intention to get round any charge of racism. In one village I visited a resident told me, "They [the travellers] used to know their place, but don't now. Another said, "Like all ethnic minorities (sic) the travelling community have a chip on their shoulder." He added bitterly that "the council bent over backwards for them," and they picked up "all the benefits."

The danger inherent in all this is that fascism is a political view that grows from the seeds of perceived injustice. The Allied powers perceived injustice to Germany at the Treaty of Versailles was partly responsible for the rise of Nazism in Germany. In France, in our own time, perceived injustice in the form of State handouts to North African immigrants has spawned the dramatic increase in support for the Front National, the French ultra-right wing party. People vote fascist when they believe the State is indifferent to the cherished traditions of their way of life. In Norfolk today, views which are very right wing are being openly expressed about rampant criminality in the county. The source of all this can be traced back in a straight line to government's refusal to tackle the issue of law and order.

"They have always come here but in the past it was just to pick fruit and they would move on to pick brussels sprouts somewhere else," said a villager. "But now they've settled here and there's no work and they steal lawn mowers from sheds. There were a few coloured people here but they were hounded out. The locals burgled their houses and abused them."

A pensioner in Emneth said, "All Fen people would have done what Tony Martin did. Fen people are independent people. I would have blown them away myself. We all wanted him to get off because they got what they deserved. Fen people would have blasted them away."

Despite the burgeoning local support, after his arrest Martin had started out with a bad press. He was described as a gun-owning middle-aged bachelor with three rottweilers for company on his remote 350-acre farm. At this point in came the celebrity publicist Max Clifford. Soon, as a result of Clifford's efforts, Martin was being interviewed in the newspapers and taking part in radio programmes. Media interest grew, and considerable national sympathy was added to the intense local sympathy for his predicament.

Much of the media attention had to be carefully constructed, because of the rules of contempt which prohibit publication of anything which carries substantial risk of serious prejudice to the course of justice. Some comment is allowed under the rules if there is a broad issue of public interest on which a case may hinge and the risk of prejudice would be merely incidental to the discussion. Although the safeguards are there primarily to ensure that the defendant is given a fair trial, it is also possible for the defence to prejudice the prosecution's case.

In the case of Tony Martin there was a huge broad issue of public interest; it was central to the murder charge and to the verdict, and it remains so to this day. It is simply, what degree of force should you be allowed to use to protect yourself and your property if intruders break into your home?

Max Clifford, who was personally incensed by Martin's arrest and was approached by Martin's solicitors to help them cope with the media, realised that he could make media discussion of this issue work in Martin's defence. Mr. Clifford waived his fee as a consultant, usually a minimum of £10,000 a month. Echoing views rapidly shared by millions of homeowners across Britain, he said he identified with Martin and hoped the farmer would escape a custodial sentence.

The strict rules governing media coverage of criminal proceedings, to remove the possibility of juries being influenced by sources outside the courtroom, did not deter Mr. Clifford, or lead him to believe he was stepping into a legal minefield. "My job will be to makes sure there is as much information passed to the British public as possible," he said.

He added: "Tony (henceforth, he always referred to Martin as Tony) cannot do interviews himself. But the media can speak to his mother, his friends, people who know about him and who care about him. That is what I will be doing." But he would not be helping the farmer to sell his story.

According to Mr. Clifford, the shootings were a tragedy for all concerned, and highlighted a problem which frightened householders had been contacting him about for years – fear of being attacked in their own homes and concern about how to defend themselves. Martin's Leicester-based solicitors, M & S, were mightily relieved at the publicist's enthusiastic interest. The partners had no training in media relations and probably very little time to get involved in it, and they were soon being deluged by the press. Michael Ballinger, a member of the firm, was delighted with Clifford's expertise "because lawyers would inevitably cock it up."

Some lawyers began to get twitchy at all this. They asked, is this the start of a new career – the legal spin-doctor? Would he inevitably go about influencing judges and juries, both of whom, after all, come from the everyday world, on behalf of his client?

Undaunted, Mr. Clifford moved the pro-Martin bandwagon into top gear. He said things like, "What Tony did was tragic, but it wasn't murder," and "If three armed people broke into my house I wouldn't make them a cup of tea."

But the fears of traditionalists that legal spin doctors would henceforth be calling all the shots were soon to be allayed. For in April, 2000, Tony Martin appeared at Norwich Crown Court to answer a charge of murder — and nothing that spin could do was able to save him.

4

THE TRIAL OF TONY MARTIN

The new millennium was well under way when Tony Martin was driven from his safe house in a police car to Norwich Crown Court. On April 6, 2000, he was charged before Mr. Justice Owen and a jury of six men and six women of murdering Fred Barras, of attempting to murder Brendan Fearon, or of wounding him, and of possession of a firearm and ammunition with intent to injure life.

To these four charges Martin answered in a clear voice, "Not guilty." He pleaded guilty to a fifth charge of illegally possessing a Winchester pump-action shotgun without a firearms certificate.

On the first day of the trial he was presented with a single red rose and the message "Stay strong, Tony," by a middle-aged woman supporter from the north of England. Every day for the rest of the trial she presented him with a new rose and a similar message.

Dressed in a dark blue double-breasted suit and blue shirt – true to form, he continued to wear only blue – and with his 3ft Teddy Bear for company, he showed no emotion as the case against him was outlined by the prosecution.

The packed court was to hear a remarkable story that touched a raw nerve across rural Britain. Attention was rapt – here was a case that provoked atavistic fears that cut across normal boundaries of politics and class an Englishman defending his castle against two burglars with 114 criminal convictions between them. Many in the courtroom must have known the sense of violation and enduring unease that a burglary leaves behind.

Opening for the Crown, Rosamund Horwood-Smart, QC, said that Martin was an eccentric who lived with only the company of three rottweiler dogs. She said: "He was vitriolic about criminals, especially gypsies, and talked of 'putting gypsies in one of his fields surrounded by barbed wire and machine-gunning them.'"

Martin had fortified Bleak House by placing iron bars on the doors and windows, she said. "He also slept fully clothed, wearing boots in contemplation of something happening." He had booby-trapped the way up to his bedroom by removing steps from the top and the bottom of the staircase and had placed ladders leading up to the roofs of his outhouses, which could be used as lookout posts.

Ms. Horwood-Smart said that before the killing in August, Bleak House was burgled in May, three months earlier, by thieves who escaped with a chest of drawers, some china and items of sentimental value. On that occasion Martin told the police he would "blow their heads off" if they returned.

"Over the years Mr. Martin and his family had undoubtedly been the victims of crime. Mr. Martin was well known to have strong views on policing matters." [This reference to Martin's family suggests that relatives lived with him. This was not so. The prosecutor was alluding to other burglaries suffered by other individuals in Martin's family].

At a meeting of a local Farm Watch group, Martin showed his contempt for the police. "During the meeting, he said, 'Out there you are on your own and you are the law.' The police were 'a waste of time.'"

A neighbour who saw Martin two or three days before the shooting remembered him referring to burglars as "light-fingered pikeys." Ms. Horwood-Smart told the jury: "He said if he caught the bastards he would shoot them."

On their arrival at the isolated farm on the night of Friday, August 20, Fearon and Barras started to make their way to a cottage which they believed to be Bleak House. In fact, it was the cottage used by Martin to house his rottweilers, one of which stood in their track growling.

"Then they were confronted by another of Martin's dogs. Fearon also became aware of a third big dog growling in the dark behind them, which was Martin's other rottweiler, Bruno. They gave up trying to burgle the cottage and backed off towards the farmhouse where they forced a window and entered the downstairs hallway."

When the two burglars prised open the window, they found the house was so run-down that at first they thought they were in a shed. Then they crossed the hall to a rear room and began filling a bag with small silver items.

The jury were told that Fearon and Barras spotted a dresser in Bleak House and began shining a torch towards it. "Fearon remembers Barras following closely behind him just before he put his bag down on the floor. He then heard a noise and shone his torch towards the stairs, where he saw a man standing halfway down. Then he heard Barras shout, 'He's got me!' at the same time as he heard a loud bang. He then made his way towards a window. He was going towards that window when he heard a second shot and his left leg at that moment went numb.

"He then heard a third bang and felt pain in his right leg and in his panic he managed to pull the whole window out of the wall."

Sobs from the Barras family in the public gallery could be heard when she added, "At that point he heard Barras say, 'He's got me! I'm sorry! Please don't. Mum!'"

The jury heard that Barras followed Fearon out of the window. Fearon, badly injured, and weak from losing blood, managed to make his way across fields heading for nearby Foreman's Cottage, home of Mr. and Mrs. Paul Leet. As he struggled along he dropped his torch, a glove by a ditch, another glove in an orchard and his baseball cap on the road. He was seen by a passer-by, who did not stop, bent double in pain. The Leets saw him on their drive and called the police.

"The gun that was used in the shootings was taken by

Martin to his mother's house and left in her lavatory," Ms. Horwood-Smart said. "Martin claimed that he had not fired the gun before and did not know how many cartridges it held.

"He said he kept it under his bed. He had gone to bed that Friday evening at around 9 p.m., having put his two rottweilers to bed and leaving the other dog, Bruno, to patrol the grounds."

Describing the burglary from Martin's viewpoint, Ms. Horwood-Smart said the farmer did not use the mains electrical system installed in his derelict house. Instead he rigged up an extension lead from a barn which he used to power his phone, fax line and two 15-watt lightbulbs – one in his bedroom and one in the hall. They were the only lights in the house.

"He said that he was wakened by noises. At first he thought that the rottweiler Bruno had got into the house. Then he saw flashes of light downstairs. He said that he returned to his bedroom and retrieved the gun.

"He loaded it until it was full. He did not know how many cartridges it held. He says he returned to the landing. He negotiated the step at the top and he says that he went halfway downstairs. At that point a torch was pointed at him. He took aim and fired a shot below the light of the torch and he continued to fire until the gun was empty."

She said that after the shooting, as Fred Barras lay dying or was already dead in the undergrowth to which he had managed to crawl, Martin had driven around his property with his gun looking for burglars. "One question you will have to consider is whether he was driving as a frightened man or an angry man in search of the burglars."

Ms. Horwood-Smart said that after the incident Martin visited the Leets, his neighbours, ahead of the injured Fearon's arrival there, to tell them he had disturbed burglars and shot at them, and they phoned the police. He then went to his mother's home and later to a hotel in Wisbech where he was arrested some hours later. The body of Fred Barras, who must have taken between 20 seconds and two minutes to die, was not discovered until 17 hours later by the police. The teenager was wearing rubber gloves, and a chisel was found nearby.

"Later Martin told police officers that he had at no time warned the intruders or given them the chance to surrender. He said he thought he would hide upstairs, but then thought, 'I have had enough,' and went downstairs with the gun."

As Martin stared fixedly ahead of him, Fred Barras's sisters, who were sitting at the back of the court with their mother and father, sobbed quietly as they heard how their brother was killed.

Ms. Horwood-Smart said it was the case of the Crown that Martin did not fire at Barras in self-defence but in accordance with his professed views that the only way to stop thieves was to shoot them. "In acting the way he did, his intent was to kill or cause really serious injuries to his victims." Martin lay in wait for the two men and shot them "like rats in a trap."

Anthony Scrivener, QC, defending, highlighted the long criminal records of the three-member gang. Barras. he said, had been sentenced to several spells in a youth detention centre. Fearon and Bark, currently serving prison sentences for conspiring to burgle Bleak House, had each spent long periods in prison for other offences.

The Crown's chief witness in this remarkable case was a burglar and, according to the police, a professional criminal. Brendan Fearon's version of what happened at Bleak House was later branded by Mr. Scrivener as "rubbish," and it certainly bears little scrutiny.

Limping into the witness box and still carrying a stick, the pony-tailed Fearon began by saying that the trio had not set out initially to burgle Bleak House, and that he had taken Barras along only "to keep him out of trouble" in Newark. He had found the 16-year-old drinking with a group of his friends and allowed him to come along for the ride. He did not explain why it was that Barras had said the previous day that he was going out on his "first big job" on Friday night.

He said he had been told that Bleak House farm had not been lived in for 100 years and was owned by a man who kept antiques. He and Barras were dropped off by Bark and were heading for the cottage where he believed the antiques were kept when they were confronted by one of Martin's rottweilers "shaking its mouth."

The pair retreated into a wooded area. "Fred was clinging to my shoulder," Fearon said. "He was frightened and crying."

With the dog snarling and barking, he said they had stumbled across what they believed was a shed – this, in fact, was Bleak House. They only realised it was a building when either his or Barras's elbow "accidentally" smashed a small window. All they wanted to do was escape from the dog, so his young accomplice used his screwdriver to prise open the window before they climbed in. They were not interested in stealing anything by this time, he said.

It was only when they found a door into the hall that they realised they were in a house, he claimed, adding that they had only crossed into a rear room to look for a way out.

Fearon maintained that he did not know how the two silver jugs and a pot got into the holdalls that were later found abandoned in the back room. He would not have stolen them because they were "junk," he said, and suggested that the farmer himself had placed them in the bags after the shooting to justify killing Barras.

When the shooting started, "I was feeling about for a window or a door. I saw what I thought was a torch flashing. I heard Fred say, 'He's got me.'" He said he turned to see an "old man" in the hallway. "I saw another flash and next thing my leg felt numb. I just went mad and ended up looking for somewhere to get out." After going through the window, he crawled away, across a field, passing out twice before reaching a bungalow.

Fearon added that he thought that he had heard eight or nine bangs, but three of them were a lot louder than the others. He came out of the witness box and pointed to his knee, leg, and groin to indicate where he was shot.

Under cross-examination he rejected Mr. Scrivener's suggestion that at least a month before he had been to "case" Bleak House. He accepted that he might have told police that he was alone because he "wanted to take all the responsibility myself – I didn't want people to think: 'Oh, you took that little lad there to be killed.'"

During evidence given about the incident in the orchard several years previously, when Martin fired at the tyres of an intruder's car, it became clear that the offender on that occasion was part of the same criminal set as Fearon and Barras.

The court heard that at the time Martin's gun licence was withdrawn, shortly after the apple orchard incident, he owned a 12-bore side-by-side shotgun, a .410 single-barrelled shotgun, a .22 rifle, and a smaller calibre shot-gun. He initiated an appeal against losing his licence, but did not pursue it. Ms Horwood-Smart said: "The Chief Constable was advised that if pursued the appeal was likely to be successful."

On the second day of the trial the jury heard that the rural community around Emneth, close to Downham Market, was beset by crime. John Spalton, a professional eel-catcher, was the man who was returning from work on the night of the shootings when he saw Fearon bleeding in the lane.

Mr. Spalton told the court: "There was this chap in the middle of the road bent over and looking a bit sorry for himself. He looked a bit depressed and signalled for me to stop. If you know that area, you don't stop unless you know someone." The area, he said, had a terrible reputation for crime. "Everyone there is worried about burglary."

Fearon, he said, was wearing a brown tee-shirt and red and black jeans, "although I soon realised that the red was blood." It occurred to Mr. Spalton that Fearon could have had a fight with someone, and that he could have taken the van off him – "it isn't much but it's what I've got."

He went on: "You don't know what they're up to.

They're either shooting each other or scrapping with each other. I thought, sod that, I'm not standing in the middle of a battle. I'm off. I phoned the police after I heard Tony had shot two of them, just to let them know I was in the vicinity. Then I heard that one of them was dead. You see the people you are up against. If you leave your mate dying in the undergrowth you must be pretty hard."

He described the area as a place where "if things aren't bolted to the ground they walk." Everyone living there needed some sort of protection, "if not a shotgun, a knife, or something under the bed."

Detective Constable Trevor Buxton gave the court details of the three burglars' previous offences. He said Barras, described as a market trader, had been convicted of assaults on police, theft and fraud and was on bail when he was killed. He had been before the courts 28 times and had served time in young offenders' institutions. Fearon had 18 theft offences on his record and had served time for burglaries. Bark had appeared before the court on 52 occasions. His offences included assault causing actual bodily harm and burglary.

Helen Lilley, owner of the Marmion House Hotel at Wisbech, Cambs, where Martin was arrested the day after the shootings, said she had known the farmer for many years. He came to the hotel at 11.30 p.m. on the night of the burglary. She said, "He appeared stressed and said there had been an incident. He came in and said the police would be coming."

In statements to the police which were read out in court Martin said he was woken by the sound of the break-in through a window.

He was aware that there were intruders when he saw a torch beam downstairs. Initially he decided to stay hidden in his bedroom. But he reached for his shotgun when he feared that the intruders would burst into his bedroom. "At that stage, I started to become very frightened, fearful, terrified," the statement said.

"The nightmare of it all was that it was like being in a

horror movie. I was thinking of the previous break-in in May and I wondered if it was the same men. I got the gun because I thought they were coming up the stairs. I thought someone was on the landing.

"I was going to stay in my bedroom but I couldn't stand it any longer. I felt someone was out there and I was not prepared to wait for the unknown." Because he could not wait until someone walked into his bedroom he went downstairs carrying the gun. He was halfway down the stairs when a torch beam swung round and shone in his face. He began firing.

"I discharged it until it was empty, then I ran up the stairs. When I fired the gun I genuinely thought my life was in danger. A torch was pointed at my face and I didn't know what was behind it. I didn't know I had hit anybody. I just thought there was someone in the house."

When he ventured back down the stairs again he could see no one.

In the statements he told police the gun was under his bed and there were cartridges in a bag in his bedroom. "I was actually sleeping with my working clothes on, with my working boots on. This is one of the oddities with me. Most women don't like men who sleep with their boots on. On the other hand it does have advantages."

On Thursday, April 13, the jury were taken on the 54-mile journey to see Bleak House, sharing a coach with Mr. Justice Owen. They walked down the 70-yard long narrow track through the jungle-like garden encroaching upon it, and around the back of the house.

The overgrown grounds at the front of the house were carpeted by daffodils and buttercups. A wheelbarrow just outside the barn contained hogweed plants and a notice had been stuck on it saying, "This is hogweed, do not touch, causes irritation." Inside the barn there were five tractors and Martin's Nissan Bluebird car. Outside the red-brick cottage where the three rottweilers were kept, old farm machinery and wooden pallet boxes were strewn around.

Bleak House and its outbuildings was made an official exhibit in the trial. That meant that from the moment of Martin's arrest on August 21, 1999, until the trial was over in April, 2000, the farm was kept under a 24-hour police guard. For years Martin had been asking in vain for police protection for his home from burglars, a request refused because of cost. Now, after a tragedy had happened and it really no longer mattered, the police were there day and night for eight months at a cost of £140,000 just so that the jury could see it as it was. The police guard was withdrawn immediately after the verdict, leaving Bleak House at the mercy of the potential burglars and arsonists who were threatening it.

Why this expenditure was incurred by the hard-up Norfolk Police for a jury visit was never satisfactorily explained. The lost time at court, the lawyers' fees involved, and the official arrangements, together with the police bill for keeping the house in mothballs for months, probably came to around a quarter of a million pounds of public money, or, according to police reckoning, another 10 or so more police officers for the undermanned Norfolk force. Why was it necessary for judge and jury to make that tedious journey at public expense, and for the police to keep the house under surveillance at such great cost, when it must have been transparently obvious that nothing very much, if anything at all, could be gained by such a visit in helping the jury to come to their decision? Martin was being tried on the issue of what happened in a few seconds on his stairway, in his hall and perhaps in his lounge on the night of August 20 the previous year – he was not, or should not, have been tried on the condition of his house. During the intervening eight months the inside of the house deteriorated, and the untended grounds looked much worse than they did on the night of the murder. If the jury needed to be shown where the staircase and the hall were, it could have been done with diagrams, as is the case in many criminal trials. It is hard to escape the conclusion that the visit was an unnecessary and expensive piece of prosecution propaganda and that as such it had no place in this trial.

Vigorous spring growth was covering the building, including all the roof and the chimney, when the jury inspected it. In summer the foliage is so dense that a detective who went to the house after the shootings told the trial he got to within 15 feet of it before realising it was a house.

The jury entered Bleak House in pairs and wearing yellow hard hats because the condition and fabric inside were considered too hazardous for all 12 to go in together. They took with them the torch which Fearon carried during the botched burglary. With police officers acting as guides, they picked their way across the ground floor, where the bare boards were strewn with cans, books, bottles, and rubble from repair work. Some of them went upstairs, negotiating the staircase where Martin had removed the bottom and top three stairs.

On the fifth day of the trial, Friday. Mr. Scrivener, defending, asked Detective Sergeant Peter Newton in cross-examination, "Is it true that someone has offered £60,000 to have Mr. Martin killed?"

Sgt. Newton replied, "We have had that intelligence. We cannot ignore something like that. We would have been severely criticised if we ignored it."

Mr. Scrivener: "Is it being taken seriously by the police?"

Sgt. Newton: "Yes."

The police, he went on, had opposed bail for Martin – unsuccessfully – for his own protection. While awaiting trial he was staying at an address known only to three or four people. The police officer agreed that because of the contract to kill Martin he might never be able to return to the farmhouse that had been his home for more than 15 years. "He would have to make his own decision whether he would ever return to Bleak House."

Mr. Scrivener: "It has been made clear to Mr. Martin that the police cannot protect him for the rest of his life?"

Sgt. Newton: "That is true."

The court was told that in February, 1999, six months before Barras was shot, about 30 farmers, including Martin, met to launch a crime-stopping initiative called Farm Watch. The idea was that farmers would pass information to each other about the activities of criminals rather than take the law into their own hands. Martin dominated the meeting with his views.

Pig farmer Peter Huggins told the court: "Tony was rather concerned about the number of break-ins he had suffered and the amount of gypsies in the area. He was having more to say than others. He felt it was a waste of time ringing the police.

"He was saying basically that it was time we started taking the law into our own hands."

Mr. Huggins added that there were problems actually contacting the police. Particular problems identified by the farmers at the meeting included incidents of theft and vandalism, and travellers allowing their ponies to graze on their land.

Mr. Huggins told the court he had bumped into Martin in Wisbech a few days before the shootings. He said: "The conversation turned to the crime situation. He asked me whether I had seen any light-fingered pikeys lately.

"It seemed as if he had got the idea that somebody was after him. He had had previous break-ins and he got the feeling that somebody was targeting him. I think he said what anybody would say: 'If I catch them in my place I will blow their heads off.' I have said the same sort of thing myself."

Anthony Bone, director of the Farm Watch project, told the court he had wanted farmers to co-operate with him and the police to combat crime. He said that at the meeting Martin gave the impression that it was a case of looking after yourself. Several farmers also expressed fears that if they had a disagreement with the travelling community "they were likely to burn you out." Mr. Bone added: "There seemed to be extreme worry among the farming community as a whole about what was going on and the inability of the law to deal with it."

Pathologist Dr. Michael Heath, who conducted the post-mortem on Barras, said the dead boy had suffered a fatal wound to the back of his chest which left a hole about two inches round. "It was extensive damage to the chest. He could not have been resuscitated by the medical team." Cuts on Barras's face indicated he had stumbled out of a window before crawling into undergrowth.

Martin went into the witness box to give evidence on his own behalf. He told the court that he was petrified when he realised that Barras and Fearon were in his house.

During his years at Bleak House he said he became more and more convinced that he was a target for burglars. He told the court that not long after moving in he arrived home one night to catch a burglar stuffing a pillowcase with trinkets, which he dropped when Martin chased him.

He said that over the years electrical items, tools and tractor batteries had been stolen from his farm. In March, 1999, a grandfather clock was taken and two months later in another raid he lost a table, a bureau and two chests of drawers. Inevitably he became more and more frustrated by police inaction and police inability to protect him.

He was close to tears on several occasions when the names of members of his family and close friends were mentioned. And he nearly broke down when he recalled that in May the previous year, three months before the shootings, his farmhouse was burgled and photos of his family stolen. On that occasion Windsor chairs he "had grown up in as a child" were stolen. "I was devastated," he said. "It was very depressing."

On the night of the shootings he had been visiting his mother's home. He returned home at 9.30 p.m. and went to bed fully clothed.

"I then heard noises I had never heard before, many different noises. Then I heard voices downstairs. I tried to avoid the situation, telling myself I was imagining the whole thing."

At first he thought the noise was either caused by Bruno, the rottweiler, or by a cat which used to sleep in his room with him.

"I had to get down to reality, that I had been broken into. I lay there for a while, didn't want to move. I couldn't move, then realised I had to move to get up."

He got out of bed and went on to the landing and saw a bright light coming up the stairs. "I became fearful," he said. He went back to his bedroom and expecting the intruders to follow, stood still.

"Then I got this terrific thumping in my body, the beating of my heart. I felt the whole room was like it." Realising he had a gun in the bedroom he decided to pick it up and load it from a bag of cartridges before going out on to the stairs.

Once on the stairs he again saw a light. "It came from the doorway downstairs. It went straight in my face. I was very frightened."

Mr. Scrivener: "Did you fire the gun?"

Martin: "Yes, I did."

Mr. Scrivener: "Did you believe you had hit anyone?"

Martin: "Not like that I didn't."

He did not know how many times he had fired the gun. He fired from the hip and aimed below the light and thought he was firing at the bottom of the doorway. After discharging the gun he went to get a torch from his car. Returning to the house he found it empty, and after that he drove around the farm.

Asked to describe how frightened he was, he told the court: "I had been through all the stages of fear, terrified, petrified, backwards and forwards."

He categorically rejected a suggestion from Ms. Horwood-Smart that he had opened fire "in anger, in retribution – you were shooting to kill or injure very badly."

In her closing speech to the jury Ms. Horwood-Smart said that Martin acted as "jury, judge and executioner" when he shot Barras. "This was not self-defence, it was murder by a man willing to take the law into his own hands," she said.

"All the evidence points to him lying in wait for Barras and Fearon after being woken by his barking dogs. This was a man who was angry, who was shooting to kill. He shot them like rats in a trap.

"He was a man who knew the power, force, and damage that a shotgun can inflict. He had that gun for one particular reason. He had that gun to use, if and when the occasion arose...to shoot any intruder who had the temerity to come in to his property, into his home, on to his land."

Anthony Scrivener said that on the night of the burglary Martin was forced to make desperate decisions. "He had suffered a number of burglaries and had been visited by a number of dangerous people over the years. He didn't want people to burgle his house. The wrong decision could have led him to suffer serious injury or death.

"The issue in this trial is self-defence. Martin knew that an unknown number of people had broken into his dark, isolated house, that night in August. He did not know if they were armed or if they were under the influence of drugs."

The intruders had not been put off by Martin's three rottweilers, said Mr. Scrivener, and were not bothered about him being in the house. "What would you do?" he asked the jury. "Say, 'hold on, chaps, can we discuss this rationally?'" In law, he added, any citizen had the right to kill in self-defence if he believed he was being attacked.

The judge told the jury, "You have to try to ascertain what was in Mr. Martin's mind at the time – what circumstances did he believe he was facing? He has said he believed he might be attacked. Was it reasonable? Should he have shouted out, should he have fired one shot, and so on?"

If they were not sure Martin intended to kill or seriously injure Barras but was inevitably subjecting him to risk of serious harm then they could consider manslaughter. "If he did not act in self-defence and all the sober and reasonable people would realise that he was subjecting Barras to some risk of serious harm, then he is guilty of manslaughter."

After retiring, the jury found Martin not guilty of attempting to murder Fearon, and not guilty of possessing a firearm and ammunition with intent to endanger life – he had already pleaded guilty to possessing a firearm without a certificate. As they returned unanimous verdicts on those charges Fearon's mother, in the public gallery, sobbed: "They can't do that."

The jury were then directed to return majority verdicts on the other two charges. After retiring for more deliberation, their foreman announced that by a majority vote of 10-2 they found Martin guilty of wounding Fearon with intent to cause him bodily harm, and guilty of murdering Barras. From the public gallery, where the Barras family and their supporters had attended the court in large numbers every day, came cries of, "Yes! Yes!" One of Barras's sisters cried out, "I hope you die in jail." Despite these emotional outbursts, Martin remained unmoved.

The verdicts, reached after a retirement that totalled 10 hours, seemed bizarre to more than a few observers. The jury found Martin not guilty of the attempted murder of Fearon but guilty of the murder of Barras. But how could this be, since both men were shot in exactly the same way, and at the same time? Curiously, they also found Martin not guilty of possessing a shotgun with intent to endanger life – yet guilty of murdering Barras with the same shotgun. Why did they have to retire a second time to consider whether Barras was murdered, when Barras was intrinsically a part of the same case, and when all his movements were exactly those of Fearon? Deeply disturbing questions arise out of this: was the guilty verdict in respect of wounding Fearon – returned after the verdict of not guilty to attempting to murder him – the result of those six men and women cowering away from the explosion of travellers' rage in the public gallery? Were the jury in such a state of confusion when they retired that they were no longer certain about what they were doing? We shall examine these possibilities in the next chapter.

Passing three sentences, of life for the murder, 10 years for the wounding, and 12 months for the firearms possession, to run concurrently, Mr. Justice Owen made some observations which seem to suggest that he was at least confused by the verdicts. He said that lawlessness in rural areas had become an issue in the case, and urged Norfolk's Chief Constable to take note of that. Then he said, "It seems to me that this case serves as a dire warning to all burglars who break into the houses of other people.

"The law is that every citizen is entitled to use reasonable force to prevent crime. Burglary is a crime and a householder in his own home may think he is being reasonable but he may not be reasonable and that can have tragic consequences."

How, one wonders, was this case to serve as a dire warning to all burglars, who incidentally, it goes without saying, break into the houses of other people? Surely the only warning the case was sending out was to householders who try to defend themselves in a State where the law has failed them miserably. The warning that was really written in the judge's sentence was: "Try too hard to protect your property while marauders are looting it and we'll jail you for life." To all burglars the signals must have appeared transparently obvious: "No one can get us now, we've got a jury's verdict as proof." This verdict was hardly a "dire warning" – it seemed more like an invitation to burglars to get on with as much burglary as they could.

And what was meant by "a householder in his own home may think he is being reasonable but he may not be reasonable"? Indeed what precisely is meant by the smoke-screen phrase "reasonable force"?

This is a phrase which has been much debated since the trial. Conservative leader William Hague called for an overhaul of the law to give "a strong presumption that in future the State will be on the side of the people who protect their homes and their families against criminals." That would be a move back towards the position before the 1967 Criminal Law Act, which states simply that anyone can use "reasonable force' in the prevention of crime, which includes defending themselves, their families and property. The question of what is "reasonable force" is left entirely to the jury.

But before 1967 the law was much more clearly in favour of the householder. If Martin had been tried before that date, he would probably have gone free.

English common law, as laid down in the legal bible Blackstone in the 18th century, said simply, "If any person attempts to break open a house in the night-time, and shall be killed in such an attempt, the slayer shall be acquitted."

A layman is surely entitled to say that it is astonishing revisionary justice that a man might go free for an act committed in 1966 and yet be jailed for the rest of his life for the same act committed in 1968.

As recently as 1924 the Lord Chief Justice said: "In defence of a man's house, the owner or his family may kill a trespasser who would forcibly dispossess him of it, in the same way as he might, by law, kill in self-defence a man who attacks him personally."

Today, with no specific guidance on dealing with burglars, jurors must try to put themselves in the mind of the householder. People under attack may take defensive action, but must not retaliate in a way out of all proportion to the assault. This is a wholly unfair burden for the jury to carry, for some people might say they would be too terrified to kill a violent intruder, even if they were allowed to do so, while others would say any burglar who breaks into their house does so at his own peril. But today, if the jury decides the level of force is reasonable, and the burglar is killed, they must then decide whether the force used amounts to murder.

Case law has established that to be convicted of murder the defendant need not have intended to kill. He must only have intended to cause really serious harm.

An attempt to define the law on self-defence was last

made in 1970 by Lord Morris in a Privy Council case when he said that a man who is attacked may defend himself but that he could only do "what is reasonably necessary."

Unfortunately, Lord Morris did not go on to define what was reasonably necessary; he left it to the courts to decide in individual cases. But in a case like the Martin case, which hangs on what is reasonable force, it is essential to give the term such strict definition. The law holds that what is reasonable force in one instance of burglary may not be reasonable force in another. In the Martin case reasonable force must be calculated on the basis of what do you do if you are alone, in an isolated house, in the darkness, and two men have broken in, are coming at you up your stairs, possibly armed (there is no way you can find out until they wound or kill you), possibly intent on killing you, at least intent on stealing your valuables and possibly intent on causing you great harm while doing so, all this happening in the darkness...

They are burglars, these men. A burglar by definition is a ruthless man. You have every reason to believe that ruthless men who break into your home in the dead of night are indifferent as to whether you live or die. They have come not once but many times before, ransacking and pillaging your home.

What is your state of mind as you sense them coming towards you in the darkness? Are you calm, or uneasy, or frankly terrified? You would be an extraordinary individual if you were not terrified. You have a gun. You may not be supposed to have a gun, but for the moment that is beside the point. Do you lay it aside and stand up and tackle these possibly armed and probably dangerous intruders in the darkness, because you don't want to risk hurting them with your gun? Of course you do not. You are terrified, and you shoot. This in all the given circumstances is reasonable force. Anything that you could do in your situation which was less than that would not be force at all.

You had a gun which by another anomaly of law you are

not entitled to have even to defend yourself in the horrific situation described here. Even under British law, where the victim of crime scarcely matters when compared to the criminal, your sentence for that cannot be more than 12 months in prison, because that is what the judge thought was right in the Martin case.

After the verdict Peter Tidey, the Chief Crown Prosecutor for Norfolk, had something to say: "Actions such as that taken by Tony Martin cannot be tolerated in a civilised society. When people break the law it is for the law to punish them, not for individuals to take the law into their own hands, whether acting out of revenge or their own individual system of justice."

Mr. Tidey did not say as he could have said, and many may think should have said, that actions taken by Barras, Fearon and Bark could also not be tolerated in a civilised society, nor that when people like them break the law, the law should punish them but does not do so adequately, which is precisely what this case was all about. We shall come across other authorities like Mr. Tidey who were to say things that fitted their particular legal point of view while leaving out the things that did not fit it. And we may come to the conclusion that it is exactly this kind of legal inflexibility, the rigid inability of any law-enforcement authority right up to a Minister of the Crown, to admit that perhaps this case showed that the law is wrong, that it is responsible for all the injustice heaped upon Tony Martin.

Mr. Tidey's view was echoed by Detective Chief Inspector Martin Wright, of Norfolk Police, who headed the murder inquiry. He said: "This country does not have the death penalty for burglary. That sounds very clinical, but I think that is what happened that night in that house." Warning the public not to take the law into their own hands, he said, "This case has been a tragedy from start to finish."

Mrs. Hilary Martin was appalled by the verdict. She said, "This is a horrific thing. It seems like the end of the world. British justice is completely mad. All Tony was doing was defending his own life, limb and property. How right-minded people can leave him to years of deprivation for what he did is totally unfair. He has been put in this position entirely through no fault of his own."

Mrs. Jacqui Leet was gloomy about Martin's future. "Gypsy families look after their own. I think he'll be killed if he goes back to Bleak House." Close to tears, she added, "We all know he shouldn't have taken the young lad's life – but they shouldn't have been there."

Fred Smith, described as representing the National Romany Rights Association, went on TV to make a remark which, if it was not incitement to violence sounded dangerously close to it. "If it was me, I wouldn't just leave him. I'd have to get some type of revenge. I've always been of the opinion it's an eye for an eye."

Meantime, Martin's solicitor, Nick Makin, said an immediate appeal against the murder conviction would be lodged.

The principal claims in the appeal would be that the judge misdirected the jury, that he failed properly to tell the jurors what constituted self-defence and that they should have looked at the question of self-defence from what Martin believed was happening. The appeal would also claim that the judge was wrong in allowing Martin's view on travellers and burglars to be presented to the jury. It would claim too that the judge erred in his summing-up by failing to point out that both prosecution and defence agreed on the most likely sequence of events during the actual shootings.

Another ground in the appeal would allege that "a fair trial was not possible in an atmosphere of intimidation of both witnesses and jury." And a further ground would claim that the jury's verdict "could not be rational" in finding Martin guilty of murdering Barras but not guilty of possessing a shotgun with intent to endanger life.

One of the first things Mr. Makin had to do after the verdict was to arrange, on Martin's orders, for Bleak House to be cleared of all the farmer's possessions. Mr. Makin's associate, Michael Ballinger, said: "The message to burglars is simply, 'Don't even think about it.'"

Richard Portham, spokesman for Martin's local support group, said, "Tony Martin has been sent to prison for a crime committed in terror."

Gavin Ashton, chairman of Martin's local branch of the National Farmer' Union, warned that the verdict could encourage burglary in country areas. "This has done nothing to put off people who initiate rural crime," he said.

But Peter Gammon, of the Police Superintendents' Association, coming back to that word "reasonable," said: "People can take reasonable steps to protect themselves and their property. But it doesn't allow you, confronted with an unknown situation, to blast out with a shotgun in a reckless manner, which clearly happened in this case."

Many Norfolk farmers found it difficult to understand the verdict and the sentence. The case had proved to them that the travelling community's criminal element was a well-drilled organisation, practising an unbridled and sinister reign of underground terror against which Martin was trying to defend his property. Their lawless methods were no better revealed than in their accusation of "cowardice" against Darren Bark for driving off when he realised the burglary was bungled, and their vow to "get him."

It had been reported that one of their "courts" put a £10,000 bounty on his head and that he had to be moved from jail to jail to escape attacks. This stands beside the courtroom information that "unknown criminals" had put a £60,000 bounty on Martin's head (some reports later put it at £40,000). There was no explanation about how on the one hand this kind of fact could be revealed and yet on the other hand how its perpetrators could remain "unknown," but we may assume that these unknown criminals could not be a million miles away from people in the travelling community. If either of these stories were true, or even if they were only partly true, where, one is entitled to ask, were the police while these outrageous monetary propositions were being bounced around to their undoubted knowledge and under their very noses? That is a question that Tony Martin asked. We shall presently see where they were, and it will make woeful reading.

And where were the Nottinghamshire magistrates? For wasn't any decent citizen of that county entitled to ask them, how was it that three young men whose combined ages added up to a mere eighty years and who had chalked up a total of 114 offences including violence, brutality, burglary and thieving – a sustained campaign of terrorising the peaceful English rural folk – were still at large and as free as air in our county?

I put this to Graham Hooper, clerk to the Nottinghamshire justices. He told me: "Magistrates imposing sentence must ensure that the penalties imposed reflect the seriousness of the offences committed. They are not entitled to increase punishment in relation to an offender because it is perceived that, upon release or completion of the sentence, he will present a more significant risk of further offending." In other words, no matter how many burglaries everyone in court knows a prisoner is likely to commit in the future – your house, my house, all 20 million homes in the UK – he can only be sentenced for the burglary for which he has been brought before the court.

Mr. Hooper refused to comment on individual sentences passed on any one of the three offenders in the Bleak House burglary, nor, he added, "was it appropriate for the magistrates to do so." This was unfortunate, because it meant that despite all the public criticism of the magistrates' sentencing policy, there will be no public accountability by the magistrates for the three professional criminals being in the state of freedom that ended in the Martin tragedy.

5

SINISTER GOINGS-ON IN COURT

Enter three travellers. They are Eli Frankham, 36, a 6ft 5in tall, 21 stone bare-knuckle boxer; his nephew Peter Chilton, 23; and a third man related to them.

The three men had gone to the trial of Tony Martin and had sat themselves comfortably in the public gallery. From there, Norfolk Police told Mr. Justice Owen, presiding, they were staring menacingly at the jury.

Because "staring menacingly" from the public gallery of a courtroom is not an indictable offence, there did not seem to be much that anyone could do about it. But the judge issued a sombre warning – not to the three travellers, but to the jury, about not speaking to anyone concerning the case, and seeking help if they thought it necessary.

Outside the court the trio denied trying to intimidate the jury by "putting the evil eye on them." Unfortunately they said a word or two too many. They said they had no connection with Fred Barras, and they were attending the trial only because it looked interesting. Such curiosity, decided *The Mail On Sunday* investigator Daniel Foggo, did not seem to have the ring of truth, so he started digging.

He discovered that Frankham and Chilton *were* related to Barras, through Barras's grandmother, Mary Dolan, 68, who was the third man's great aunt. He also discovered that after Frankham and Chilton had both been charged with an attack on a pub barman, two years previously, and before they were brought to trial, prosecution witnesses were complaining that they were being threatened by unnamed persons.

One witness told Daniel Foggo: "We reported everything to the police, but their response was limited. At one point they put a patrol car outside our home, but that lasted only about three days. We asked for an escort to the trial, but we didn't get one."

Another man, Edward Dolan, was also charged over the pub attack, but the case against him was dropped because he was already serving a three-year prison sentence for another offence by the time the case came to court.

The court was told that the incident, in the Princess Victoria pub in Walpole St. Andrew, four miles away from Tony Martin's farm, was a singularly brutal affair. On July 18, 1997, Frankham, who had been styled as heir to the title of King of the Gypsies, strode into the bar with Peter Chilton, who was then aged 20. They forced the barman, Ian Madder, to the floor and pelted him with beer glasses, splitting open his head. This horrific scene was watched by Mr. Madder's sister Carol, the licensee, and many of her regular customers who were in the bar.

Despite the complaints of the witnesses, on June 26, 1998, Eli Frankham was sentenced to 15 months in jail and Peter Chilton to nine months for violent disorder and unlawful wounding.

Knowing the facts of that case, we can ask, why was it that less than two years later, when they had been let out of jail, these two men turned up in the public gallery at the trial of Tony Martin? Was it out of simple curiosity, as they said, or was there some other purpose in it?

The police, who had all the answers, apparently decided there was some other purpose in it. On April 23 officers armed with batons and CS spray watched Frankham as he tried to enter the court and then ejected him. It seemed that court passes used by Frankham and Chilton were taken from two other travellers.

Turned away by the police, Frankham spoke to reporters. He protested: "It's true I'm a big bloke, but I wasn't trying to intimidate the jury. I went to see the trial because it had been on the telly. I had a legitimate interest in attending, the same as everyone else. I found myself surrounded by no less than 30 officers and they had unclicked their CS canisters ready for action. I had to walk away."

Chilton added, "As soon as we sat down the case was stopped and the lawyers started talking about a bounty on Martin's head. We weren't there five minutes before the jury got sent out. I felt I was being looked at, but then I was looking at other people. I was looking at the jury some of the time, but that's what you do in court, isn't it?"

If the police had any doubts about the presence of the two travellers – and they must have had, or why eject them? – why was the trial allowed to continue when everyone was well aware of what had been happening in the public gallery? The police response was bland: "Two people were told they had to leave the building after stealing passes. They seemed to be there with the intention of causing trouble."

Once again we are left with that uneasy feeling that the show must go on, that come what may someone must go to jail, preferably the softest target, which in this case was the man in the dock.

Norfolk Police knew all about Frankham and Chilton, and they must have known what the trouble was that they claimed the two men were intent on causing. For they did not dispute that witnesses in the 1998 trial of Frankham and Chilton had reported a string of incidents, but insisted: "No formal complaints were made of intimidation. The witnesses all attended court and gave evidence."

What was going on at Tony Martin's trial, in this British court of law? Evidently something sinister, something that the public did not know about. From the outset the case was surrounded by tight security and the jurors were given numbers so that their names would not be revealed. Presumably as a result of what the police had told the judge privately, during the trial he warned jurors that if they were approached about the case they should immediately dial 999.

In my forty years of association with British courts as a journalist, covering some of the most frightening murder cases in the history of crime, I have never heard a judge give that sort of warning to a jury. And indeed, why dial 999? That suggestion would imply that the police from their experience would know that the juror was in immediate and serious danger and would need instant police protection.

Could a jury really be expected to listen to a trial in these circumstances and then deliver a fair verdict? And if the answer to that question is no, then the trial should either have been stopped or there should have been a sufficient number of arrests to remove all possible danger to the jury. But none of these things happened.

So what was going on? Someone asked Peter Tidey, the Chief Crown Prosecutor for Norfolk. You may remember that he was the official who had said in relation to Tony Martin after the verdict, "People who break the law must be punished." He replied: "I'm aware that there was one incident during the trial at which there was communication between the judge and the jury. Precisely what that was about I have no knowledge of at all. If there is a complaint that an offence has been committed then the constabulary is going to have to investigate."

We shall get no help from Mr. Tidey, so let us look elsewhere. The day after Martin's sentence a woman claiming to be one of the six women jurors who tried the case called a local radio station and said she had been threatened. She told staff at Radio Broadland in Norfolk that she felt under pressure to give a guilty verdict because of "possible repercussions" and said the decision would remain with her "for the rest of my life."

The radio caller made her allegations at 7.45 a.m. during a phone-in about the trial when the overwhelming sentiment was in favour of Martin's right to protect himself.

The mystery caller did not go on the air, and on the advice of lawyers Radio Broadland at first declined to make any comment. When they did, they said they had no way of telling whether the woman caller was genuine. "We have no name, no phone number, no way of identifying the person."

Although the conversation was not broadcast, it was later reported to listeners by disc jockey Rob Chandler, who as soon as the call was received handed over the microphone to one of his colleagues and spoke to the caller in private.

Mr. Chandler said: "We have just spoken to one of the jurors and they do not wish to be named or come on air, but we can report some of the things this person said.

"I think the most powerful thing is that the last eight days have changed their life. This person now feels frightened to leave their house. The most poignant thing I think they said was that in Tony Martin's situation they would have done the same thing, opened fire on the intruders and paid the consequences."

The BBC were also reported to have taken a call from the family of a male juror who said members of the jury felt "stared at" by people in the public gallery.

Told of the Radio Broadland call, Martin's solicitors immediately got in touch with the radio station, sensing a situation which, if it were substantiated, would overturn the verdict.

Nick Makin, Martin's solicitor, said: "We don't know if the radio call was a hoax or was genuine and we are doing all we can to ascertain that. If it turns out to be genuine, it is incredible news. We are now asking for any information from any member of the jury who feels that he or she may have been intimidated."

But even before that call, a separate inquiry had started into an attempt at jury nobbling, a specific attempt to influence a juror during the trial.

After the judge's warnings to the jury that they must inform the police if they felt in danger of being coerced, one juror did phone the police. No details were given, but it was thought that the juror was concerned about someone loitering near their house. Some jurors had already mentioned to police that they had been "eyed' by four men as they entered court. Things went from bad to bizarre when Norfolk police then declined to comment on these stories, saying that any claims of jury interference were handled by the Lord Chancellor's Department.

The Guardian, reporting in its issue of Saturday April 22 the story of the alleged woman juror's call to Radio Broadland, said, "It is understood that the juror said she had been warned to convict Martin ... It was reported that she said she had received threats." Phrases like "it is understood" and "it was reported," which do not quote a source are not good journalism, especially when the same report then went on to say, "But yesterday a spokeswoman for the station said the caller had not spoken of being 'intimidated, pressured or nobbled.'" If that spokeswoman was correct, then *The Guardian's* earlier statement in the same report, "It is understood that the juror said she had been warned to convict Martin," must have been incorrect.

Even so, here was a variety of serious allegations any one of which should have been immediately and thoroughly investigated and which collectively were a prima facie case for a miscarriage of justice.

We must remember that all twelve jurors came from Norfolk and were doubtless aware of the background to the case, of the persecution of rural Norfolk folk by burglars and thieves identified with some sections of the travelling community. The woman caller, if she was a jury member, was saying to the radio station that she and other members of the jury were so terrified that they felt they had to find Martin guilty for fear of the consequences to themselves.

The "threats" were probably inferred rather than spoken

outright; none the less there may have been an awareness among the jurors that all was not well. They were told in court that there was a price of £60,000 on Martin's head, they may have known that there was a price of £10,000 on Darren Bark's. They were Fenland people, they would have known from whence these dark threats came. Then they were told by the judge to dial 999 if they felt threatened in any way. They were given numbers, not referred to by their names, in order to mask their identities. There were suggestions of aggressive eye contact with two traveller relatives of one of the victims who were escorted from the court, and another juror apparently so distraught that he or she set alarm bells ringing at sight of someone outside their house. Whether that loiterer was bent on mischief or not is of no account – the juror's reaction was a symptom of the climate of fear that ruled the trial of Tony Martin.

Given all this, with their knowledge of rural Norfolk, where some of them might be living in isolated places, is it any wonder that one woman juror said, "We did not want to be empanelled to try this case"?

Did she know what the *Observer* newspaper alleged it had already found out and reported upon in its issue of April 30? "The harassment and intimidation of witnesses and jurors ... was part of an orchestrated campaign which began just days after the shootings," the newspaper declared.

"Sources within the gypsy community say that friends and supporters of Barras used contacts to find out information on the whereabouts of potential witnesses as well as of Martin himself.

"The travellers were so successful in their attempts to track him down that Martin's bail was revoked after just a week and he was returned to prison 'for his own safety.' It was the activities of this same group of supporters that led to Martin's first court appearance being transferred at the eleventh hour from King's Lynn to Norwich magistrates court."

Under gypsy custom, the newspaper went on, all attacks must be avenged. "Although gypsy society has its own system of settling disputes, with punishments ranking from fines to banishments, little is known about the kind of judgements made where the perpetrators of crimes are non-gypsies."

It was believed that a gypsy court, known as a *kris*, had already passed a death sentence on Martin. According to the *Observer*: "'The case was never expected to come to court,'" said one source. 'There were those who believed it would have been sorted out long before.'" The newspaper report went on: "Once it was clear that the trial would go ahead, the supporters of Barras are alleged to have set about intimidating potential witnesses."

It is not therefore with the benefit of hindsight that anyone should ask why the Norfolk law-enforcement authorities, with all their expertise about these disturbing local conditions and their inability to cope with them, allowed this case to be tried in Norfolk by a Norfolk jury? Would it not have been much fairer to Tony Martin to have removed it to the Old Bailey, where it would have been heard by a jury of Home Counties residents, far removed from fears of travellers' threats, real or imagined?

Over the weekend following the verdict, the Crown Prosecution Service was shown a transcript of the radio station interview. It was their job to decide whether any unlawful pressure was placed on any of the jurors.

The CPS spokesman said, "We are not an investigating body and from that point of view, were there any investigation to be carried out, that would have to be by the police."

The CPS report and the transcript was then sent back to officers of Norwich Crown Court who, in turn, handed the evidence of the juror's complaint to the Lord Chancellor's office.

The Lord Chancellor's office is directly responsible for the running of the courts. If it believed there was evidence of unfair pressure or wrongdoing, its next logical move in this bureaucratic game of murder would be to ask the police to investigate.

This apparently did not happen. Instead, two months later, we learned of the entry into the case of yet another law-enforcement agency – the Appeal Court. After the police, the CPS, the Lord Chancellor's office and Norwich Crown Court officers, it was learned that the Appeal Court would become the fifth tribunal of the people to weigh in with a view.

The Lord Chancellor's Department announced that Appeal judges would now decide "whether and in what terms" jurors could be questioned over the claims of intimidation. This would mean that they might have to go into the witness box to answer questions about the reasons for their guilty verdict.

Professor Michael Zander, a law specialist at the London School of Economics, thought that the only similar example of such a happening had been in the civil courts. "There was a civil case once when all 12 members of the jury swore affidavits that they had said 'Yes' when they meant 'No.' But that was done by the litigant's solicitor. In this [the Martin] case the court itself would authorise the process. That as far as I know would be breaking new ground."

In fact it had happened before in a criminal case, and in recent times. This was when jurors were quizzed in the infamous "ouija board case" at Hove Crown Court in 1994, when it emerged that four members of a jury had used a makeshift ouija board to "get in touch" with the two murder victims in the case during a drunken session in a hotel. The Appeal Court decided to direct that affidavits be taken from all the jurors, after which a retrial was ordered.

On June 19, 2000, three Appeal Court judges sat at a hearing in London and, on an application by Mr. Anthony Scrivener, representing Martin, they agreed that the Martin case jurors should be written to and asked to answer certain questions "as soon as possible." They ruled that the questions addressed to the jurors should not be disclosed by the Press.

Lord Justice Rose told Mr. Scrivener that the court was sympathetic to the idea that they should be asked one or two questions. But, he added, "We are not sympathetic to them being set an exam paper."

Mr. Scrivener agreed that there should be a limit to the number of questions the jurors could be asked.

Lord Justice Rose said: "Then one will know whether there is, or may be, something in the point. If there is, it may be necessary to take further steps. If there isn't, it can be forgotten.

"The court directs that the registrar writes to the jurors, emphasising that we don't want to know anything in relation to their deliberations on the verdict. The registrar will also stress that the writing of a letter doesn't imply any wrongdoing on their part. The jurors will be asked to answer these questions as soon as possible."

This again was mildly disturbing. No one had suggested before this that the jury were guilty of any "wrongdoing." The only possible wrong they could have done would have been to return a verdict against their conscience because they felt pressurised. The mere suggestion that it must be emphasised that they had done nothing wrong could suggest that they might have done something wrong – that is, returned a verdict they knew was not the true one. This might immediately put a juror answering written questions in a position where he or she felt compelled to defend their decision, even though they had some doubts about it. So here was yet another stage at which the trial verdict should have been thrown out as unsafe, and Tony Martin set free.

In review, what had happened here was that a defendant was sentenced to spend the rest of his life in prison after being found guilty as a result of something which was undefined in law – reasonable self-defence; by a jury which now had a large and very unusual question mark over its head, who were about to be asked secret questions by judges (who would first of all go off for the long law summer vacation) about matters associated with their verdict; and all this at a trial where, as we are about to see, possibly a dozen witnesses were too scared to give evidence on the defendant's behalf.

How just was any of this? Does it have any similitude with the British idea of fair play? How could any criminal trial have been surrounded by such a dubious set of circumstances in a country that prides itself that its legal system is beyond reproach?

For all that, the Appeal Court move was doggedly hailed by Martin's legal team as an important victory on the road to a full appeal. Application for leave to appeal, we had once been told, was scheduled for as early as May. Then it was June. Then it was July, with the full appeal by September. In fact, leave to appeal was granted at the end of July and the appeal was finally scheduled for October. But October came and went, and so did Christmas, 2000, and there was still no date fixed for the appeal.

Martin's solicitor Nick Makin said: "We welcome the fact that the Court of Appeal has instructed that the case will be listed for appeal once they have received responses to these questions. I feared the judges would say no to the questioning because it would create a precedent. Tony is frustrated at being inside prison and desperately wants to get out and resume his life. We are confident this will happen."

The Appeal Court could handle the jurors; what it could not handle was the witnesses. On April 27 an unnamed "farming friend and neighbour of Tony Martin" told *The Times* that he had declined to give evidence for the defence in the murder trial because he was threatened not once but four times. One man told him: "We are coming for you."

The potential witness said that rural life in that part of Norfolk was dominated by fear of crime, and added, "You are at the mercy of the travellers and local villains."

Nick Makin then announced that up to ten defence witnesses who would have supported Martin's fear of rural crime declined to appear in court "because of the atmosphere of intimidation." Several of them dropped out when told they could not give their evidence from behind screens, in order to cover their identity. Martin's lawyers wanted some of these witnesses to give evidence which could counter the prosecution claim that Martin had an exaggerated fear of crime and a vendetta against gypsies.

"We had a substantial number of witnesses decline because they feared they would be hurt or their property torched," Mr. Makin said. "One of the witnesses who did appear only agreed to do so after we made special security arrangements.

"Quite frankly, it illustrates the fact that the area around Tony Martin's home was like a frontier town – a lawless place where the police didn't go. People were, and still are, genuinely afraid."

After Martin's arrest a would-be witness said that he had received death threats. On one occasion a car drew up near his home and a man shouted, "We'll deal with Tony Martin first and we're coming for you next."

The ten refusals were in fact 12, because two other potential witnesses mentioned in a report in the *Eastern Daily Press* the previous day were dealt with by Michael Ballinger, Mr. Makin's colleague. According to the Norfolk newspaper those two potential witnesses had fired shotguns at intruders they found on their farms and had suffered previous burglaries, much as Martin had.

Both men lived near Martin's home at Emneth. One who gave a witness statement said he had received death threats from travellers after the fatal shooting of Barras. The other would be prepared to give evidence at Norwich Crown Court only if he were allowed to do so in camera. This, as one would begin to expect about anything enhancing the case for Martin's defence, was not permitted. In this trial the police, on behalf of the prosecution, were allowed to spend a quarter of a million pounds keeping Bleak House under wraps for a jury visit that had no particular merit, yet up to 12 defence witnesses failed to give evidence because no one could find the money to protect them.

Witnesses and jurors were not alone in being threatened. A report on April 21 claimed that there had been anonymous calls to burn down Bleak House as well as threats against the life of Darren Bark, the getaway driver. The report did not say to whom the calls were made. The threats were being made against Bark apparently for leaving the scene after the shooting.

John Kendall, a solicitor representing Bark, who was in prison for the Bleak House burglary, said in a statement on April 20: "Darren would like to extend his most sincere apologies to the Barras family for his involvement in this tragic incident."

Nick Makin soon had his hands full again after the Radio Broadland phone-in by an alleged juror. A few days after Martin's sentence, a member of the jury – one of the six women members – told him that officials at Norwich Crown Court had attempted to block jurors from passing on information about intimidation. She said that court staff had tried to dissuade her from contacting Martin's lawyers with vital information that could be central to his appeal.

This allegation followed unsubstantiated reports that court staff had discouraged witnesses and jurors from passing intimidation evidence to the defence team. Mr. Makin said, "Had this woman juror not been so persistent they would not have found us. We are now considering lodging a formal complaint with the Lord Chancellor about the court staff."

Mr. Makin would not comment on what the juror said because Martin's formal application for leave to appeal was lodged only the day previously and he did not want to jeopardise the juror's evidence. Then another juror surfaced to allege intimidation during the trial – this time a male juror.

Roger Farrant, a producer with Norwich-based TV station BBC *Look East*, said their sister broadcaster, Radio Norfolk, had received an anonymous call from someone who knew a juror. Mr. Farrant had then made contact with a relative of the juror.

Mr. Farrant said: "We talked about how the jury member had said that a number of jurors felt intimidated because they were aware they were being stared at in court. He felt particularly anxious as he was leaving the court each day. He felt vulnerable.

"He wished he had been able to listen to the evidence from behind a screen so that nobody in the court would be able to identify him, and his relative said that was the view of several members of the jury."

Told about this on Wednesday, April 26, the Lord Chancellor's Department, said that it had yet to receive a complaint from a juror.

Three days later yet another statement from the Lord Chancellor's Department announced that the court manager of Norwich Crown Court, Mike Haw, had issued a letter to all staff the previous week in response to allegations, instructing that details of defence solicitors must be given to inquirers. The spokeswoman confirmed that Mr. Haw had spoken to a juror following the trial and said, "He also took the opportunity to explain to the juror that anything that was said within the jury room cannot be disclosed to a third party. If the juror wanted the solicitor's details they were given them."

It should be noted, however, that not everyone was ready to believe that the jury was intimidated. Tony Joynes, Fred Barras's uncle, speaking on Radio 4's Today programme, asked, "How could anyone intimidate them? There was only his mother and his two sisters there, and his dad. How could they have intimidated that juror? I don't believe it." Mr. Joynes appeared to have missed the point, though, that the intimidation claims centred not on close family members but on other members of the travelling community who turned up in the public gallery.

An anonymous letter in the *Eastern Daily Press* from a man claiming to be the father of one of the jurors, also insisted that the jury and the witnesses were not intimidated. The letter-writer complained of media bias in favour of Martin which had led to the public being ill-informed.

"I understand the wave of emotion that has swept the country in support of Tony Martin's defence of his property," he wrote. "I too whole-heartedly agree that it is every man's right to do so. However, the more serious issue was not the defence of his property, but whether he was acting in defence of his life when he killed Fred Barras. That is what the jury had to decide from the facts put before them."

But the real issue here is not a fifty-fifty discussion on whether or not the jury were intimidated by an outside party or parties – the real issue is whether there was the slightest shadow of suspicion that intimidation was present. Two jurors had apparently felt that they were intimidated and the inference that must be considered is that they may have voted in a certain way inside the jury room in order to avoid the consequences of intimidation. The only correct thing to have done at this point was to release Martin pending an inquiry in public, for if we are jailing people for life in a situation where there is even the faintest suspicion that the jury are in fear of reprisals we are practising banana republic law that is rotten to the core.

It goes without saying, too, that anyone suspected of attempting to intimidate the jury should have been immediately arrested and charged.

None of these things happened. Nick Makin continued quite properly in the circumstances to speak with great circumspection. Even so, the public were left believing it was at least possible that Martin did not have a fair trial.

Indeed, this was to be one of the claims in Martin's appeal – that he could not receive a fair trial because of the "atmosphere of intimidation of both witnesses and the jury." The main ground for the appeal, however, was to be that the judge "substantially misdirected" the jury during his summing-up.

Michael Ballinger, of the defence team, said that after

the trial there had been "an aggressive atmosphere" throughout the nine days and added, "We are concerned about the jury being nobbled. There was something that happened during the trial that was a cause for concern. Unfortunately we cannot discuss details of that at the moment.

"We cannot be sure at this stage if the call to the radio station really was from a juror but we would certainly not be surprised if it was because of what we were aware of during the case. I would appeal to any juror who felt intimidated to make their concern known to Norwich Crown Court."

Then in mid-August came another disturbing revelation, again from *The Mail On Sunday's* investigator Daniel Foggo. In his report Foggo said that two jurors who had replied to the Court of Appeal's questionnaire claimed that they were not comfortable during the trial.

One juror had confirmed that he was "intimidated" by the heavy gypsy presence in court and felt "relieved" by the guilty verdict, a comment suggesting he may even have altered his verdict to appease Barras's supporters. Another juror had reported that she felt "generally afraid" by the highly-charged atmosphere in the courtroom.

None of these reports would give any satisfaction to any member of the public who believed that British justice is inviolable. Jurors in apparent fear, an aggressive atmosphere in court, complaints about eye-to-eye contact, court passes being passed on to people "intent on making trouble"...how could any of this be equated with incorruptible justice? And if troublemakers with criminal records were identified by the police within the precincts of the court as people possibly intent on intimidation – or perhaps even attempting to pervert the course of justice, for which theoretically the maximum penalty is life imprisonment – why were they not locked up, instead of just being told to leave the building? I have seen people brought before the judge and sent to the cells for far less cases of contempt than this. Why not in this case? No answers were provided to any of these questions, giving rise to the feeling that a very nasty smell hung over the trial of Tony Martin, and it persists to this day.

6

ONLY GOD HAD A CLEAR VIEW

The first year of the new millennium appeared to have left summer back somewhere in the last century; it was cold and a wrestling wind was blowing when I set out for The Fens at the beginning of July. A few miles outside Wisbech I stopped for refreshment and remarked to the innkeeper, "I have come to follow the footsteps of one of your local heroes."

"Who's that, then?"

"Tony Martin."

Silence. The only words he said to me after that were, "Good day."

Wisbech. After the travellers settled there, conditions in the town deteriorated to such an extent that the council set up special sites for them, providing concrete walkways and proper sanitary facilities, persuading them to colonise squalid and dangerous housing estates. As a result private property prices plummeted, and householders particularly felt betrayed.

Now, despite the imposing confidence of its Georgian buildings, there is an air of desperation about the place, as if the community has been abandoned by the outside world. On the streets there is a visible dysfunctional underclass; the civility of the town's architecturally attractive public spaces has given way to an atmosphere of transgression and menace, of violence and crime with an edge of savagery.

The pathology has extended across three decades – years in which a network of camaraderie spread out from the travellers settled in Newark northwards to the travellers settled in Wisbech and The Fens. Along the way there are occasional caravan groups at the roadside, many of them belonging to this community of people who once made a vital contribution to the nation's economy and became embittered when there was no work for them after the market declined.

After Wisbech I headed north into Norfolk. A map of Fenland shows The Fens reaching across the three counties of Norfolk, Cambridgeshire and Lincolnshire and disappearing into The Wash. But the most northerly Fenmen, those who are north of Wisbech and therefore closest to The Wash, dispute this. They are the Marsh people, and they claim to be different from the Fen people. Different in what way? They fall silent at the question. Pressed, they will only say, "Different." Tony Martin was a Fenman, for Emneth is south of Wisbech. He wasn't a Marshman. He was *different*.

I asked, is this something to do with snobbery, something perhaps to do with the proximity of Sandringham, the royal estate up in the north of Norfolk, an hour's drive from Wisbech, in the country of the Marshmen? I asked this because I noticed that the grassy side of the main road leading to the royal estate is built up along its edge, and then ditched, and eventually I discovered why: it is to prevent travellers parking their caravans there. So is it because they may be allowed to cause havoc to the residents around Wisbech, but they must not be allowed to cause any trouble to the royal family?

Silence to that, too.

There is one perceptible difference in the terrain between the Marsh and The Fens – a difference in soil. After the last ice age, as the ice melted the land around, The Wash sank and at times was covered by the sea. The sea left a large swamp area inland of The Wash, with a brown silt ridge close to the seashore. When this land was drained, the silt soil provided, and still provides for the Marshmen, the most fertile agricultural land in England. Over the years, further inland, dying vegetation turned to peat, which is the rich soil of The Fens.

The Fens are all about drainage, reclamation work that began in the 17th century under the auspices of Dutch engineers. They dug long straight "cuts," or drains, to take the water to the sea. But as the land was drained the peat shrank, allowing the water back in. Then wind pumps, and, in the 19th century, steam pumps, allowed man to control The Fens again. It is not total control – the land continues to shrink and continues to sink.

Fenmen, Marshmen, call them what you will, for if there is a difference it is indistinguishable to the casual observer, there is no doubt that the environment has fashioned them. Living under their big sky on their pancake-surface, chilled by the wind from the North Sea amid the potatoes and sugar beet that stretch like battalions to a horizon so uninterrupted and distant that it hurts your eyes just looking, their battle with the water they almost stand upon has created them distinct creatures of Nature. They are resourceful, tenacious, reserved, thoughtful. They speak their minds openly, for there are no hills or mountains to bound their thoughts. They have all the moods that water has. Such a man is Tony Martin.

The first thing that strikes you when you finally see Bleak House for the first time is that it is there at all. The approach, from the Outwell road, is down an unmarked, overgrown track. The first building that comes into sight, described as the cottage, is on the right. It is almost covered in verdure, and is much more of a house than a cottage. Beyond it and on the same side is a shed, and opposite both these buildings, on the left side of the track, are open fields. At this point anyone approaching the cottage could be forgiven for thinking that this was Bleak House, and if that were so they would not go on any further.

But Bleak House is farther down the track, lost in dense undergrowth. In front of it is a small patch of short grass that must once have been a lawn. Giant shrubs reach up on both sides seeming to clutch at the sky, forming the shape of a long building. Inside this dense foliage, hogweed and ivy growing rampant out of fertile Fenland peat, is Tony Martin's red brick, slate roofed farmhouse.

Two months after the verdict on Martin, friends and neighbours along the border dividing Norfolk and Cambridgeshire who evidently did not share the view of *The Times* newspaper that he was "a racist with a squalid lifestyle and unbalanced personality," arranged for the 14 windows and four doors of Bleak House to be sealed by half-inch thick steel plates bolted to the brickwork. The aim was to keep out intruders and frustrate criminals who were threatening to burn down the place. The steelwork, which cost Martin's friends £6,000, is welded and layered and fixed in such a way that machinery would have to be used to open it up. The plates are battleship grey and stand out sombrely among the green. The brickwork can hardly be seen, so that the plates seem as if they are floating in the air. Martin's friends then used heavy equipment to dig deep holes around the grounds – traps into which the unwary intruder might fall. One of them said: "These are the lengths you have to go to in the Fens to defend a friend's property."

Behind one of the steel plates, in the lounge of the house, is the final place of confrontation of two individuals with deep prejudices. When Barras and Martin came face to face it was inevitable there would be a tragic outcome. Martin, with his detestation of burglars, was goaded into violence against the criminals he believed were persecuting him. Barras, at 16, thought he was beyond the law, and viewed householders like Martin as easy pickings.

Outside, at the front elevation, it is possible for the first time to get an impression of the size of the house, which must once have been a grand place. On the ground beneath one of the windows covered by its steel plate are the remnants of the window frame through which the frenzied Brendan Fearon leapt, followed by Barras in his death throes. Fearon ran through the jungle beyond the small clearing; Barras staggering and unable to see in the dark, fell into the undergrowth on the left of the clearing and died there.

A track, like a jungle path, leads round to the left side of the house, so difficult to negotiate that it is almost dark. This leads to a clearing at the back of the house. On the far side of the building at this point there is a double garage.

A sealed back door and the garage face into a sort of clearing, strewn with rubble which includes an abandoned black Rover 2000 saloon car with a registration plate from 30 years ago, with its boot lid gaping wide open. The car belonged to Martin's father Wally, who died in the early Eighties. In the undergrowth around the sealed door there is a broken lavatory pan and an old and rusting refrigerator.

The clearing narrows on to another track through less dense undergrowth. Rounding a bend in this track a lane comes into view, fifty yards ahead. There are some low sheds on the left and beyond them a mound of earth and rubble. On the mound are two discarded police cones and a discarded rubber glove, used for taking away evidence. This man branded as eccentric for his untidiness had his house turned over by policemen who could not be bothered to take away their rubbish.

The track arrives at a gate, or what passes for one. There is no sign on the gate, no indication that it may lead back to a house. The gate has one horizontal bar and one diagonal and it swings on indolent hinges. It is not fastened because there are no fastenings. Beyond the gate is the narrow, quiet, lane, hardly used.

Around Bleak House there is silence everywhere, broken only occasionally by the sudden rising of a startled partridge in the tall trees that close in on all sides of the building coffined in greenery. The place is at once beautiful and sad, made beautiful by the weeping yellow rays of sunlight that somehow find their way through the foliage, and sad by the proximity of death.

Several things become clear. First, the house is so buried in its jungle that it is almost worth paying £100 to someone who can tell you how to find it. Whoever gave that information to Darren Bark must have sat down and sketched a detailed diagram and written copious notes; the burglary must therefore have been premeditated and well-planned.

Second, the 70 miles journey from Newark in Nottinghamshire to Emneth Hungate would also have had to be described in detail; the route is torturous.

Third, when Fearon and Barras left the getaway car on the Outwell road, they could not have mistaken the cottage, which they saw first, for the farmhouse, because there are clearly two properties and the burglars who informed them would have made the distinction clear.

Fearon said that he first heard the three rottweilers growling in the cottage. In fact, two dogs were in the cottage and one was roaming free. With only the light of a torch to guide them, when they heard the dogs growling they could not have intended, as Fearon said they intended, abandoning the burglary. If that idea had crossed their minds, the obvious thing would have been to retrace their steps fifty or so yards to the safety of the Outwell road. They must therefore have checked that the two rottweilers were secure in the cottage before they went on through the undergrowth, in the knowledge that there was a house to be burgled there.

They came to a window, smashed the panes and used a screwdriver to prise it open. At this point there was absolutely no possibility even in the darkness that they could have mistaken Bleak House for an outbuilding, as Fearon suggested. Even by torchlight they would have seen the front door, which, without its hard grey steel plate, is an impressive piece of carved wood. They were inside the house for ten minutes, in the hall and in the lounge for sure, and they had probably traversed the entire length of the house in their search for plunder before Martin's arrival on the staircase.

Martin was to say that after hearing the sounds of the break-in, the smashing of glass and the screwdriver prising open a downstairs window, he did not know what to do. He was petrified. He lay in terror for some moments, got up, then went back to retrieve his gun from under the bed. He found some ammunition in the dark and loaded the gun, probably with five cartridges. He then crept across his bedroom and negotiated his way to the staircase.

By now the two burglars were well inside the house. They had begun to fill their holdalls and were examining a piece of furniture when Martin confronted them. Everything they did, from the moment they left Darren Bark in the car until they broke into Bleak House and were surprised there, points to a ruthless, calculated burglary, planned meticulously and only failing at the last moment through the efforts of the homeowner to defend himself and his property.

Beyond the undergrowth that surrounds the house are Martin's orchards, lines of well matured fruit trees. In the spring Helen Lilley arranged for the neat meadow grass between the trees to be cut. Already, though, one healthy-looking tree had gone over on to its side. Other friends had vowed to try to keep the farm running in its owner's absence – this looked at first glance to be a formidable task.

Is it possible to hypothesise exactly what happened when Martin confronted the two burglars in Bleak House that August night? Some things are beyond dispute – that Fearon was shot in the legs and the groin, Barras in the back. We have Martin's word for it that as he stood on the stairs of his home he was suddenly blinded by a torch turned on to his face from the hall. At that point he fired, below the line of the torch beam. Time and again he insisted that he fired only from the stairway and from nowhere else. He did not know what he was firing at, or if he had hit any intruders. He did not say he heard Barras cry out – it was only Fearon who said he heard his accomplice. The two men had already put silver objects into one of their holdalls so that in the split second between when they were disturbed and before the first shot was fired they might have been reluctant to abandon their loot.

The man in charge of the murder investigation, Detective Chief Inspector Martin Wright, did not believe Martin's story that he fired from the stairs. "His version of the events differs from common sense," said Inspector Wright. "There was shotgun residue in the lounge of Bleak House, and to put it in fairly basic terms he would have had to shoot round corners three times to have achieved the injuries on Fearon and Barras that were consistent with his account."

What the police officer was attempting to establish was that Martin advanced down the stairs more in anger, less in self-defence, and pursued the burglars through the house firing his shotgun – in other words, he had passed the boundaries of what law-enforcement authorities believe is how far you can go to defend yourself reasonably against burglars in your house in the dark.

This argument is unsatisfactory on two contradictory counts. First, it does not take into account that a man driven by naked terror may advance with his gun without any awareness of what he is doing and may not remember what he has done, such may be the state of his fear-crazed mind. This is a phenomenon well known among terrified soldiers in battle. Sometimes it is even known as bravery. Are we really to define the difference between freedom and a life sentence in prison on the basis of a few panic-stricken steps taken by a man in such circumstances? In the cocktail of extreme emotions that Martin must have experienced in those few seconds is it really possible to sort out the difference between anger and stark fear, and to say that one and not the other must have been uppermost in his mind and that therefore he is a murderer?

If Martin was in a state of terror he must have been acting in self-defence, but how does shot residue in the lounge prove that he was *not* in a state of terror? It would be hardly surprising if there were shot residue all over his house. After all, he was firing in fear in the dark – what was he supposed to do, wait to see if the fire was returned before either dying from returned fire or himself firing again? If he walked around his house blazing away in the darkness all that proves was that he must have been beside himself with fear. The police view only makes sense if we can say that in a totally irrational situation we would all act perfectly rationally.

Second, the police view not only differs from Martin's, it also differs from Fearon's. The burglar said at Martin's trial that he first saw Martin, "an old man," standing in the hallway. But when police took him to Bleak House before the trial they videoed him there, and on that film he said that after seeing the flash from Martin's gun, "I heard a noise and my leg felt numb. I saw an old man *standing on the stairway*. I just went mad. My arm went through a window. I just ripped it out." Whichever version was right hardly matters, for in all the circumstances Fearon in his panic could be forgiven for being confused about where Martin was standing. What matters is that he did not say he was aware of being pursued around three corners into the lounge by a blazing gun, or that he was running through the house trying to escape from continuous gunfire.

Chief Inspector Wright also found it "somewhat disturbing" that when Martin was asked to account for his illegally held shotgun he replied, "I woke up one morning, went to my car and the gun was lying on the back seat with a note from a well-wisher to the effect that the weapon would come in useful."

Chief Inspector Wright commented, "To be frank, that isn't the type of thing that happens very often, is it?"

Of course it isn't. It is the type of thing someone might say in order to protect someone else from whom they have obtained an illegal object. All it seems to say about Martin is reinforcement of the view that the police were failing to protect rural Norfolk people who were therefore obliged, legally or illegally, to obtain weapons to protect themselves.

Chief Inspector Wright enlarged on his case against Martin in a Channel 4 documentary screened in September – his second TV appearance on the Bleak House tragedy. This appearance was trailed a fortnight earlier by the media, claiming that his comments would infuriate Martin's supporters. One of these comments, almost too bizarre to be true, was reported thus: "There's a lot of prejudice against travellers and burglars." Those of us who are prejudiced against burglars waited breathlessly for confirmation of this as the programme came on, but in fact it turned out that Inspector Wright never said that at all. Or at least he never said it in the screened version.

Even so, he revealed himself as a man with a disarming way with words. Barras, regularly referred to as Fred, was "at the lower end of criminality – the lower end, petty thief type of level." The chief inspector told us that "this was probably Fred's venture into another division of criminality." The thief caught stealing apples from Martin's orchard before the Bleak House tragedy was three times referred to as a "male," and once as "this gentleman" – what he was apparently doing in Martin's orchard was not stealing but "taking apples." The journey made by the three burglars from Newark to Emneth was "this venture." It could not have been the inspector's intention to attract an impression that he was on the side of the burglars and against Martin, but this kind of phraseology speaks for itself; it also suggests a police attitude that is bound to upset the citizens they are supposed to protect.

In the media preview to the programme we were told that Inspector Wright was going to say other things which on the night he did not say. One report said: "He will tell viewers, 'I don't think the public heard the full facts. And those who did aren't bothered. They do not like burglars.

'After the trial many individuals in the media told me they thought it was the right result, but when the papers came out the other line was taken. I think they printed what people wanted to hear.

'I am proud of the investigation, which was professional, objective and fair [the investigation was led by Chief Inspector Wright], and I was pleased with the result. I wasn't happy the police were put on trial. We want to serve the public and I'm not comfortable when we are criticised unfairly. I myself received 40 to 50 threatening letters.'"

In the TV programme the inspector dwelt heavily on the prosecution's ballistic evidence at the trial, which is supposed to have condemned Martin as guilty beyond doubt. He insisted that the actual "crime scene" was the lounge. He had come to the "sinister conclusion" that Martin must have advanced down the stairs because the cartridges extracted from the right barrel of his shotgun were found in the lounge, between a point near the door at the foot of the stairs and the lounge fireplace, indicating as we have seen that he could not have been firing from the stairs unless he was firing around corners. Inspector Wright conceded that it was pitch black but said nothing at this point about Martin's obvious state of panic; in fact, he told us, "it must have been terrifying for them [the burglars] in the pitch dark."

Because blood and tissue were found by the window at the exit point and by the back door the police were "fairly comfortable" that the burglars were beginning to exit from the house when in the complete darkness "they were hit in the legs." Nothing here about a terrified victim still having enough sense to aim low so that he did not kill, to fire at the legs, or where in the darkness he thought the legs would be; nothing here to suggest that Martin had no idea how many of them there were, whether they were staying or fleeing, or whether they were armed and likely to kill him. "It was pitch black but he knew there were burglars in there," said Inspector Wright – words that surely speak as well as any others in Martin's defence.

"He [Martin] by his own admission didn't hear any shouting, no cries of pain," Mr. Wright continued. But why should he have done? As we have already seen, there is no reliable evidence that there was any shouting or cries of pain in Bleak House that night. The only person who says he heard Barras scream out was Fearon, and he did not even say that until nearly 24 hours after the event. The words, "He's got me! I'm sorry! Mum!" if they were said at all were only heard by Fearon and it is unreliable testimony because first, Fearon has been established as an untruthful person and second, if he had indeed heard those horrifying words it is almost inconceivable that he would not have stopped, turned, and done something to help his obviously stricken teenage friend, if not at that moment, then certainly at the moment of his arrest within the next hour.

Fearon told the court that the silver objects placed in his swag bag found in the lounge at Bleak House must have been put there by Martin after the shooting. There is no way of proving whether that is right or wrong, apart from the fact that the balance of probability is against it having happened like that. If Martin did not place the objects in the bag, then Fearon's intention in saying that he did must have been to make matters better for himself, and correspondingly worse for Martin. Suppose Fearon also invented Barras's dying words, with the same object – to make matters worse for Martin (but not realising at that time that it might actually make matters worse for himself)? There is no way of proving whether that is right or wrong, either. It comes down simply to this: should we believe Fearon? The question is rhetorical, because Fearon has changed his story; he is not a man who regards the truth as sacrosanct. That is why there is no reliable evidence that there was any other sound in Bleak House that night other than the firing of Martin's gun and the ripping out of the window.

Were there any redeeming features that might have given the vulnerable homeowner some cheer? We learned that Martin had told the police about his May, 1999, burglary. "That has resulted in someone being charged and is awaiting trial," Chief Inspector Wright said. Martin reported the burglary within hours of its happening, but there was no comment on why it had so far taken one year and four months for that defendant to come to court, during which time Martin, the victim, had been arrested, tried and sentenced. The defendant surfaced finally at Norwich Crown Court on November 24. His name was Christopher Webster, 41, of Ellistown, Leicester. He denied conspiracy to burgle but his plea of guilty to handling property stolen from Tony Martin was accepted. The court heard that Webster recommended to Darren Bark that Martin's farmhouse was "a good place to burgle"—more evidence of the criminal fraternity's conspiracy to rob and terrorise Martin. Webster was jailed for 14 months. The burglars in this case were never charged.

Despite one protestation to the contrary, it was hard to believe that this police officer had any sympathy for Martin. "It [burglary] is a most despicable type of property crime, you know. But that's a different subject altogether, you know." He cited two instances of the farmer's behaviour which he did not appear to like. In one he recalled the trial evidence of a witness who said Martin had driven around at night without lights on his vehicle looking for travellers who he thought had stolen a milk float. In the other instance, "Martin's own admission is that he lay all night by his barn waiting for someone to come who he thought was burgling his barns." These episodes, according to Chief Inspector Wright, indicated that "there does seem to be a track record of Mr. Martin actually sorting things out for himself, you know."

It was left inevitably for a friend of Martin identified only as Paul to point out yet again that people were in fear of burglars "because the police are unable to control the situation." Paul added, "I've shot at undesirables," reinforcing what we all knew – that Norfolk had degenerated into a county so ill-served by its law-enforcement agencies that its rural homeowners were compelled to take the law into their own hands.

The question whether the police should be involved in

this sort of television programme, especially with an appeal pending, might have occurred to some viewers when Chief Inspector Wright, remarking upon the rubble-strewn floors of Martin's home, said: "Bleak House must have looked to the burglars like a derelict house. There could be no substitute for seeing the unique nature of how Mr. Martin lived."

An observation merely, or a criticism? Certainly a touch of criticism might be read into it. Certainly too a great deal had been made of the way Martin lived, and the anti-Martin camp's stance has always been that because he did not live like other people he was suspect. This is a dangerous way to think. We were told several times after the trial that Norfolk Police were upset by press and public criticism of their part in Martin's arrest, trial and conviction, but it cannot be any part of the duty of the police to appear in a television entertainment programme in order to try to redress the balance in their favour.

Nor should a police officer be giving voice to the sort of dismissive reductionism made by Chief Inspector Wright in this unfortunate programme: "He [Martin] wasn't threatened [sic]. He didn't shout a warning. He didn't fire a warning shot. He effectively went up to these people and shot them. It's as simply as that."

It wasn't as simply as that and it wasn't like that at all.

In Wisbech in July it was suggested to me by supporters of Tony Martin that Barras was mortally wounded as he stooped to pick up his holdall with its contents of plunder after the first shot was fired. If that were true he might have received the fatal shot in his back that was intended for his legs – in other words, Martin, despite his state of terror, was firing low, as he maintained that he was all along. When someone is firing low, their intention, as everyone knows, is not to kill. It would have been natural for Barras on hearing the first shot to have turned away, receiving the shotgun pellets in the back. The suggestion that he was deliberately shot in the back is difficult to support when it is remembered that all this was happening in the dark, and that the man with the gun was, according to his own testimony, "petrified." No August night light filtered into Bleak House; outside the dense foliage would have made the exterior pitch black, ensuring that inside there was no light at all, except for Fearon's torch.

It is clear from Martin's next action – that he drove round his farm looking for burglars – that he had no idea he had hit anyone. Even if Barras did cry out, "He's got me!" and Martin heard that cry, since there was almost immediately no trace of the burglars Martin had no reason to think that Barras was dead or even seriously wounded. The reason why he next went to Redmoor, his mother's house in Elm, in a state of alarm and confusion, and left the gun there was, fairly obviously, because he knew that he had used an unlicensed and illegal gun to defend himself, and for that he was going to be in trouble with the police.

Not a word of this suggests premeditated murder. That Martin spoke violently about burglars in the months before the fatal shooting is, as we will continue to see, fairly commonplace among victims of burglary. That he "booby-trapped" his house to defend himself against burglars has been argued as an indication of vengefulness – it might just as easily be argued as an indication of common sense. Martin lived alone, isolated, half a mile from the nearest house. He wanted only peace and quietness. He was deliberately targeted as easy pickings by thieves and violent men living in another county in another part of England, 70 miles away. He suspected as much; he knew they would come again and even told the police they would come again. He knew he would receive no protection from the police. Why should he not have booby-trapped his house in all these circumstances?

He kept a gun – but so do huge numbers of Norfolk farmers. Get close to them in a pub and they will soon admit that the weapon is as much for self-defence as anything else. He kept rottweilers – so do huge number of Norfolk farmers. In fact, *all* the Norfolk farmers I spoke to while researching this book kept fierce dogs. And they were not keeping them as pets. Not one of them had any confidence at all in the county police to protect them from violent nocturnal marauders.

In the months leading up to the shootings at Bleak House Martin was doing exactly what most other Norfolk farmers would have done in identical circumstances. The reason was simple: they had lost all confidence in the police to protect them. The known facts about the shooting itself offer absolutely no evidence that Martin shot to kill, or even to seriously wound.

The last argument I have heard employed by those who remain unconvinced is that this was a case tried by a British jury which, having heard all the facts, decided Martin must be guilty. That argument presupposes that juries are faultless. During the past decade a number of important jury decisions have been overturned either on appeal or on subsequent inquiry, and considerable sums of public money have been paid out to victims of wrong decisions made, for whatever reason, by juries. The argument that suggests the jury has the clearest view and therefore must be right is unrealistic and deeply flawed.

In *Waterland* children ask the Fenland lock-keeper: "Why are the Fens flat?" And the lock-keeper's face takes on a wondering and vexed expression and he says, "Why are the Fens flat? So God has a clear view."

On the night of August 20, 1999, when Tony Martin got out of bed and gunned down the 16-year-old burglar, only God had a clear view.

7

'I COULD HARDLY BREATHE
FROM FEAR...'

The verdict of the six men and six women provoked an
angry reaction from millions of people, and it was
greeted with horror by Martin's many supporters across
the country. The reaction was in sharp contrast with the
mood of optimism which had pervaded the defence team
when Martin arrived in court on the last day of the trial,
when a court official passed over a bundle of letters of support to add to the hundreds he had received every day.

People in Emneth shook their heads in disbelief. A
woman who moved to the village from Watford the previous December, said, "The thefts round here are terrible.
You cannot leave your lawnmower out. There is a large
travelling community here and I hate to feel this way
towards them because we are left-wing, but cars and lorries are stolen. We have been surprised at the crime level –
it's just so senseless."

Another resident who did not want to be named, said: "I
have a lot of these travellers near me and I have had a lot
of burglaries. I'm very sorry that the farmer has been
treated in this way. Like many other people I could have
been in the same situation. If I had a gun I might have
fired off a warning shot, and since my aim is hopeless I
might have made a similar mistake."

Malcolm Starr said: "I'm absolutely devastated by the outcome and to be quite honest I think the whole country will be genuinely gobsmacked. If burglars were put away for longer then they would not have been there and they would not have been shot."

Sir Michael Lakin, Bart, of Cirencester, was equally disturbed by the outcome of the case. For most of his adult life he had lived abroad, frequently in times of criminal turbulence. "I attribute my survival in rural areas to a well-stocked armoury," he declared. "While burglary, rape and murder were routine problems for less well-protected neighbours, I was left unharmed. A couple of warning shots will deter all but the most enthusiastic criminal."

Sir Michael believed that the Government was guilty of "crass stupidity" in its attempts to disarm the people. "It has shown itself to be incapable of protecting the rural community, but denies it the right to do so itself. Responsible citizens should be encouraged to own shotguns for their own defence, and should show their outrage at not being able to do so at the ballot box."

David Owen, of West Kirby, Wirral, wrote to the *Sunday Telegraph* on April 30: "The first duty of any state is to protect its citizens from harm. States have evolved from local arrangements whereby a strong man would offer protection to neighbours in return for tithes. Our State has gradually abdicated from this responsibility and transferred it on to the law-abiding citizen, who is increasingly treated like a criminal because of the actions of a minority, yet prevailed upon to protect himself despite having already paid the State to do it for him.

"This is a tacit admission by the State that it is no longer able to perform its primary function, yet the citizen who takes unilateral action when attacked is punished for its (the State's) failure.

"Not only has the State failed Tony Martin by failing to restrain a known active criminal, but by giving liberty to Fred Barras in the certain knowledge that he would re-offend, it also failed him."

Martin was taken to Bullingdon Prison, near Bicester, Oxfordshire, and placed in the hospital wing "for his own safety" – a phrase which means that besides being unable to control their burgeoning population of burglars, British law-enforcement agencies are unable to control the men they put in jail.

Bullingdon houses 700 prisoners, including murderers and rapists. Security is tight and there is a strict regime, as befits a prison holding violent and dangerous men. The experience might initially have been too much for many strong men, but Martin showed that he could cope. He passed his first days there listening to the radio, reading the newspapers and watching television. He was allowed to move around and go to the day room.

He said, "I've been told that some prisoners have been shouting rude things at me, but I haven't heard them. The only appalling thing is that they wouldn't let me bring my Teddy Bear. They seem to think it could be stuffed full of drugs. Otherwise I'm nowhere near as frightened of my life now as I was when I was living in Bleak House."

He added: "I believe I was right to stand up to those men who broke into my home. I killed him and I'm sorry I did – but in the same circumstances I would do the same again. I don't think I had any alternative. It was me or them."

He challenged other householders to ask themselves what they would do if they awoke one night to find criminals looting their home.

"What happened to me happens to other people all the time," he said. "It even happened to George Harrison [the former Beatle] who spent a fortune securing his house. Someone still gets in. A lot of people have told me they would do the same as me. Of course, what people say they'll do, and what they actually do when it comes down to it, is very different."

Pictures of Martin taken while he was being held in the prison's hospital wing, showed that stress was turning his thinning hair almost silver. A prisoner said, "It's pretty tough for him in here – quite a few villains and especially the gypsies have got it in for him. But the officers try to make things as painless as possible for him. They can't understand why he is under lock and key with all the rest of the scum in this place."

Martin told Malcolm Starr, visiting him in Bullingdon Prison in late April, that he was "absolutely astonished" he was found guilty. Mr. Starr said, "Tony is angry that a jury could convict him." Martin was particularly surprised at the jury's verdict because he regarded the summing-up by the judge as favourable.

"He felt the jurors were completely confused," said Mr. Starr, who first met Martin four years previously when the two men joined a satirical campaign to have the police station at Wisbech knocked down and turned into a car park because a car park would be of more use.

He said Martin was in good spirits, buoyed by letters of support from all over the country and the backing he was getting from prison officers and even from other prisoners.

While the two men were talking to Martin a woman visiting her husband in the prison approached the farmer, shook his hand, and said, "You shouldn't be in here." Mr. Starr added, "All the prison officers I spoke to said they would make sure they looked after him. But I, and least of all Tony, cannot lose sight of the fact that this man has had his freedom taken away. Prison is a terrible place for him.

"He is occupying his time by trying to reply to all the letters he has had. But he is finding it difficult to get hold of writing paper, envelopes and pens. He likes Basildon Bond and if anyone out there can send him some, I'm sure he would appreciate it."

But in an emotional conversation with Max Clifford, Martin said, "I took the ultimate stand against criminals and now I'm forced to live with them. Many of them hate me. I'm not one of them – they see me as a toff, a member of the establishment. It goes against everything they stand for."

The next time Mr. Starr returned to visit Martin at

Bullingdon he found his friend's prison conditions had changed. With the customary insensitivity that most of the public authorities involved had shown throughout the case he had been given a new cell-mate: a burglar.

The irony wasn't lost on him, Mr. Starr reported. "A burglar isn't his ideal choice for a room-mate and some may say it's rubbing salt into the wound. However, he knows he has to get along with the man. I think they are doing so after a fashion, although they accuse each other of being awkward at times."

On this visit he found Martin depressed. His friend was missing the annual blossoming of the wild flowers in a meadow at his home.

Mr. Starr reported: "There is practically no garden at Bullingdon Prison apart from a strip of lawn and he yearns to see his favourite 20ft laburnum tree and delphiniums at his home. But some of his friends are sending him photographs of the flowers in his garden.

"He has had more than a thousand letters and cards of support and they really do cheer him up. He cannot understand though what he is doing in jail and I had to reassure him that neither can 95 per cent of the British public."

A somewhat different account of Martin in prison was presented in a new report a month after the verdict. It was described as coming from a prison source – which could have been a prison officer or, more probably, a recently released inmate. It said: "They've put him on the same landing as two gypsies. He's very lonely and is obviously aware he is a target."

According to this source, Martin spent 20 hours a day lying on the metal bunk in his 10 ft by 8 ft cell. "Every time I've seen him he's just been lying on his bunk looking at the ceiling. The TV's been switched off and he hasn't been reading.

"Initially he went from cell to cell introducing himself, but that didn't go down too well. No one wants to know him. People don't want to associate with him in case he gets done over.

"He still looks like a farmer in his prison clothes. He either wears purple tracksuit trousers and a grey top, or blue jeans and a white striped shirt.

"He has a huge chip on his shoulder. The only sign of remorse he is showing is that he's inside. Even the prison officers dislike him because he expects to be looked after better than any other inmate. Unless he changes his attitude he'll fall foul of somebody."

Martin, according to this source, was on the first floor, the upper of two landings, in the jail's E-wing which houses vulnerable prisoners – including sex offenders and bullying victims – and inmates rewarded for good behaviour.

His cell was above a kitchen and communal area with pool, table tennis and bar football tables where prisoners are allowed to gather every night.

The long hours of inactivity and strict confinement were said to be proving especially tough for a farmer used to the outdoor life. Describing his 24-hour routine, the report said that after 8 p.m. he was locked in his cell but had control of his own lights. At 8 a.m. the cell was unlocked so that he could collect a bacon and eggs fried breakfast and a cup of tea from the kitchen downstairs. Prisoners eat the meal back in their cells and are given five tea bags and milk sachets for the day.

At 9 a.m. prisoners with jobs went to work while the others were locked in the cells. They were allowed out briefly to fill a flask with hot water. At 11 a.m. Martin was allowed to stroll around the exercise yard for an hour.

At 1 p.m. prisoners were let out to collect a set lunch – typically fish and chips and an apple – from the kitchen which again they had to eat alone in their own locked cells. At 4 p.m. they were allowed out to fill their flasks again. Then at 5 p.m. the cells were unlocked for them to eat a cooked supper – often lasagne or roast chicken and apple pie or rice pudding – in their own or a friend's cell on the unit.

After supper inmates were allowed to roam freely during "association time" when they could make phone calls or play games and chat together until lock-up around 8 p.m.

Those who are working in the jail are paid £10 a week but jobless prisoners, like Martin, get £2. 50. He was also allowed to spend £10 a week of his personal cash (he arrived at the prison with £1,000 of his own money) on extra food, tobacco, stamps and phone cards.

The report from Bullingdon said Martin was initially given a single room in the prison's health centre. The centre is staffed mainly by contract nurses and the more relaxed regime is regarded as the jail's "soft option." But he lost the privilege after he phoned a newspaper.

During his early days at Bullingdon Martin wrote a moving letter to his 86-year-old mother which gives the lie to some reporters' descriptions of him as "a very unpleasant character." It said:

"Dear mother, I do not want you to worry – that will not do you any good. You must realise there are terrible things happening to people every day all over the world.

"I have always used that as a tool to fortify myself against other terrible happenings and I am not aggrieved and extremely strong.

"I know people are appalled out there and in fact the people who work in my new house [his prison] are all very sad and surprised.

"I have never held high hopes in the eight months because to fall from there is a long drop.

"I did become very hopeful during the trial especially after what the judge said. But we'll never know why the jury came to the decision they have.

"They found me not guilty initially on some of the charges. They did not find me guilty unanimously, so we ended up with a 10 to 2 verdict – I can't explain it as it would take too long and I don't fully understand it myself.

"Some who know may explain it to you – but I feel Tony Scrivener [his barrister] did his best and is a nice man. I feel I should have said more in my own defence, who knows?

"I am disappointed I brought a bear with me [a reference to taking one of his Teddy Bears to prison] but they will not let me have it.

"It is a lovely time of the year and you must continue to enjoy your life. I realise I am most fortunate.

"I am a very happy man because I have found a safe house for my dogs, which I felt was paramount not to let them down. I am happy they are in the best of hands.

"As I speak farmers are being murdered in Rhodesia [Zimbabwe], people are starving in Africa which is now different to Belsen considering we are able to feed them especially with our over production of food.

"I see a man in his early thirties, whose marriage has gone wrong, killed himself and his two children. So you see things are not so bad. I do feel for you as we all can't realise what has happened – events have overtaken us.

"I have had many letters from good people over the last eight months and know I will get another avalanche soon. You see letters do give me great fortitude. I am sure you will meet many people who will talk about me in the future.

"I have some wonderful photographs of my dogs – I have always loved my dogs and ended up being over fond of Daniel, who has had a few problems in the kennels.

"I feel he is now mending and is in normal hands and well loved. I wonder if they miss me?

"Who knows? I suspect as long as they have plenty of attention they will take to anyone. I will finish now as I want to get this letter off to you as quickly as possible.

"My best wishes to Aunt Joan, my favourite aunt.

"My best wishes – your ever loving son Tony."

Hilary Martin, who was being comforted by her son Robin, described the letter as "quiet and humble." What surprised her, she said, was the lack of anger in it. "I'm beginning to pull myself together now and I feel I've got to be strong to help him," she said.

She had not been able to see him since he was sentenced,

"because there is so much going on with the legal aspect of it, the lawyers are going like bats out of Hades," and because she was in poor health.

She said she was determined to fight for her son. "Poor Tony. A man's liberty is at stake. He's not mentally very strong. He must feel terrible because he is not the sort of person to be shut away. He did all his own farmwork and liked to be in the open air. I do accept that it is a tragedy that a young man's life has been taken, but it is not Tony's fault.

"The young lad should have been looked after by his own mum, not be 70 miles away from his home. Why do they blame Tony for something they have caused? He was merely defending himself against thieves and vagabonds. They are evil. If he had not acted as he did they would have kicked his head in. The worst thing about the verdict is that everyone was telling him he'd get off.

"I'm disgusted about the way it was presented in court that Tony had booby-trapped his house. That's rubbish. He was a terrified man. He was in a state of fear and when he shot the gun was not quite stable.

"I feel terrible, but I'm also very angry. I'm going to chivvy everyone up. I always have to do things myself."

A revealing interview with Martin was published in the *Daily Mail* on April 29 after their reporter Angela Levin became the first journalist to speak to him in prison by telephone. He told her that the reason why he shot at the intruders in Bleak House that night was "a combination of instinct, self-defence and absolute fear.

"I didn't intend to kill anyone. I didn't think about shooting anyone in the back, legs or anywhere else. I didn't actually see anyone at all. I was terrified. My mind went blank and my actions were purely spontaneous."

Ms. Levin described Martin's voice as "modulated, with each word precisely and carefully pronounced. Despite the occasional flash of irritability, he sounded calm and self-possessed." She thought this was partly because the enormity of his life sentence had not yet sunk in, partly because he felt buoyed up by the tidal wave of public support.

Martin told her: "I usually sleep with my clothes on, because the house is cold, but also because I'm lazy. I know I'm only going to put the same things on the next day and it saves time.

"It also stops me worrying if the dogs jump all over me. I certainly wasn't lying in wait for anyone. It's also rubbish to say that I hate gypsies. I don't hate anyone. The only thing I hate is being terrorised.

"Just as I was thinking about going to sleep, I heard a car drive up outside. I thought whoever it was would circle around, perhaps get out and wander about a bit just to wind me up and then, because they knew I was at home, go away. It had happened before, but this time it was different. They stayed.

"Suddenly a feeling of absolute terror swept over me. It was hard to think straight. It came to me that I couldn't just stay where I was. I must do something. It was pitch black. I could feel someone's presence. I could hardly breathe from fear...

"When you are faced with something like that, it's like being on the edge of a precipice. If you do nothing you risk being pushed over the edge and getting killed. If you choose to turn around and face things, you have to fight back. It's a natural instinct and what seems to be happening now is that laws are being created to go against man's natural instinct."

Describing the years of burglaries he had endured, Martin said he started to feel particularly fearful in 1994, after the apple orchard incident.

"Only someone who has been robbed could understand just how violated and dirty it makes you feel. I became increasingly despondent, depressed and even suicidal. Although people describe me as a loner, I'm not really. I just don't like mixing with people when I feel moody or low.

"I was also worried about leaving the house in case I was robbed when I was out. Gradually my anxieties turned to pure terror. I was regularly threatened. I'd be working on my own farm and strangers would come down my driveway shouting, swearing and generally threatening me."

Angela Levin had little doubt that the attempted burglary was the final straw for "this frightened man at the end of his tether." He was, she said, a man who, despite a certain eccentric bravado, had become increasingly scared of the regular stream of tearaways who seemed to delight in threatening a middle-aged bachelor of failing strength.

If you have any doubts about that view, listen to the phrases of this victim of serial burglary..."Suddenly a feeling of absolute terror swept over me...It was pitch black...I could feel someone's presence...I could hardly breathe from fear " – then remember that in this state of stark terror in the darkness as his house was about to be ravaged and his life perhaps put at peril, he acted instinctively and was sent to prison for the rest of his life for it.

Peter Cadbury, the chocolate tycoon who has endured almost a dozen burglaries at his home in rural Hampshire and is an active supporter of householders' rights to defend themselves, donated £1,000 to the Free Martin Campaign. The 82-year-old millionaire said, "I think the whole thing is utterly astonishing. This verdict gives criminals the licence to rape, murder and mug householders in their home. It's all quite awful. All householders must be allowed to protect their homes if necessary."

Mr. Cadbury said that he had recently had dinner with a number of senior police officers. "I asked them, 'What would you do if I injured a man who had broken into my house in the middle of the night?' And they told me that no matter what the circumstances, they would charge me. One of them added, 'You wouldn't need to worry, because a British jury would almost certainly acquit you.' He was quite cynical about it." As a matter of fact, both items of advice offered by these particular senior police officers were wrong.

Others also stumped up cash in protest at the Martin verdict. A retired banker was so outraged by it that he phoned *The Sun* newspaper and declared he had pledged £50,000, a third of his entire capital, to help fund the farmer's appeal. He bellowed down the phone, "Get this man out of jail now. Tony Martin should not be behind bars. It is a disgrace."

But while the Victims of Crime Trust said Martin's conviction was another example of making criminals out of crime victims, John Wadham, of the civil rights group Liberty, said householders should use only minimum force to protect their property. "The right to life, even of criminals, must be respected."

That was also a view held by Gill Marshall-Andrews, chairwoman of the anti-firearms campaigning group Gun Control Network – created in the wake of the Dunblane tragedy.

She said, "All the evidence shows that you are six times more likely to be involved in a gun incident if you keep guns in your house. In other words, someone in your family is much more likely to be shot if you insist on having firearms to hand, whatever your reason. The hallmark of a civilised society is one in which people hand over the right of self-defence to the State."

Which inevitably invites the rejoinder: the hallmark of a civilised society is also one in which the State performs that job properly. If it fails, it has no other option but to hand that right back to the people.

In his prison cell, Brendan Fearon appeared to have a Pauline experience. He set down his feelings about what happened at Bleak House and sent them in the form of a letter to his local newspaper, the *Newark Advertiser*. Prisoners sometimes do this in the hope that it will reveal a brighter image of themselves – it rarely works. In the case of Fearon, who was described in the media as "a petty crook," and by DCI Wright as "a professional criminal," it only served to reveal him as naive.

He now claimed that Barras was taken along only because the teenager badgered them. Fearon saw Barras on the day of the burglary outside a shop with 20 other boys. He decided to take Barras with him to stop him getting into trouble with the other teenagers.

"They appeared to have been drinking which I do not approve of as it will only lead to mischief," he wrote.

"The driver picked us up and off we went. I didn't know where we were going as I had never heard of Bleak House before. When we got there I told Fred to stay in the car. I was walking towards the 'empty' house and when I was about 500 yards from it I stopped.

"It was then that I noticed Fred was there. I told him off and demanded that he go back to the car."

Then, he said, they were attacked by the three rottweiler dogs and climbed inside Bleak House to escape. They hung around inside for about 10 minutes before the house was lit up by a blast from Martin's gun.

"We both went mad with pain and panic and tried desperately to get out of there."

After describing his escape, Fearon wrote, "Acknowledgement of causing the death of a little boy shames me and whatever I say or do will not bring him back now. This keeps my eyes wet at night and my head hung in shame by day. I feel my stupidity has gone too far.

"To this day, I regret taking him as he would still be alive today. I wish it could have been me instead of Fred."

He wanted everyone to know that Tony Martin acted excessively by shooting at them. "I also think Martin was a timebomb waiting to go off. Don't get me wrong. I do think an individual has a right to protect his property to a degree.

"But I don't think I would have done what Tony Martin did. To fire that often seemed excessive. For all he knew we could have had some innocent reason to be there."

Soon after the sentence, during the growing campaign to win Martin's freedom, members of the burglary gang's families were asked for their comments. The farmer received some faint support and sympathy from two unlikely sources – from Barras's grandmother, 68-year-old Mary Dolan, and from Fearon's father, Joe Fearon.

Mary Dolan said, "I never wanted him to get life. I didn't want to see another life destroyed." Although she thought the sentence was wrong, she thought the farmer had to be punished for killing her grandson. Some of her sympathy seemed to evaporate as she went on, "He has destroyed all our lives. It was murder and they have done him for murder. You can't shoot people like that."

Joe Fearon, who during several interviews maintained an admirably dignified stance, was more positive. He thought justice had been done for his son. "A 16-year-old boy lost his life over a bit of silver. It is such a waste. I feel sorry for Martin. It was his house, his home, and they should never have been there. He was protecting his property."

He said his son still awoke during the night imagining Fred's screams as he was shot. "Brendan's lucky he wasn't killed. He's in jail but he's recovering from his injuries and we'll have him back one day. Fred is never coming back."

Fearon's mother, Glenis, said she had "mixed feelings" for Martin. "They shouldn't have been there," she said. "But he shouldn't have kept shooting. I know what Ellen Barras is going through."

Meanwhile, in another letter from Bullingdon Prison, Martin again rejected the prosecution's claim that he hated travellers. He said he had once let a traveller who was being hounded by other farmers in the Emneth area use his land.

He claimed he was on good terms with the gypsy community. "I have known plenty of travellers since the 1960s and I've drunk tea with them outside their caravans." He said that when he raised this point with his defence team they did not want to know.

In a later interview he added, "The worst thing I've done is actually to live in my own house. I should have got out. I can't live there any more because of the number of burglaries and attacks I've suffered."

George Hoyles, the Spalding magistrate, does not believe that Martin should have got away with the shooting, but thinks there were good grounds for a manslaughter verdict. Mr. Hoyles would have been satisfied with a term of imprisonment.

"He lived alone, and that probably acted against him," Mr. Hoyles told me. "Most farmers around here are married. A problem shared is a problem halved, a problem not shared is a problem doubled. We've all been burgled around here. It's something you learn to live with. I report incidents to the police and I make sure they log each crime that happens on my property, so that the crime is reported. But they don't do anything and there isn't anything else I can do about it in my position."

Mr. Hoyles has watched travellers illegally coursing hares on his land and has had his car rammed by them. He keeps a rottweiler, two Jack Russells, geese (the species that saved ancient Rome from invasion), and guinea fowl, which are also extremely noisy when alarmed, simply in the interest of self-defence.

In Wisbech the mood was not nearly so philosophical. A 40-year-old builder who preferred to be nameless, talked about the rampant crime. He said, "The whole town is screaming out for help and we ain't getting any. The police do nothing. People are too scared to go to court." Pointing to a livid scar on the side of his head, he said, "This came from a run-in with the travellers three months ago, back in January. We were in the Spread Eagle, and one of them smashed my wife in the face. I went over to her and three of his traveller friends jumped on top of me. I had a glass smashed over my head.

"I said to the police, can you guarantee my safety if I take this to court? They said no. I asked one of the travellers if he could identify who hit me and he said, 'I can't tell you that. I've got kids.'

"The pub landlord tried to take it to court and he got threats. He locked the front door and they smashed the window and walked in through that. Everyone's living in fear. The pub we're standing in now has been shotgunned – the travellers blew the windows out with a shotgun and then came in and smashed the bar with a baseball bat. That was because the landlord refused to serve them."

The landlady of another pub said, "My husband and I have no comment. Running the business we do, we can't afford to."

The woman who was punched in the face said, "The police won't go after the travellers. If they go to the sites they just tell them that the man they're looking for has moved on. Everyone lives in terror that they'll come round to your house. Tony Martin was right to shoot the two that came to his farm."

A 50-year-old man said, "I admire Tony Martin. I'd have done exactly the same thing, but worse. I'd have made sure I shot them both. A man's home is supposed to be his castle, so why should they rob him? I know Tony Martin, I've drunk with him. He's a lovely man. God help them if they came round to my place.

"I'm ex-army, I've been in situations where you have to shoot. Believe you me, you go by instinct. You say halt, they don't halt, you fire. You should not be condemned for your instinct. Tony Martin is innocent. He deserves a medal. It's about time justice opened its eyes to the situation."

A young man said, "Travellers can be scary. A lot of people really hate them. They just go around stealing things. They don't talk like normal people – they talk differently. They've got their own codes, they just sound like idiots."

A factory supervisor said, "In Alabama or Tennessee Tony Martin would have been elected mayor."

And a taxi driver who said he would not normally pick up passengers from five of the seven pubs in the town centre, commented, "I've never come across a place like Wisbech in my life. It's a horrible place. I now live seven miles outside town to get away from the crime. The only crime the police in this area seem to be interested in is motorists. I've had a parking ticket at one o'clock in the morning when there's a fight going on round the corner."

Wisbech purred with delight, though, when Home Office Minister Charles Clarke announced that the town was to receive some government money to help it reduce its alarming burglary figures. The cash was allocated in the second round of bidding from the government's £50 million Reducing Burglary Initiative Fund.

A bid for some desperately needed cash was put in before the Martin trial by the Fenland Crime and Disorder Burglary Task Group. Applicants were allowed to bid up to £100 for each domestic burglary and attempted burglary and the amount awarded to the Fenland team, £17,000, was the maximum permitted. Three areas of Wisbech had suffered well over the national average of burglaries – 54 per 1,000 households for the last three years – and this was the basis for the bid. But the latest figures appeared to show that in the previous 12 months there had been a reduction of 44 per cent in the number of houses being broken into in Fenland. If that good story appears to militate against Martin's initiative in defending himself against burglary, a note of caution needs to be sounded: these are crime statistics and, as we shall see, compilers of crime statistics do not always want to spoil a good story for the sake of the truth.

Trevor Bracken, a supervisor for Fenland's Crime Reduction Unit, said: "Despite the recent successes we are having, this money will be used to reduce the figures still further. Hopefully though, these [latest] figures will reassure the people of Wisbech that the chances of their house being broken into aren't as great as they perceive.

"The big problem we have in Wisbech particularly is the fear of crime and the reality is that it isn't that bad. But people are convinced it is everywhere."

How does one spend £17,000 of taxpayers' money to deter burglars? Some of it was already earmarked to fit new locks, house alarms and technical security equipment alongside a campaign to raise the awareness of home security.

Malcolm Starr said he could not criticise the £17,000 windfall, but the cash could not make up for the response of the local police to requests for help. "You can't buy enthusiasm," he said.

8

WHAT THE PAPERS SAID

Should Tony Martin be locked up for life?" That was the question headlined in *The Sun* newspaper, whose sales, in excess of more than four million copies a day, are greater than any other national newspaper in the land, immediately after the verdict. Readers were invited to phone in at 10p a call. A few days after the question was asked, *The Sun* reported that its first wave of calls from respondents numbered a staggering 189,556 – of whom 183,342 thought the verdict and sentence were wrong.

In the next few days the number of callers steadily rose to around 270,000 – by any stretch of the imagination an astonishing reaction to a courtroom trial. This news was conveyed to Martin in Bullingdon Prison. He said, "This is the sort of support that keeps me going. Ordinary people out there know I am not a murderer."

The Sun's readers insisting that Martin should not have got life outnumbered those who agreed with the sentence by nearly twenty-five to one. Only 10,800 out of the total of 270,000 thought the sentence was justified.

According to David Yelland, the newspaper's Editor, the reason was simple and heartfelt. "They don't feel safe and they don't know what they would do themselves if a burglar came into their house. They don't think Martin is a hero. A lot of readers don't like him but wonder if the police would be there to protect them. They used to feel they were."

One caller, an 82-year-old woman pensioner who the newspaper refused to name in order to protect her identity, said that she was so scared of burglars that she took an illegal pump-action shotgun – the same kind of shotgun that Tony Martin had — to bed with her. She had an alsatian dog to guard her, and kept her mobile phone at her bedside in case intruders cut her phoneline. Frail, and only five feet tall, she lived alone in a village in the South of England where she has been burgled four times.

She said, "I'm telling you now, if anyone comes into this house again they're not going out alive."

Her first and most horrific burglary was 13 years ago when two men burst into her house, tied her up with wire and threatened her with a shotgun and a machete. She said, "They tried to steal my diamonds and warned me they'd shoot me if I called for help. It was terrifying."

She told the newspaper that she was now so frightened of being attacked in her home that she stayed awake all night, only feeling safe enough to go to sleep at dawn. She usually woke some time in the afternoon to relive the whole nightmare experience all over again. As a result she had lost two stone with worry over the past year and now weighed only seven stone.

She also said that she hated leaving her house because she was frightened of running into intruders when she got back. Like Tony Martin, she had turned her house into a fortress with double and triple locks weighing down the front and back doors, and bars masking the windows.

"I really am afraid to go to bed at night," she said. "I'd shoot anyone who tried to break in now. What choice have I got? They'd never get out of my house alive – they shouldn't be here in the first place. My son is begging me to move somewhere safer but I don't see why I should be driven out of my home by criminals. They've already robbed me of my sleep.

"I won't give up my home to these people. But it seems

we are fighting a losing battle and no one wants to send in reinforcements. We have a lot of gypsies around here and I'm sure they're behind a lot of the crime."

The old lady's predicament was put to Norman Brennan, a police officer who heads the support group Victims of Crime. The law, he said, stated clearly that shotguns should be kept locked away.

He added, "I don't support what this lady is doing but I understand why she is doing it. Legally she's wrong – but morally, how many people wouldn't do the same thing? Her actions really are a terrible indictment of the British criminal justice system."

Some of the other callers among the colossal number who condemned the sentence had some interesting comments. Father of three Michael Carey, of Bermondsey, London, asked fellow protesters to march on Downing Street. He said, "There are so many people feeling angry about this."

Dr. Stanley Robinson, of Stafford, called Martin's conviction "a gross miscarriage of justice." He insisted, "Any right-thinking person would feel the same."

Martin Morley, who runs a Leicester scaffolding company, said, "The injustice of the verdict is the only topic of conversation at the moment."

Drinkers in Forest Gate, East London, were raising cash for Martin's freedom campaign. John Cullen, landlord of the Forest Glen pub, said, "We've already got around £1,400 in less than a week. All my customers are mad about what's happened to this farmer and want to help him."

A mother of three, Bev Sargent, of Peterborough, said, "Mr. Martin's sentence stinks. I would go to prison to protect my children if anyone ever broke into my house."

Peter Lenton, of Kettering, said, "I was in tears when I heard about the conviction. I just couldn't believe it. I've been burgled too and I know what he must have been going through."

Ron Blount, 55, of Derby, backed Martin's claim that

the police were hopeless in dealing with such cases. He said, "It took them 20 minutes to answer a 999 call when my wife's car was being vandalised. The police have given up – and it's getting to the point of anarchy." Defence of private property was also much on the mind of Dorothy Woolford, a disabled 81-year-old, of Milton Keynes: "I'm living on my own – how am I supposed to protect myself? Surely everyone has the right to do what they can."

Pensioner Gladys Sansom, 78, of Lowestoft: "Please do all you can to get Mr. Martin freed. If people are not permitted legally to defend their own property what the hell are we supposed to do? It's not right that he's in prison." And Victor Bull, 53, of North London: "This man has to be freed."

Dave Evans, 29, of Worthing, Sussex, described Martin's sentence as ludicrous. He reasoned, "Suppose the Queen was being burgled and a bodyguard shot the burglars dead. He wouldn't be facing the same charge. There are double standards in this rotten country."

Some of the relatively tiny number of callers who said that Tony Martin got what he deserved were also quoted. Denise Ryan, 27, of Epsom, insisted, "You can't take the law into your own hands." And Thomas McAllister, 25, said, "He's taken the life of a 16-year-old. It wasn't necessary – he's a grown man. He could have done something else to protect himself." Mr. McAllister did not specify what else it was that Martin could have done to protect himself.

The Sun's Sunday companion paper, the *News of the World,* also asked for readers' views about the Martin case. The paper polled 1,001 readers, of whom 749, or 74 per cent, believed the farmer should not have been jailed. Only 24 per cent, 239 readers, said his life sentence was the right punishment. Thirteen did not know. The newspaper's columnist Richard Stott seemed indifferent to the majority of the readers' views when he described Martin as "a sad, pathological loony who is now locked up. And quite right, too."

Here, then, was a cross-section of Englishmen and women, giving its huge majority view to the Fourth Estate that the law was wrong and that the sentence on Martin was barbaric. Most of them were over fifty, a number of them were considerably older than that. What makes such people call a newspaper and express such concerns about the impotence of law and order and police and State inability to protect them in their homes?

The answer is not hard to find – it is fear that is uppermost in the minds of homeowning Britons when they lock their doors at night – fear that whatever happens if they are burgled they will end up on the losing side.

When *The Sun* was announcing its readers' poll findings, I was in Italy, researching another book. One evening I dined with a retired English barrister who is now living in Tuscany. Anxious to know whether British lawyers might disagree with the vast majority of their public, I put it to him as provocatively as I could that the verdict and sentence on Tony Martin were a disgraceful reflection on the state of the British criminal justice system today.

His reply surprised me. "I absolutely agree with you," he said, unperturbed. "If Martin is guilty of anything it is manslaughter. The law of the land should always try to keep in step with public opinion; although perforce it has to lag a little way behind it. This case proves that the law must be changed as quickly as possible."

Another lawyer, Shaun Evelegh, of Seaview, Isle of Wight, thought that on the evidence he would have found the force used in the Martin case close to the edge, but still within the bounds of reasonableness.

"The bigger problem lies with the officers of the law; the police, the lawyers of the Crown Prosecution Service and magistrates. Some of these appear to be unable to see the difference between chalk and cheese when deciding respectively whether to investigate, prosecute or decide a case involving reasonable force. A presumption, as a starting point, that any force used in self-defence or defence of one's home was reasonable would go a long way towards correcting such myopia."

This was also the view of Max Clifford. After the verdict he said, "Anyone involved with convicting Tony Martin for murder should hang their heads in shame. What has happened to him may be the law, but it is not justice.

"Tony defended himself against aggressors and he ends up getting a life sentence. Nobody condones murder but if, God forbid, you are ever in his situation you will understand his terror.

"He had turned to the police in the past for help and protection but got none. So he had to protect himself. The criminals who broke into his farmhouse were very well aware of this lack of protection. As a result they did as they pleased. It is a common story all over the country.

"How can his actions be seen in the same light as Kenneth Noye? Can anybody justify to me how these two men received the same sentence?"

Mr. Clifford said the British public had reacted with "horror and outrage" to the charge. He had never known a similar reaction to an event, although he had been involved in some extremely high-profile and controversial events in his career.

"I have seen a vast number of letters from people saying they live in fear of criminals invading their homes. The Tony Martin case has highlighted what a huge problem this is and Jack Straw should sit up and take notice.

"When someone's house is broken into they are often frightened for the rest of their lives. Every time a floorboard creaks, or something rattles, they are literally petrified. This is the sentence criminals such as those who broke into Tony's farmhouse pass on people all over Britain.

"Tony Martin turned to the police for help and protection. It was not forthcoming. This meant he had a choice of running away or defending himself. He did the latter. No more or less. That is why I will continue to do all I can to get him the justice he deserves."

The Mirror's Chief Crime Correspondent Jeff Edwards

took the diametrical opposed view, although, he said, he could understand the outrage felt by the murder. He had no sympathy for the "weasel-faced burglars" who were shot – they were "parasitic scum" who should have been in jail.

He argued that once people were allowed to start shooting, anyone would get shot, from the anti-social neighbour to the wife's suspected lover. These people would be invited around, then slayed by the house owner, claiming they were intruders who had surprised them in the dark.

To this rather stretched view Edwards added a back-up that was much more alarmingly elastic: "Let's not forget as well that Martin was by no means normal, reasonable or rational...By anyone's standards he was a nut...Frankly, he was like a bear living in a cave."

Jeff Edwards had other dubious views. "Barras was shot in the back, which seems to indicate he was running away at the time. And if you do that, under our legal system you are guilty of murder." The first statement clearly indicates doubt, so the second statement, which is dependent upon the first, would suggest that because there is doubt Martin was not guilty of murder. The meaning probably is that if you shoot a man, then under our legal system you are guilty of murder. Although that isn't true, it was precisely the charge of murder which was causing the outcry.

Jeff Edwards was also concerned that the farmer did not seek police help after the shooting. "You might have thought if he had nothing to worry him, Martin would have called the police." Others did call the police, but "Martin made no attempt to contact them himself."

Why didn't Martin call the police? It seemed like a fair question. Martin answered: "I didn't call them straight away because my brain was in a muddle and I couldn't think straight."

That seems like a fair answer. It would not be unreasonable for someone's brain to be in a muddle, preventing them from thinking straight, if they had just gone through the sort of horrific experience that Martin had gone through. He had no idea he had shot anyone; he thought he had scared off a couple of burglars. On the basis of his experience with the police, and on the experience of most other people in rural Norfolk, too, he would have been justified in thinking it would be a waste of time anyway to report the incident.

Tina Weaver, *The Mirror's* deputy editor, discovered her readers were not so bullish as *The Sun's*, and sought to avoid "a knee-jerk, emotional reaction."

British newspapers have a visceral instinct for courtroom murder dramas, which besides being reported at great length in the news columns, provide work for their columnists. *The Sun's* tough, uncompromising columnist Richard Littlejohn launched a broadside into Britain's sub-standard police force. His comments were perceptive and in tune with public opinion, as the comments of a good columnist should be. He said that despite what chief police officers boasted to the contrary, "vast chunks of the nation are now 'help yourself' areas as far as burglars and thieves are concerned." Readers' e-mails on the Martin case, he said, made depressing reading. "So many of them detail police negligence and dereliction of duty, contrasting their complete indifference towards burglary and car crime with their heavy-handed obsession with minor motoring offences."

He went on: "The police only police those who consent to be policed. Their idea of 'community' policing is turning a blind eye to petty crime and drug dealing.

"The top brass [of the police] seem interested solely in advancing their own careers by sucking up to *The Guardian* readers in the Home Office and pandering to their obsession with the politics of race and sex and the rights of criminals."

Littlejohn then turned his guns on the governance of Britain, which "bears absolutely no relation to the values, beliefs and best interests of the overwhelming number of people who live here. ... I have never known a time when the ideological gap between government and the governed was quite so cavernous. Nor when politicians have shown such contempt towards the paying public."

Next to this outspoken column was *The Sun's* editorial. The people were rebelling, it said, against politically correct policing. "They do not necessarily support Martin [this was curious, since more than 75% of *The Sun's* 270,000 readers who phoned in about the Martin case did seem to be supporting him]. They do not necessarily think it was wrong to jail him. But they feel threatened. They don't feel safe in their own homes. They don't think the police are protecting them.

"The mistake the Government has made is to allow a situation to develop where the criminal is perceived to be as protected by the law as the victim of crime. Tony Blair's Government is not entirely to blame. The policing in this country has been heading in this direction for decades."

The *Daily Mail* argued that Barras did not deserve to be shot, but his was not the only tragedy. Martin faced years behind bars for the way he reacted to a "gross and frightening intrusion" into his own home.

"In hamlets and remote farmhouses all over the country, there are countless people who today wonder how they would have responded in such circumstances...whole swathes of rural Britain have been all but abandoned by the forces of law and order...country dwellers have become fair game for thieves...are the politicians listening?"

The best-selling novelist Frederick Forsyth let loose the dogs of war in an article in the *Daily Mail* which targeted those responsible for years of soft-on-criminals philosophy. He declared that the tacit contract between the governors and the governed in Britain, which was for the governors to defend and protect, and the governed to pay for those services, had been broken by the governors.

"About 20 years ago, a new Left-liberal, trendy, progressive ethos began to invade the Law and Order Establishment, moving swiftly from the civil servants, who dominate whoever is in charge of the Home Office, through the Lord Chancellor's department which nominates the judges, down to the magistrates and the police leadership.

"The new philosophy would have it that the citizen was a tiresome whiner, with his obsessions with the safety of his body and his property. Since rigour had not eradicated crime, it was clearly all society that was at fault.

"The criminal was not really bad, just a creation of an unjust society that had deprived him in early years and thus created its own pitiable slave, like Shakespeare's Caliban in *The Tempest*.

"The criminal should be reasoned with, not punished, and certainly not sequestered. A thug should not be given a second chance, but if need be, 50 chances. Insidiously, inexorably, our liberal establishment inverted centuries of morality by sympathising with the criminal rather than the victim."

In the meantime, said Forsyth, no one gave a thought for the victims of crime, those coming home to find their cherished home violated, robbed and trashed. "We entered the age of the can't-touch-me thug."

The real villains of Bleak House, he said, were "the magistrates and judges who allowed the burglar gang of Bark, Fearon and Barras still to be at large after a total of 114 convictions.

"If they had done their duty to us all, there would have been no raid on that isolated farm...What Bleak House has done is simply expose the tip of a long-growing iceberg of resentment, anger and sense of betrayal; a dull, fuming awareness in us all of a broken contract. And it was not us, the people, who did the breaking."

Alongside this was the *Mail's* leader, describing Mr. Blair's condemnation of William Hague for daring to articulate public anger over the failings of Britain's criminal justice system as "outrageous."

"Tony Martin is no hero ... Yet there are countless decent, law-abiding people who understand only too well why he became so fearful and obsessive," said the *Mail*.

In his column in the same newspaper, Peter McKay expressed his contempt for "the snivelling, more tolerant than thou, creeps in the press who have no answer to the problem of habitual crime other than accepting it.

"We are all got at by the drumbeat of propaganda which makes excuses for criminals; from the families and friends who swear they are innocent – or good boys who steal because they are bored – to the intellectuals who say we should focus not on punishment but on 'social forces' which make them commit crimes."

After the Martin verdict the distinguished former editor of the *Daily Mail*, Stewart Steven, recalled, in his column in *The Mail on Sunday*, an occasion a few years ago when he was downstairs at his home watching television while his wife was upstairs in a bedroom being held at knifepoint by a burglar.

Mr. Steven wrote, long after that event, when passion was cooled, "To say I could have killed her assailant, who frightened her half to death and made off with her jewellery box, would have been an understatement."

Here was a ring from the past in a different form of Tony Martin's words, held against him at his trial, but with the same sort of meaning: "Next time I'll blow their heads off."

Mr. Steven continued, "We were victims. We felt defiled and our lives were changed for ever and for the worse... Once we had been frightened of nobody. Now we're frightened of everyone. This is what this man had done to us and if I met him tomorrow I would wish to ensure that I was equipped with a rusty pair of gardening shears to inflict upon him some unmentionable indignity."

Unless Tony Martin won his appeal, Mr. Steven wrote in April, 2000, he would be in prison for a very long time. That was wrong, and the fault could be laid at the door of politicians for their insistence on mandatory sentencing in murder cases.

"Let us vow that the same sort of politicians who made that law are simply not allowed to stoke up the emotional temperature again so that they can heap error upon error, injustice upon injustice, and thus create a fearsome place...a society in which fear rules over reason."

Columnist Dominic Lawson also recalled waking up to find an intruder in his home. "My senses were scrambled. I was incapable of reasoned thought. I simply panicked."

Mr. Lawson suspected that the vast bulk of the public did not believe in the concept of "reasonable force" at all. "What we really think is this: why on earth should I be required to use 'reasonable force' in defence of my home and family against burglars? Have they behaved reasonably? Hell, I'll be as unreasonable as I damn well like."

A few weeks after the Martin trial the *Daily Telegraph's* Editor, Charles Moore, told a conference that there was a growing and alarming dissatisfaction among readers of his newspaper – ordinary people in middle Britain – with the performance of the police. "There is a feeling," he said, "that bad people have rights and possibly even sympathy from our institutions, while people who do the right thing get into trouble."

The Times appeared to have made up its mind that it did not like Tony Martin. Writing in the issue of April 21 Simon Barnes, who lives in East Anglia, said, "The troubling thing is that he seems to have been condemned because he is a deeply unpleasant man, rather than for his actual crime." How is it that a man who lives alone in an old farmhouse and wants to protect himself against the serial burglaries which are tormenting him, who speaks out against the thieves and burglars from whom the police are supposed to protect him but fail to do so, suddenly becomes "a deeply unpleasant man?" There is plenty of evidence from those who knew Martin that he was a bit eccentric, but not a single one has ever described him as "a deeply unpleasant man" – a phrase which might even be interpreted as a polite rendering of the description of Martin used by the burglar fraternity, "a fucking old nutter."

This unnecessary and unfortunate phrase apart, Mr.

Barnes echoed much that was deep-seated in the minds of country-living people as well as farmers. He was worried for his family and for his pregnant mare. What was he to do if he found an intruder on his land?

"Assuming I have the opportunity to get to a telephone, it will take the police a good 15 minutes to get there, even if there is a car available at the nearest stations in Halesworth or Saxmundham. So, according to this judgement – well, burglar, it's your next move, isn't it? And you have a leisurely time in which to make it."

How could Mrs. Barnes defend herself against attack if Mr. Barnes was away? With a saucepan, or the kitchen knives? Should she take her chance on waiting for the police, or hoping that the jury is in a good mood?

"I ask these questions not in a rhetorical or argumentative sense, but because I want to know... There seems to be no rules of engagement. There is only a general feeling that crusty landowners are a bad thing. This is a legitimate point of view, but we need something better than liberal angst in a bad situation."

Weighing up the pros and cons of country living he came right to the nub of public anxiety: "The Martin judgement appears to open my front door to invaders. Could we have it spelt out in simple words what is acceptable and what is not? Reasonable force? An invasion is not a reasonable situation."

The Times also published a letter from Lord Ackner on April 26, the first sentence of which appeared to suggest he was unaware what hundreds of thousands of British people, and probably millions, were thinking. "Among those who have criticised the result of the trial of Tony Martin there must be few, if any, who thought his plea that he acted reasonably in self-defence should have succeeded," declared this law lord.

Few, if any, my lord? Could this really be true? But it wasn't all bad news. Claiming to know "what seriously concerns that public," Lord Ackner told *Times* readers that it was "first, the automatic conviction of murder if exces-

sive force is used in self-defence, and secondly, the dispro-
portionality of his punishment – automatic imprisonment
for life – the actual length of his imprisonment being determined not by a judge but by a politician, in private ... The
sentence of life imprisonment being mandatory, mitigation
was irrelevant."

The Scotsman was violently anti-Martin. The farmer was
a "murderous obsessive," with "few soul-mates in the
Highlands, or in many of Britain's rural areas." Quite how
the newspaper came to that conclusion three weeks after
the verdict, when most of rural England was resounding
with anger over the life sentence, is anyone's guess; one has
to assume that the news from England had not yet reached
Edinburgh.

According to *The Scotsman*: "Martin's crazed desire to
gun down an intruder was an isolated thing, specific to his
own damaged condition." The newspaper then went on to
list "some conditions held in common" by the country
areas of Scotland and England. These included disappearing police stations, and rural living becoming a little more
dangerous. Many country areas were being targeted by
organised gangs attracted by the isolation of premises –
and by the an absence of CCTV. "Thieves have been stealing to order, with sheep, tractors and expensive quad bikes
topping their lists, despite a Farm Watch scheme."
Grampian Police were "responding to public concerns,"
but "vast areas with sparse populations and many holiday
properties which are often empty continue to attract the
travelling criminal."

Anything to worry about in Scotland? Apparently not.
But the report indicated that there was some sympathy
from a Janet Home, described as chair of the Northern
Joint Police Board, who conceded that, "It's not nice when
someone's house or premises are broken into."

The Guardian did not want Martin made into a hero.
There was, said the newspaper, understandable public
sympathy for a 54-year-old farmer, living in a remote
Norfolk house, defending himself against a gang of three

much younger men. The burglars' crime had few extenuating circumstances. It was not spontaneous but deliberately planned. The trio went fully equipped, with a holdall for the swag, binbags, chisel, torch and gloves. All but one of the windows of the farmhouse were barred. It was that one window which the burglars broke through to gain entry.

"But Mr. Martin is not the hero which the tabloids are likely to make him. He broke a fundamental rule of civilised society: rejection of the use of unnecessary and undue force."

There was no explanation why someone has to keep to the "rules of civilised society" while being attacked by people who had thrown all the rules away. Martin, this limp piece ended, "must be appalled by the murder of a boy."

There is a pattern distinguishable here: the tabloids and their readers are vigorously pro-Martin, the broadsheets, rather less so. We should not however confuse this with the tabloids' traditional stance that public affairs cannot be properly explained, that institutions, laws and regulations are all boring, and that the reader can be engaged only by playing on his emotions, often and cleverly enough to get him to continue buying the paper. The Tony Martin case transcends that underlying view that the reader can only pick up impressions rather than grasp the truth, for this reason: just as many of the people who read tabloid newspapers as read broadsheets have either themselves been victims of burglary or are close to those who have. They did not need their newspaper to tell them that Martin was wrongly jailed – they had bitter first-hand experience of exactly how he felt, and they phoned in to say as much.

There was also plenty of evidence in the broadsheets that their readers were just as much behind Martin as the readers of the tabloids – it was the broadsheets' opinion columns that sometimes took a neutral or an anti-Martin stance, no doubt mindful that a greater percentage of their readers than those of tabloids belonged to the counter-culture ravaging British society which believes, among other things, that criminals are simply deprived people. All the newspapers bore evidence that the Martin trial articulated the angry mood of the country's householders.

Not all newspaper columnists make trenchant or valuable commentary – some produce stuff that is chewing-gum for the mind, and they were unable to increase the flow of saliva even for the Martin case. They did not appear to know what to think, so they wrapped up their offerings in vague words and phrases and some of it was poor stuff. W. F. Deedes, a former newspaper editor, opined, "If police and property owners are going to match the power of these predators – a growing proportion of them rendered desperate by misuse of drugs – they will have to work closer together."

Deedes asked if the police could spare time to guide him into the right steps to take to defend his property. Could insurance companies be persuaded to levy premiums in relation to the steps he then took? He was "opposed to this dependency culture which presupposes the police are wholly responsible for protecting my back door. It is a gift to burglars." His readers must have wondered, as he himself must have wondered, where all this was leading to, and they must have sighed as thankfully as he himself must have done, when he moved on to his next item: a description of the delights of drinking coffee and nibbling chocolate chip cookies in the first class lounge of King's Cross railway station.

Terry Waite, whose qualifications for writing a newspaper column are rather less incised than Deedes's (Waite sprang to fame after being kidnapped when he was Archbishop Runcie's special envoy, and spending some years as a hostage) reported that no one in his village supported villagers taking the law into their own hands. No one? Here surely was a good news story, for if that were true Waite's village, bordering lawless Norfolk, was conceivably unique in East Anglia. Eschewing this possible scoop, the columnist went on to tell a story about a man he had seen lynched before his very eyes after a robbery in

Uganda, which is certainly a long way from Emneth Hungate.

To this day, Waite said, he doubted if the unfortunate victim was the thief. Waite tried to interfere before the lynching began and was curtly told to move away. He can still hear the sound of breaking bones as they beat the unfortunate and possibly innocent man to death.

"After that experience I certainly don't want to see summary justice and, thank goodness, we haven't yet got to this state in Britain," declared this weighty writer. But, he warned ominously, "there are signs of unrest in the countryside." There may be other signs that some newspaper columns are not performing any worthwhile function beyond filling in the space between the news.

For all of the commentators, though, the issue was a difficult one to handle. Quentin Letts wrote in the *Daily Telegraph* that the Martin case was "unsatisfactory" for a couple of reasons: first, Martin was a poor martyr, because he had no gun licence and "an imperfect grasp of most of the decent rules of engagement;" second, the judge's claim that the case would "serve as a dire warning to all burglars" was absurd – burglars would be "laughing like foxes who have just seen hunting banned."

The situation was complicated too because any conservative line that newspapers wanted to take was too often upset by the strength of public feeling – newspapers, of course, are aware that they should listen to their readers. According to a MORI poll in *The Mail On Sunday* 70 per cent of people thought that the life sentence for Martin was too harsh; 86 per cent thought the law was too lenient to burglars, and 96 per cent said people should have the right to defend their property. By any pollster standards, these were huge numbers.

In truth, though, some of those newspapers that traditionally would have been expected to trumpet a liberal line were much less tolerant than they might have been. In an excellent piece in the *Sunday Times* Melanie Philips complained that "public policy is dominated by penal reform-ers who routinely characterise ordinary people's concerns as driven by prejudice and vengeance."

She attacked the Government for a "refusal to distinguish between right and wrong behaviour by making whole groups of people victims (women, asylum seekers, single parents) and defining other groups (white people, men, the middle classes) as oppressors so that they can never be the victims of anyone in the designated victim classes. This leaves people feeling bitterly powerless and disenfranchised."

In *The Guardian,* columnist Hugo Young took a somewhat different view from the newspaper's editorial stance when he described Martin's life sentence as an "outrage," placing him on the same level of wickedness as the Yorkshire Ripper. Mr. Young advocated the abolition of mandatory life sentences for murder which "nullifies the grades of stigma between a desperate act of domestic violence and contract murders by a professional killer." Another *Guardian* columnist, Mark Lawson, pointed out intriguingly that the newspapers most reluctant to support women who killed in self-defence were quickest to back Martin.

Interestingly, among all the newspapers that did not support Martin, or who were critical of his action, not one had an answer as to what to do in his predicament. Ten times burgled or attacked on your own property, driven to distraction, alone and afraid and in a state of terror when two men with long criminal records burst into your house in the dead of night...what do you do?

Those who implied you should shoot and ask questions afterwards at least had an answer. Those who said you should not do that were all unable to say what you should do.

Aware of the Fourth Estate's universal dilemma, the *Daily Telegraph* seemed to get some relief from the fact that the Press were not the only ones with no answers to the problem. It reported, "A week after his conviction, the outcry over the case of the Norfolk farmer Tony Martin shows no signs of dying down. Worryingly, neither the Government nor the police appears to have a clue as to how to respond."

9

A MURDER IN THE NEIGHBOURHOOD

There is an oft-quoted admonition that those who do not learn from history are condemned to repeat it.

After the purgatory suffered by Tony Martin, should he have learned something from history? Should he have readied himself for any eventuality in his lonely farmhouse? Should he have expected that he might have to defend his life against burglars? Or were his protection methods simply over the top, the reaction of someone who, as so often described, was eccentric?

Let us see.

No one knew the Fenlands much better than Martin. He knew about the thieves, the burglars, and the travelling community. He had started prep school in the area at the age of six. That gave him half a century of familiarity with The Fens.

The point is important, because long-standing residents of The Fens recognised something chillingly familiar in the Bleak House tragedy. Something like it had happened in the vicinity once before. On that occasion three burglars were also involved, the victim was also a Norfolk fruit farmer with a 300-acre farm, and it also happened at Emneth. Tony Martin was 22 years old at the time and from local farming stock, so he would have known all about the brutal killing of 62-year-old farmer John Auger, whose land almost abutted Bleak House farm.

The year was 1967 and in the course of the trial of the three burglars at Hertfordshire Assizes, Detective-Superintendent Wallace Virgo told the court that crime had become so bad in the Wisbech area of Cambridgeshire that terrorised residents had armed themselves with shotguns and other weapons for protection.

The police officer was giving evidence at the trial of David Warden, 22, of Wisbech; Barrie Cooper, 26, of Sutton St. Edmund, Lincolnshire; and Patrick Collins, 28, of no fixed address.

John Auger was taking his dog for a late-night walk when the three men, wearing stocking face masks, attacked him. One was carrying a shotgun. They clubbed him unconscious with a two-foot jemmy, using "considerable violence," and bound and gagged him. Then they broke into his rambling home where they attacked his wife, Isabella Auger, 59. She was also tied up and her mouth was gagged with sticking tape.

The thieves stole Mr. Auger's 4 cwt safe and made off with it in the farmer's pick-up truck – unaware that the safe was empty and that the key had been missing for two years. They left behind the owner's collection of porcelain, clocks, furniture and other antiques completely intact.

Mr. and Mrs. Auger were found later by their daughter Audrey, 32, who returned home at about 11 p.m. Her father was already dead, her mother survived the ordeal. When it was discovered that the phone lines to the Augers' house had been cut, a farm worker's son ran to a neighbour's home to call for help. Police later found the stolen pick-up truck abandoned in Wisbech and the safe in a nearby river.

The burglary in which John Auger died was the third attempted theft from his Emneth home in 12 months. After the last attempt, six months previously, when he chased off the thieves with a shotgun, he refused to keep money in his house.

He also changed and strengthened all the locks on doors leading to the four rooms containing his collection which, he claimed, was one of the finest in East Anglia.

After the killing Mr. Auger's brother said the dead man's fortune was worth about £100,000. "But he was a generous man and local charities were never turned away when they needed funds."

The three burglars were initially charged with murder, but in court they were found guilty of manslaughter. They were jailed for a total of 39 years.

But that was not the end of this bizarre similarity with the Martin case. In the summer of 1967, just after the trial of the three burglars, a potential prosecution witness, Kenneth Holman, fled into hiding from his home in Lynn Road, Wisbech. Mr. Holman was eventually caught by the police and jailed for three months for failing to attend the Assize court to give evidence.

Twelve days later he was brought from jail to Hertfordshire Assizes again. The judge, Mr. Justice Glyn-Jones, who had sent him to jail, now told him: "I am satisfied you were intimidated. I believe you were not the only one in this case who was intimidated. It was foolish of you not to give the reason when you were first before me."

The court was told that Mr. Holman fled on the day before the murder trial after receiving letters threatening him if he gave evidence for the prosecution. One of the letters, made up from newspaper cuttings, read: "Don't do it on Tuesday. The only way is killing. Run fast, don't stop."

During the murder trial Mr. Holman's wife was also due to give evidence for the prosecution but she too failed to appear. Mr. Justice Glyn-Jones said: "This is not the first time I have had wicked men who are charged with serious offences of which they are guilty, who will go to great lengths to intimidate witnesses. It could have been done by someone else acting on behalf of these three men, because they were in custody at the time."

The unfortunate Mr. Holman's jail sentence was then

altered to 12 days and he was discharged.

Here in the Auger case, right on Martin's doorstep, was a 32-year-old warning that Martin could not have forgotten when he was robbed time and time again by burglars. These men, he knew, could be dangerous, they were men who would stop at nothing. Burglars had already brutally killed one of his neighbours almost on his own doorstep. Had he not taken steps to protect himself he might not have been labelled an eccentric, but he would certainly have deserved to be labelled a fool.

Here, too, in the same case is clear evidence of intimidation and rampant lawlessness in the Wisbech area, causing the residents to take up arms to protect themselves, just as 32 years later there was suspected intimidation in exactly the same area. What, one wonders, was done in those 32 years to prevent this recurring? What will be done now? Is witness intimidation endemic in Wisbech? Who is responsible for it? How many arrests have been made? How safe is any conviction in any case that has anything to do with Wisbech or its surrounding villages? These are questions that need to be urgently addressed by law-enforcement authorities if the administration of justice in Fenland is not to be regarded as a three-ring circus.

Another case across the other side of the country was to show that Fred Barras was not the only serial recidivist let loose by magistrates on the law-abiding public.

Two months after Tony Martin had been packed away for the rest of his life, on June 20, armed raider Scott Griffiths, aged 28, accompanied by at least one other person, burst into the village post office and store at Wolverley in Worcestershire. As was the case with Fred Barras, this job was to be Griffifths's last.

The criminal career of Scott Griffifths, who lived on a council estate at Wollaston, near Stourbridge, West Midlands, had followed a familiar pattern. He first came to the notice of the police at the age of 17 when he was involved in a spate of thefts from cars in the Stourbridge area. Magistrates were told that he had turned to crime after losing his job as a plasterer in 1989. The following year he was given two years' probation for burglary and in 1995 he was jailed for 21 months for causing actual bodily harm to a man he thought had assaulted one of his brothers. He was cleared of a second assault in a pub.

A magistrates' court banned him the same year for drink-driving. He was subsequently stopped again by police and this time admitted driving while banned. The court sentenced him to three months' imprisonment to run concurrently with his 21-month sentence. He was also banned from driving for a further three years. Police were aware that on his release he had become increasingly involved in drug dealing.

At the time he barged his way into Wolverley Post Office he was on remand for the latest in this catalogue of crimes. On that occasion he had been given bail despite being caught red-handed in a Wolverhampton hotel room with six 0.5g wraps of heroin. Quite what the magistrates imagined a young thug like Griffifths with his horrendous criminal record, a drug dealer caught with a supply of drugs, would do with his time when they set him free in these sort of circumstances defies speculation, but none the less they set him free.

Wolverley has a population of 2,000 and it has the kind of sleepy setting that would mark it out for a travel brochure illustrating the attractiveness of rural England. Its tiny post office, tucked away between cottages and a pub, is about the last place on earth which anyone would imagine would be targeted by an armed gang. But that is because most people still do not have a concept of how rural England has changed.

In fact, the post office, run by 50-year-old Richard Watkins, had been raided twice before. It looks like the softest of targets. Mr. Watkins usually worked alone, serving newspapers and sweets in between running the post counter. Sometimes he was helped by his elderly mother, Iris, or his sister Sue.

He must have known what was going to happen as soon

as Griffifths came in brandishing his sawn-off gun. But this time Griffifths did something none of the other raiders had done – he hit Mr. Watkins across the head with his gun to make him open the locked door to the postroom.

Mr. Watkins did not hesitate. He grabbed a conveniently placed knife and plunged it once into his assailant's chest. Griffifths fell dying and an hour later his young life ebbed away.

Whose side are you on? Why, the side of Richard Watkins, of course. But hang about. You can't be, because of what happened to Tony Martin. Surely the law according to the Tony Martin case says Richard Watkins murdered Scott Griffifths – after all, he didn't have to stab him to death. And the mandatory punishment for murder is life imprisonment. So let's see what happened.

Immediately after the incident police were summoned and Richard Watkins was asked to give his version of events. He was then allowed an overnight respite to recover from shock. Later, asked what was happening, a police spokesman said, "Mr. Watkins is being treated as a witness and a victim."

If you think that is a bit different from the treatment meted out to Tony Martin, wait...

Three hundred yards down the road from Wolverley post office lives Sir Michael Davies, a retired judge who adjudicated in some of the Old Bailey's highest-profile trials. He said, "Richard did what 99 per cent of the population of this country would not have the guts to do.

"If he were to be charged over this criminal's death and he came before me, I would make sure the case was thrown out at the first possible stage. It was a classic case of self-defence."

There was no analogy as far as this distinguished former judge could see between this case and the case of Tony Martin.

"Richard was staring into a shotgun. He didn't know if it was loaded. He could hardly say, 'Excuse me, sir, I must telephone a legal friend to find out if it is all right for me to defend myself.' He didn't have time to think, 'I have a knife. Is it all right for me to use it?'

"He is a gentleman and a very gentle man. The post office is his life. He works seven days a week and takes one day's holiday a year.

"I think it is 95 per cent certain that he won't be charged. If he is, no jury would convict him. I don't think they would even need a judge to address them."

With the post office and store having to close indefinitely, Sir Michael suggested a fund to help the Watkins family through what might be hard times ahead. Many other villagers were hoping after the killing that the family members would not decide that they had had enough and close down.

John Wardle, 78, chairman of the parish council at Wolverley, said, "Richard is a brave man. He did what an Englishman would be expected to do – which is to stand up to someone who is threatening his life and property. It's not only the village who should be grateful to him, but also the nation."

John Gretton, a parish council member, said everyone in the village respected the Watkins family. "They have kept the shop and the post office going while others have been closing," he said. "It is a mainstay of village life."

Dr. Roderick Summers, the retired GP who attended to Mr. Watkins's wounds immediately after the attack, said that had Griffiths's accomplices taken Griffifths to Kidderminster Hospital, less than two miles away, he might have survived.

"He had a single wound to his chest. He could have been bleeding to death or it might have punctured a lung. Either way, there was a good chance that he might have lived with immediate medical attention."

No one could be found at Wolverley to condemn Richard Watkins's action, not even God's representative in the village. At the midweek Communion service at St. John the Baptist Church, Wolverley, the vicar, the Rev. Geoffrey Shilvock, 53, said prayers for Watkins and his family. "I'm afraid we didn't pray for the man who died," he said. "I don't think the congregation were ready for that. Forgiveness will come later."

We are certainly now a long way from the Newark vicar and that lovable rogue Fred Barras. But perhaps everyone in Wolverley had plenty to say because their lives had not been blighted by robbers; they did not live, like the people of Wisbech and rural Norfolk, in a state of fear about speaking out.

It is difficult to imagine, though, how the analogies between the Watkins case and the Martin case could have been overlooked by Sir Michael Davies. Griffifths, like Fearon and Barras, was a burglar. Like them he had a long criminal record. He was of the same generation as Fearon and Bark. He picked out what he thought was a soft target, as did Fearon, and he took along accomplices, as did Fearon. Watkins had a convenient killing weapon handy, as did Martin. Both Watkins and Martin are bachelors, both run their own businesses. Both Watkins and Martin had been burgled before. Martin, just like Watkins, was in no position to phone a legal friend on the night of August 20, 1999, when two men barged into his home. Nor did he have time to think as two burglars came into his hall in the darkness, "I have a weapon. Is it right for me to use it?" As Watkins probably was, he was in a state of terror. Like Martin, Watkins killed his tormentor. In both cases the accomplices turned and fled, leaving one of their number dying. In both cases the burglars who were killed were on bail, awaiting trial on other charges, and both were drug users.

Many would say that Tony Martin was every inch a gentleman and a gentle man as Richard Watkins – both are withdrawn, dedicated, self-effacing people and no doubt both have other gentlemanly qualifications. But in the reporting of the Watkins incident there is a hint that the case is not analogous with the Martin case because Watkins was a gentleman. One unfortunate construction that could be put on this is that because people in Wolverley claim that Watkins was a gentleman, and because we already know that Martin was considered to be an eccentric, the eccentric should go to jail for life and the gentleman should be freed. Anyone who thinks Martin has been wrongly treated could not possibly want Watkins to be tried and sent to jail. But if Watkins was not to be tried and jailed, then Martin was entitled to claim that he has been dealt with by lynch mob justice.

Watkins was not tried. On the same day in July that it was announced that Tony Martin had been given leave to appeal, the police announced they were taking no action against Watkins.

If Watkins indeed was a gentleman and Martin an eccentric and never the twain shall meet, that is a non-analogy, albeit a slightly spurious one. There is one other non-analogy in these two cases that is more sinister. In the Watkins' case one of the burglars was a drug-pusher, in the Martin case the burglars were gypsies. There is a good deal of evidence that the police do not pursue all crime complaints against gypsies, and no evidence at all that they are nearly so lenient with drug-pushers. Once again questions are raised: was Martin sent to jail for life because he killed a gypsy and the jury were frightened of gypsy reprisals? And is it a case that when we are looking at two criminals, one a gypsy and the other a drug-pusher, we regard the second much more severely than the first? Or, put another way, is killing a gypsy considered a far worse offence than killing a drug-pusher, because the gypsy has a large body of support behind him and the drug-pusher has none?

Another worrying aspect of the Richard Watkins case is that courts seem to think that a homeowner who arms himself with a knife and uses it to inflict a lethal wound is acting in a reasonable manner to defend himself, while one who uses a gun is not. But of course using a knife is something that only happens during a fight, and most homeowners do not want to get into an armed fight with intruders. A gun, which is much safer for the homeowner, appears to be disallowed, while a knife isn't.

If that seems improbable, let's look at some cases. John Campbell, aged 25, grabbed a kitchen knife when two men with pepper sprays and a baseball bat attacked him in his London flat in 1995. One of the men, Brian Firmager, aged 32, was beating him, so Mr. Campbell stabbed him. Firmager later died of the injury.

When Firmager's accomplice, Tony Garrard, 34, was jailed for six years for aggravated burglary, the Recorder, Brian Higgs, told him, "Thugs who attack householders cannot be surprised when their victims fight back." Police decided not to charge John Campbell.

Another burglar, 6ft 4in Patrick Halcrow, armed himself with a pickaxe handle, tear gas, knife and chisel before breaking into a house in Wicklow, Essex. The house belonged to the parents of Dean Davis, who stabbed Halcrow when the intruder attacked him. A coroner ruled that Halcrow had been lawfully killed, and no charges were preferred against Dean Davis.

John Graham, 53, tackled an armed burglar breaking into a neighbour's flat in Brockley, London, in 1996, stabbing and killing him. His solicitor told reporters: "He would like it to be known that he does not think of himself as a hero. He is mindful of the fact that however violent and criminal were the intentions of the deceased man ... his death had inevitably left his relatives to mourn his loss."

It was announced by the police that Mr. Graham would not be prosecuted.

Another burglar-killer who wasn't armed with a gun and wasn't charged was Nick Baungartner, a 57-year-old Hungarian-born self-employed contractor who laid tennis courts. When Mr. Baungartner encountered burglar Robert Ingham in his five-bedroom detached home in the village of Ockbrook, near Derby, in December, 1996, there was "a violent encounter." During the fight Mr. Baungartner strangled Ingham, who was 22 and 6ft tall.

An inquest jury later returned a verdict of accidental death on the burglar after deciding that Mr. Baungartner used reasonable force to defend his home.

In the horrific fight to the death in his £300,000 house Mr. Baungartner suffered severe cuts and bruises and a broken wrist. Later he claimed he was left traumatised and unable to work, so he took his case to the Criminal Injuries Compensation Panel. A couple of weeks after Tony Martin's sentence it was announced that he had been awarded a substantial sum. How much? That's another legal secret. You, who must pay the bill, cannot be told.

Mr. Baungartner said, "I was a victim – and Tony Martin was a victim too. The law is not strong enough. Burglars don't get locked up until they do it again and again. This would not happen in America. The law must do something or it will happen to other people who just want to be left alone.

"I have not been able to work for four years. I still have pain in my wrist and in my face where I was kicked and punched.

"I feel sorry for Tony Martin. He had to put up with burglaries for years and had to turn his home into a fortress. They kept coming back, and the police did nothing.

"Maybe he shouldn't have killed that boy, but I understand why it happened. He was protecting his property. I have had people shouting abuse at me, too, but I did what everyone else would do. So did Tony Martin."

His solicitor, Simon Hale, said, "The compensation settlement was a fair one. The damage can never be adequately compensated by money but he is pleased with the outcome and now wishes to put the whole incident behind him."

All these cases leave an idea in one's mind that if you get to grips with a burglar, strangle him or knife him, thereby killing him, you are likely to fall within an acceptable definition of reasonable force. One wonders just how many householders in Britain will be comforted by that thought.

What the law will not give you any points for is taking what most people would regard as reasonable steps to protect their homes without having to engage in armed combat with intruders. In 1995, after being stabbed on his doorstep, and having his flat burgled three times, Richard Pownall, aged 27, fortified his home in Miles Platting, Greater Manchester, by wiring a metal gate behind his front door to mains electricity. He was arrested and spent six months on remand under 19th century laws introduced to stop landowners setting fatal traps for poachers. He was eventually freed on probation.

If, while he was sitting in his cell in Bullingdon Prison at the beginning of his life sentence, Martin read about the case that came before Judge Hugh Mayor, QC, sitting at Peterborough Crown Court, on May 4, he might be entitled to claim that he had been very much singled out for judicial lynching. On that day at Peterborough was told the story of the burglar who came away with much more than he bargained for when he broke into a house. A broken wrist, fractured elbow, cracked ribs and a cracked skull to be precise – all administered to him by his irate victim, Lee Gapper, the owner of the house.

After hearing how the burglar, drug addict David Summers, was punched and beaten with an aluminium baseball bat by the terrified householder and his lodger, a judge told him it served him right – the burglar, that is, in case anyone is losing the thread.

"They used reasonable force," declared Judge Mayor, jailing the burglar for a year. "You brought it on yourself, and I have no sympathy for those who receive hurt while committing a crime."

But Mr. Gapper, 20, and his 21-year-old lodger George Goodayle, were arrested, handcuffed and locked in a police cell for 12 hours after Summers accused them of assault. They were later released following a police investigation.

After the case Mr. Gapper, a self-employed builder from Peterborough – just 40 miles from Bleak House – compared the plight in which he found himself with that of Tony Martin. "I think what happened to that Norfolk farmer was a disgrace," he said. "I was told if anything happened to the intruder who broke into my home I could be looking at manslaughter. I was petrified at the time."

Mr. Gapper said he kept the metal baseball bat in his bedroom for self-defence. "I think 90 per cent of England has something to use to defend themselves, but I never thought I would use that bat. I acted out of fear. I'm no angel, but I'm not a violent person."

That burglary occurred on a February morning in 2000, two months before Tony Martin went on trial. Mr. Gapper recalled: "I was in bed when I heard this banging of the window downstairs. At first I couldn't think what was happening, then I heard the door being smashed in downstairs. I woke up George, my lodger, and raced downstairs. At first all I could see was the shadow of this man in an empty bedroom, but as he turned to face me he lifted his arms above his head and I saw he had a spanner in his hand.

"I was face to face with him for a split second before he ran past me, and I just hit out. I thought he could have hit me. I hit him first in the back of the head and then twice about his body."

The lodger, George Goodayle, then punched Summers three or four times. "He deserved what he got," he said.

Mr. Gapper said, "I could feel my adrenaline taking over my body. I could have killed him. Afterwards I was still shaking, but chased him barefoot out of the house into the street."

The two men gave up the chase as Summers fled to his home in the city, where police found him being treated by his mother for a head wound. He admitted the burglary but told the court that it was not planned, and had been carried out to fund his drug habit. He broke into the house, he said, by smashing a window in the back door. He had thought the house was empty because no one came to see what was happening when he banged on the front door.

Summers was released on unconditional bail, only to go thieving again less than three weeks later, when he stole some bed covers from a shop.

Passing sentence the judge told him there would be no reduction in his prison term for "any hurt you may have received in a failed attempt of a citizen to arrest you."

But Lee Gapper is now unsure whether he would attack anyone breaking into his house again. "Maybe knowing what I know now, about what happened to Tony Martin and myself being put under arrest, I think I would still use force, but I would try to pin him down. If I had no choice, if my life was in danger, then I guess I would do anything. Anyway, I don't regret what I did on this occasion."

Most allotment holders have some knowledge of thieves who break into their sheds and steal their tools. Most are aware, too, of how crimes on allotments are treated with studied indifference by the police, notwithstanding how debilitating they are to allotment holders, who are generally not well-off people.

A pensioner, Ted Newbery, of Ilkeston, Derbyshire, was charged with the attempted murder of Mark Revill, aged 21, during a break-in at the shed on his allotment in 1988. Mr. Newbery was cleared but in 1995, seven years after the charge, he had to pay Revill £4,353 damages after the Appeal Court ruled his action was "out of all proportion to the threat posed."

Mr. Newbery, now aged 88, said, "I have nothing but sympathy for Tony Martin. He was well within his rights to shoot at these people. Everyone has a right to protect their home.

"These men had no business being in that house. People don't realise how frightening it can be in that situation. Like me, Mr. Martin was all alone in his property and must have been terrified."

Twenty-four hours after the Martin verdict, middle-aged Kent farmer Jon Pritchett packed his bags, put a one-way ticket to Australia in his pocket, and left Britain for good. Six years previously Mr. Pritchett had been woken in the early hours by an alarm rigged to his bedroom which told him that, yet again, burglars were in the warehouse where he stored the wine from his vineyard. He strode out into the night shouting, while the two thieves crouched in the darkness were laughing, clearly unabashed by Norwich Chief Constable Ken Williams's advice to shout as loud as you can if you want to scare them away.

The laughter stopped, though, when Jon Pritchett fired his shotgun into the ground and into the air.

One of the thieves was on the warehouse roof and took much of the blast from one cartridge, while the other was peppered with a few pellets. They were whisked off to hospital, where their wounds were treated. When they were eventually brought to court they were given two years' probation.

Jon Pritchett, though, was arrested, locked up in a cell for two days and arrived in court almost a year later to face charges of causing grievous bodily harm and one of using a firearm with intent to endanger life.

Recalling the case, he said, "There wasn't a word of sympathy for me and my predicament. I was the wrong-doer. I was strip-searched and DNA tested. The strain of being treated like a criminal in the run-up to my trial took its toll on all my family. You will understand why, after what we have been through, all our sympathies are with Mr. Martin."

After a few more years Mr. Pritchett decided to leave Britain. As fate would have it, his plane ticket was booked for Friday April 14, the day after Martin was sentenced.

He told reporters: "We leave tonight. Another few hours and you wouldn't have caught us this side of the world. We are going to a country where I am confident that victims of crime who try to defend themselves do not end up being treated as criminals."

He was probably right about that. Australia's legal system leans more towards the American attitude to self-defence than the British attitude.

In June, two months after the Martin trial, a farmer walked free from Lincoln Crown Court after being accused of shooting at and wounding the teenage member of a gang hunting foxes in the early hours on his farm at Stewton, Lincolnshire. The judge halted the trial and ordered the jury to find the farmer not guilty. He said: "I take the view that firing a .22 rifle in the dark and pointing it at a vehicle is an extremely stupid thing to do. But there was no evidence that the teenager would be protruding out of the Land Rover."

The case was highlighted by Mrs. Hilary Martin as being not unlike her son's. She said: "Although he was charged with the more serious offence of murder, it is in effect no different. My son shot blind. He had a torch shone in his face and shot into a darkened place. It seems to me that the judge in the Lincolnshire case has more common sense. He's more realistic and aware of things going on in real life. In my view he directed the jury correctly."

10

IN THE LAND WHERE
THE GUN IS KING

One of the millions of people who found the Tony
Martin verdict incomprehensible was the veteran
Hollywood superstar Charlton Heston.

Although at 75 he is no longer the strapping Ben Hur of
yesteryear, Heston would still present a formidable adversary for a burglar. He is 6ft 3in, 14 and a half stone, and
has a voice that comes like the roar of a lion out of the pit
of his stomach. He is the president and a keen supporter
of America's National Rifle Association and a virulent
opponent of any kind of tighter gun control.

He has no doubts what his reaction would have been
faced with the dilemma that Martin faced at Bleak House.
"If someone broke into my house I would shoot them in a
second," he says.

Heston has the weaponry to do just that. He owns six
firearms, two of which are antiques.

"I've got a hunting rifle, a shotgun for clay pigeon
shooting, which is fun but I don't do much any more.
Then I've got two pistols which I keep for self-protection.
In America, if someone breaks into your house, you can
shoot them. And I would do that in a second if my wife

were back there sleeping and someone broke in."

His antique guns are two silver pistols which once belonged to Thomas Jefferson. "They were given to him as a present from a friend." The pistols are kept in a case on the wall of a corridor in his Beverly Hills mansion, and both are in perfect working order. In Britain he would be jailed for keeping this kind of weaponry.

Heston has always been a fiercely political animal, like Ronald Regan, Shirley Temple, Clint Eastwood, and plenty of other famous Hollywood names. Once a moderate Kennedy Democrat who marched with Martin Luther King in the 1960s in support of the black freedom movement, his politics are now more right-wing.

In the 1990s Heston was courting controversy when he spoke out vociferously against any kind of gun registration in America, after a series of incidents in which schools and schoolchildren were targeted by gun-crazed criminals as well as other gun-slinging children themselves.

Gun ownership in America is controlled by law, but not very well. Registration is not the problem, Heston maintained, the problem is that the current laws are not being enforced. His views were opposed by President Bill Clinton, a supporter of much tighter gun-control laws, and by millions of American moms alarmed by playground shoot-outs. He has received numerous death-threat letters and the influential actor-director Spike Lee has even suggested that Heston should be shot through the head with .44 Bulldog. This would appear to make Lee a supporter of gun-shooting, but the remark was made in the context of shooting the opposition to get rid of it. Lee even went so far as to suggest that the weapon used to execute the veteran actor should be a .44 Bulldog. For the uninitiated, this was the type of gun used by the serial killer known as Son of Sam.

Like many members of rural American families, Charlton Heston grew up in an atmosphere loaded with guns. As a boy he regularly went hunting in Michigan with his father, carrying his own gun. When he was nine, and already a good shot, his parents gave him a .22-gauge rifle as a Christmas present.

Today the veteran actor takes his eight-year-old grandson Jack on shoots. Jack began by accompanying his father and grandfather on clay pigeon shoots, to get the hang of it. But he is not yet allowed to carry a gun.

"The important thing is to teach kids how to handle firearms safely," said Heston. "Jack has been taught he cannot touch a gun yet. But he has been shown how a gun works and what it can do."

Charlton Heston's view about this is firmly entrenched. "It's not the guns that kill, it's the maladjusted kids." President Clinton's proposal to implement gun registration, he claims, would be a violation of the American Constitution's Second Amendment which gives all Americans the right to bear arms. Furthermore, he insists, gun registration would be pointless. "If car registration doesn't reduce road deaths, which are significantly higher than deaths by shooting, then what chance would gun registration have?"

While there is a growing debate in the United States over its deadly romance with firearms that kill 35,000 people a year, polls show overwhelming support for the killing of intruders, even if there is uncertainty that they are armed. Such is the pervasive fear of trigger-happy robbers that juries regularly refuse to convict householders who shoot them.

Tony Martin would almost certainly not have gone to jail if he had killed a burglar in the United States. Homeowners there have virtually unchallengeable rights to use firearms to protect their property.

Even though there are wide variations in the laws of the 50 states, in the most liberal and pro-gun control states such as Massachusetts and New Jersey, the prosecution of someone in Martin's position would have failed. According to John Baker, professor of law at Louisiana State University: "It would be very difficult in any state to convict a homeowner even of manslaughter if he shot a burglar who was burgling his home."

In 1992 a Louisiana jury acquitted a man of manslaughter after he shot dead a Japanese student who arrived at his house in fancy dress looking for a Halloween party. The defence argued successfully that he had justifiably thought his life was in danger. This is the sort of verdict that stops such a killing entering the statistics for US murder rates – currently 10 per 100,000 citizens, or 25,000 a year, mostly resulting from gunshot wounds. The UK's rate is 1 per cent per 100,000 citizens, or 500 a year.

The most celebrated case of vigilante action was that of Bernard Goetz, 37, an electronics technician, who shot four black teenagers on the New York underground. He claimed that he had armed himself with his "equaliser", a revolver acquired illegally in Florida, after being mugged. The jury cleared him of attempted murder.

But as most regular visitors to America know, the truth is that huge tracts of the States, the vast area that rolls below the wing on a flight from New York to California, are free from serious crime in a way that is unimaginable in all but the most remote British hamlet. Crime in the States is almost exclusively confined to predictable areas in big cities – for instance, New York's Lower East Side, New Orleans outside the French Quarter, the barrio of south central Los Angeles. I have regularly stayed in Southern California with friends who would never dream of locking their front door when they go out. James Langton, the *Daily Telegraph's* New York correspondent, wrote that he does not lock the doors of his house or even his cars parked in the driveway, and that his wife often leaves her handbag on the front seat of her car in the driveway.

"The wholesale looting and pillaging that plague almost every corner of Britain simply does not occur here in the US," he said.

Mr. Langton moved to America from Stoke Newington, in north London, where his car stereo was stolen three times in a year, the last time when it was in the house and taken in a burglary that stripped everything of value from the ground floor. In his first home in New Jersey people went to bed with open windows and unlocked doors and the garden centre left its geraniums unattended on the pavement every night.

Why the difference? Mr. Langton suggested one reason was that America sends six times as many people to prison as Britain – although this is largely because of an ineffective war against drugs. Another reason was possible a highly visible police force. Still another was that Americans are law-abiding people. They generally don't take what they haven't earned.

"One of the few times they get seriously jittery about crime is travelling abroad, Britain and the continental countries being no exceptions.

"When a CBS London correspondent described Britain in a report as 'one of the most violent societies in the Western world,' he elicited a wave of indignation from a country that perceives America as riddled by violence. But crime, as Britain understands it, does not exist in America."

Chester Mirksy, Professor of New York University's Law School, was not a supporter of Charlton Heston's views, and referred to the 1999 Columbine High School massacre in Colorado, America, in which 12 students and a teacher were murdered by two gun-toting pupils.

"I live in a society which is armed to the teeth and where the culture of 'shoot first and ask questions later' is deeply ingrained," he said. "With Columbine very much in our minds, the way that tragedy illustrated how easy it is for kids to get guns here, gun-owning freedom isn't an approach that I would personally recommend. And it is one that Britain has tended to resist because it doesn't consider an armed society to be a civilised society."

In America it is considered to be self-defence if a house-holder attacks an intruder he finds in his grounds. Police are extremely reluctant to prosecute in such cases. The only time a charge may sometimes reach court is if the intruder is shot in the back, as Barras was. But even then most US juries would probably clear the householder. After that he may however be sued by the victim's family – the law will not protect him from such a civil action.

Millions of Americans fiercely defend their right to carry arms in a tradition that dates back to frontier days. Where law-enforcement doesn't work, they maintain, the citizen has an inherent right to defend himself against aggression. The same argument was used hundreds of years ago in Europe, where citizens in Renaissance times carried a sword or a dagger in their belt to defend themselves. Carrying arms in Britain and other European countries became less of a habit until it was not a habit at all as law and order prevailed, and citizens could rely on felons to be arrested and punished with the full force of the law.

Today, as everyone knows, felons are no longer arrested and punished with the full force of the law. And in Britain there is no Amendment to a Constitution giving Britons the right to anything, since there is no written Constitution. Until recent times Britons could own hand guns, although gun laws were stringent and were vigorously enforced. Then a madman ran amok in a school in Dunblane, Scotland, killing 16 children and a teacher.

Unfortunately for thousands of people who enjoyed shooting within the confines of a gun club, the killer, Thomas Hamilton, was a member of such a club. Knee-jerk legislation prompted by pressure groups in the wake of the Dunblane shooting, tore the heart out of gun clubs across the length and breadth of the land, when their members, who had broken no law and were innocent of any crime, were given a period of time to surrender all hand guns and give up their sport. This was despite the fact that no one could deny that British gun clubs were run by sportsmen who put safety above all else and who were therefore a danger to no one. After Dunblane, thousands of innocent people were punished by the British Government for the crime of just one man. After Dunblane, armed crime statistics have not gone down.

Britain's firearm laws are now the most stringent in the

world and permit no ordinary householder to own a gun for self-defence. Target shooters cannot even have a .22 calibre target pistol for use in the Olympic Games unless it is kept abroad.

Shotgun ownership must be certificated, and a shotgun can only be used for vermin control, game shooting or target shooting. It must be kept securely locked up when not in use. Owners of rifles and high-powered air rifles have to be certificated and must satisfy the police that they have good reason for possessing the weapon. They also have to be people of exemplary character. The certificate for target shooting requires membership of a Home Office approved club with a shooting range, and for game shooters, use on land approved in advance by the police. Ammunition purchases are regulated and recorded on the certificate.

No such draconian reaction exists in America, where Charlton Heston complains only that the gun laws are simply not properly enforced. "We have 22,000 federal gun control laws in America, yet the police arrest violators but don't imprison them," he said.

In Richmond, Virginia, under a new law backed by the National Rifle Association and supported by Heston, anyone with a felony record caught carrying a firearm is immediately jailed for five years without trial. Heston is delighted with the result of that legislation. "Within a year the crime rate dropped 50 per cent. Now other cities are following suit."

In 1999, in the latest gun-horror story to come out of America, a six-year-old child shot dead a fellow schoolmate. In the wave of revulsion that followed, the National Rifle Association was accused of fanning gun violence, and one of the accusers was seen to be President Clinton himself. The NRA promptly launched a series of television commercials in which Charlton Heston was seen implying that Clinton had lied in his misrepresentation of the NRA. The President's response was to denounce the NRA as a "ruthlessly brutal lobby" that voters were unlikely to believe "even with Moses reading the script" (a reference to Heston's Hollywood career as a superstar of biblical epics).

Heston scoffed at this. "The NRA spends a million dollars a year every year solely on teaching gun safety for small children, so a kid doesn't walk into a hall and pick up a gun that is loaded," he says. "There is no government agency that has even touched that issue. If other people spent more of their money on the same sort of objective, you wouldn't have had that six-year-old killing another."

In the unlikely event that someone in America is initially charged with murder in a burglar-killing case, as soon as self-defence is raised as a defence issue the charge would be second-degree murder, which does not carry any mandatory sentence. There have been degrees of murder in America for more than a century, it being recognised that some murders are much worse than others. Yet in Britain there is still no discrimination in murder – any murder is treated as murder and carries a mandatory life sentence.

Defenders of this absurd law invoke the "tariff" system, a device which generally ensures that a life sentence is not for life. The serious flaw in the tariff system is that it happens behind closed doors – it is not justice if justice has to be seen to be done. In any event, why should a man who is being sentenced to life imprisonment afterwards be told that it won't be life, that it will be, say, only six years? That is not only senseless, but it is manifestly cruel. It remains little short of astonishing that British law has reached the twenty-first century without recognising that a man with a broken heart who kills his girlfriend in a failed suicide pact is a slightly different case of murder from a man who strangles fifteen people, boils their bodies in saucepans in his kitchen and flushes the sludge down the drain.

Even in Europe the law is not so savage as it is in Britain. Under German law, for instance, someone who kills another person in a similar situation to the Martin case can be acquitted so long as the person can show he acted to prevent an attack against himself or someone else. This of course is precisely what Martin did.

This is the case even if the defendant went beyond the boundaries of what was necessary to defend himself. The defendant would have to convince the court that he or she was sufficiently afraid, shocked or in a state of confusion to have reacted in such a way to a clearly perceived threat. Section 35 of the German criminal law grants citizens the right to defend their property with "the appropriate means."

In Belgium the penal code recognises a general right to self-defence. "Justifiable homicide" is allowed in cases "dictated by necessity" in defence of oneself or someone else. It has to be proportionate to the threat, and does not apply if only property is at stake. There is no special law for self-defence against burglars inside one's home.

A test-case is currently in the Belgian justice system. Wouter Tyberghien, a jeweller living in West Flanders, is awaiting trial for killing a burglar. Aiming from an upstairs window at a gang of thieves who were smashing their way into his jewellery shop, he fired five shots from a revolver and 10 shots from a hunting rifle. His arrest set off a petition for his release, aggressively sponsored by the opposition parties which had been accusing the government for some years of being soft on crime. Tyberghien is now on bail.

In France it is harder to predict what would happen to a Tony Martin. In a case from 1902 which defines French practice on the defence of property, the owner of an estate who had mined the banks of his lakes was found not guilty of the injuries caused to poachers who subsequently tried to steal his fish. But in another case, the owner of a country house who set up a booby-trapped radio during his absence and killed a burglar was charged with murder.

French law on self-defence is consequently vague and depends almost entirely on jurisprudence. The law permits any victim of crime to defend himself "as long as the means of defence employed are not disproportionate to the gravity of the attack." The law also allows any person to use force "strictly necessary and proportionate to the crime" to protect his property from thieves. It is made clear, though, that this is not an excuse for "wilful killing."

The question of what would have happened to Tony Martin in other civilised countries begs another question: what chance would there be for Messrs. Barras, Fearon and Bark to be still at large in other countries given their appalling criminal histories? Here the record of France is abysmal. Like the British, the French do not know how to handle the problem of multi-recidivism, and do not seem to understand that serial delinquence leads on to major crime and even murder. As a result nothing sensible is done to check young criminals in their formative stages. Nor is the average Frenchman much good at obeying laws – among Western European countries, France is the one where you are most likely to be run down on a pedestrian crossing.

For example, on Friday, May 12, 2000, a month after Tony Martin was sentenced, 20-year-old Abdelaziz, from Nacre, a district of Méru which bears comparison with Newark's Hawtonville estate, appeared before a court at Beauvais on ten different charges. The first series of offences occurred in the two weeks between March 7 and 21. They were theft from a hardware shop, damaging an apartment block hall, mugging, robbery with violence and driving a car without a driving licence or insurance.

The second string of offences happened between April 3 and 21: breaking into an educational institution, armed violence, threatening to kill, defacing the wall of an apartment block and breaking a shop's illuminated sign. For all these offences Abdelaziz was "sentenced" to visit an "expert psychologist" within thirty days. Not surprisingly, he didn't turn up for the appointment.

The day after his "sentence" Abdelaziz caught the train from Beauvais to Méru. He didn't bother to buy a ticket, so when a travelling ticket inspector joined the train Abdelaziz was peremptorily ordered to get off at the next station. On the platform he began to bombard the train with stones picked up from the tracks, breaking windows and injuring passengers. He then broke the window of the train driver's compartment and beat the driver over the head. Despite his injury, the driver decided to apply full steam to distance his train as rapidly as possible from Abdelaziz. The next station was Méru. The driver stopped the train there and refused to go on. Three hundred passengers were left stranded on the platform.

Abdelaziz was arrested within a few hours on the strength of a description given by a disgruntled passenger. On Sunday May 14, two days after his "sentence," he was brought before a magistrate who, ignoring expert advice given in court, placed him under a form of judicial supervision that allowed him to walk free immediately from the court again, provided he kept away from Méru.

Three days later he was back in Méru. During the night of May 17–18 he broke three shop windows in the centre of the town, damaged eleven private cars parked in the streets and three others parked in the courtyard of the police station, threatened to kill police who moved to restrain him, was arrested and escaped. When he was finally arrested again in the morning of May 18 he was carrying a knife. He is at last in detention at Amiens. A vast amount of public cost and public inconvenience was thus caused by the actions of two magistrates who seemed not to know that the first duty of a responsible State is to protect its citizens from aggression.

Although Abdelaziz's crimes were different in character from those of Barras, Fearon and Bark, in France the general judicial attitude towards the young criminal is very similar – no matter how many offences appear on the charge sheet the magistrates appear to think that the recidivist has only to be released into the community and somehow he will go straight and merge unnoticed into mainstream society. As everyone but the magistrates knows, that is almost always the exact opposite of what happens.

"There is an enormous gap between what we feel should

be done to people like Abdelaziz and what the magistrates do," a senior French police officer told me. "All too often they release into the community young criminals who are obviously dangerous or have the propensity to be dangerous."

He might have had the same view about some of the magistrates in Nottinghamshire. For what is any community of law-abiding people to expect from Abdelaziz, Barras, Fearon, Bark and all the others like them unless they are locked away, long before they become recidivist, and rigorously educated to behave properly and not released again until they have satisfied that criterion? That is what the political rhetoric "tough on crime, tough on the causes of crime" really means.

France has identical inner city problems with its schools as Britain has, giving rise to a worrying increase in child crime in the sort of environment that breeds young criminals like Fred Barras. Andy Trotter, the Metropolitan Police deputy assistant commissioner, said, "We are trying to explain a phenomenon. We are seeing more and more youngsters getting involved in crime. It is perhaps increasing confidence, it is partly that there are more targets and, perhaps, it is a breakdown in family structure."

Metropolitan Police officers called in researchers to try to identify possible links between children's expulsion from school and their involvement in crime. They were seeking an explanation for what has become in parts of the capital a "lost" generation of children for whom crime is a way of life.

"Our fear is that we now have hundreds of kids committing tens of offences, whereas in the past we had tens of kids committing large numbers of offences," said Mr. Trotter. The Met launched a crackdown on mugging in the capital in May, 2000, in a drive to stem the wave of youth crime.

As we have seen with Fred Barras, however, the involvement of children in crime spreads far beyond the capital. Early in 2000 police in South Yorkshire arrested a five-year-old and a nine-year-old for trying to rob an elderly lady of her handbag. Both were freed because they were below the age of criminal responsibility.

One country where Tony Martin might have been one hundred per cent safe from prosecution is South Africa. Even under the new liberal constitution, hailed as one of the world's most enlightened, it is unlikely that he would have seen the inside of a courtroom, let alone a cell. By the same token, it is almost inconceivable that any criminal breaking into a home in South Africa would do so unarmed.

Had Martin shot and killed an intruder who had broken into his home in, say, Johannesburg or Cape Town, he would have been cautioned by the police that he could face a charge of "culpable homicide" – which in Britain is manslaughter.

"But such is the backlog of similar cases it would be unlikely that it even came to court," said a Johannesburg lawyer. "Most likely, unless he had a long record of similar offences, the brief would gather dust and he wouldn't hear anything more about it.

"In the unlikely event that he did get to court on a charge of culpable homicide, he would probably walk away with a suspended sentence or a fine. Such a case would be unlikely to make news even in the local newspaper, let alone become a national political issue."

In a recent case in Johannesburg a young man was awakened by an armed burglar entering the bedroom where he was asleep with his wife. The husband pulled his 9 mm pistol from under his pillow and shot the intruder dead. Police who investigated the case did not even warn him that he might face charges of culpable homicide.

"They were most sympathetic," the husband said. "One black officer even gave me the name of his cousin who specialises in cleaning bloodstained carpets."

Two weeks after the Martin verdict a British businessman who shot dead an armed robber as he fought off a gang at Nairobi's Jockey Club was told by police that they were treating the killing as self-defence. The four-strong gang took Bob Holt, 52, the chief executive of the club, which runs Kenya's horse racing, and his staff hostage at his office.

They stole money and jewellery before one man forced Mr. Holt into a back office to open a safe. But the gunman became angry when he discovered the safe was empty and forced Mr. Holt to lie on the floor while he beat his legs with his gun barrel.

"He wanted me to lie and face the floor, but I wouldn't. If I had turned over like he said I think he would have shot me," Mr. Holt, who is a former aide to Robert Maxwell, said.

The robber left the room briefly to tell his accomplices there was no money, giving Mr. Holt time to draw a gun from his jeans pocket. He killed one robber instantly and hit another at least once. The other gang members fled with their wounded friend, firing wildly as they escaped.

"When they waved a gun in my face I had a feeling like an electric shot go through me," Mr. Holt said. "When I got a chance I had just a split second to react or they might have killed us." The police told him, "There is no problem here. It was self-defence."

He had no regrets about firing. "If you carry a gun you have to be prepared to use it," he said. Nairobi is in the grip of a crime wave. With Kenya's economy crumbling and high-level corruption rife, shootings and robberies are regular occurrences. In retaliation, vigilantes – tacitly encouraged by an over-stretched and underpaid police force – often take the law into their own hands. Street lynching of suspected criminals is common and those responsible are rarely brought to justice.

Police feared the robbers, or their gangland bosses, might try to take revenge on Mr. Holt, and stepped up security at the Jockey Club. A security advisor at the offices said, "We don't expect them to come back, but if they do we will be prepared."

The point about comparisons with countries like the

United States, Germany, Belgium and South Africa is that we think of them as part of our highly-developed civilised world, a group of leading nations which set an example to the rest of the world, a group of nations with whom we in Britain feel we share a common bond. We share our economic views, our political views, our views on how we think other countries should behave on the international stage, our views on democracy and our views on morality.

Why, then, should there be such a diversity of view among us about a legal case like that of Tony Martin? Surely it must be fundamentally wrong that, if Martin happened to live in another country in every way the equal of Britain, the view of what he did under extreme duress should be regarded in Britain in an entirely different way from the way it is regarded in that equally civilised country. Justice cannot be justice unless, at least in the civilised world, there is some equality in it. Whatever else you may call it, to put Martin in jail ostensibly for the rest of his life in Britain, and perhaps not even to charge him in America for exactly the same offence, cannot be justice. We are not dealing with rocket science here – we are dealing with common sense.

The irresistible inference is that one of these two civilised countries has got it very wrong. Which one? Most of the top echelon of British lawyers would have no doubt about that – if it's British, it must be right, so it's murder. Americans, on the other hand, shake their heads in disbelief at the sentence on Tony Martin. It must be self-defence, they say.

Could it be that real justice for Tony Martin lies at least somewhere between these two polarised views?

11

THE PROBLEMS OF
THE POLICE ...

Ken Williams, the Chief Constable of Norfolk, made his much-quoted comment about his lack of resources to police Norfolk immediately after the Martin trial. There were no excuses; it was a plain statement of fact, as honest as it was unsatisfactory.

Thereafter, Norfolk Police drove their case along as if all their wheels had come off. Besieged by angry county residents about inadequate policing, the Chief Constable advised anyone who was confronted by a burglar to scream.

"Really shout and make a lot of noise," he said. "My experience tells me after 37 years as a police officer that most people burglarising a house are actually quite terrified at their actions and frightened to death at being disturbed. Any disturbance, any noise, would have terrified them [the Martin burglars], and they would have exited the premises fairly quickly."

Mr. Williams, a man with a university degree not in law or criminology or some such other discipline related to catching criminals, but in Social Science, had agonised over what he would have done if faced with the Bleak

House burglars. Would he have screamed himself?

"You can never put yourself in the position of Tony Martin," he said.

Reactions to the "shout and scream" gaffe were predictable. "The advice will astonish the isolated communities targeted by thieving thugs who often think nothing of using violence," said *The Mirror*. "Tony Martin acted out of frustration and fear familiar to villagers the length and breadth of Britain. These people have one simple demand. They do not want platitudes, they want police officers."

A pensioner who phoned a newspaper, Ken Wilton, of Edenbridge, Kent, launched into a bitter attack on Mr. Williams. Mr. Wilton, 72, said, "His advice is the advice of a moron. I wouldn't even put him in charge of traffic. What are you supposed to do if your nearest neighbour lives miles away? I would do the same as this farmer. If anyone broke into my house I'd kill them."

In prison, Tony Martin was told of the Chief Constable's comments. He responded: "He must be bananas. In the country most people, including me, are much farther away from their neighbours than shouting distance." In fact, Bleak House is half a mile from the nearest habitation.

Sixty-six year-old Barbara Bentley, of Mansfield, Notts, told a newspaper: "I've never heard anything so stupid. Doesn't the Chief Constable realise that people are isolated in these places – who the hell is going to hear? If I had a gun I'd use it."

In Norfolk, police believed that one of their biggest difficulties was trying to persuade people that while rural crime was on the increase, in their view it was not out of control. They believed their task was made more difficult because the effects of a criminal act ripples much further in rural areas than in towns.

Mr. Williams said, "It is important to get this into perspective and while there are clearly community concerns it is very easy to exaggerate them."

Worse was to follow. On April 25 two weeks after the Martin trial was over, the Chief Constable reported that his officers were facing a torrent of abuse. He was "shocked at the ferocity of the public backlash against the life sentence," which had sparked a flood of abusive phone calls to police switchboards.

But why should he have been shocked? Here, it seemed, was a senior police officer who was distinctly out of touch with the views of those whom he served.

Mr. Williams used the opportunity to get back on to his hobby horse. "But I feel that good will come out of the Martin case, tragic though it is. The Government must now listen to calls for extra funding and extra resourcing."

Norfolk Police, he went on, had always done everything possible to protect the public with the limited resources available. "If you could see the state of some of our staff who are having to receive grossly offensive and vulgar telephone calls directed at the constabulary and myself, you would be horrified," he said. "To suggest that we are complacent or that we don't care are things I find wounding and grossly offensive."

He defended his officers' investigation of the case as "utterly professional" and impartial and added, "We have done our duty in a wholly proper way. We are not here to make value judgements about crimes we investigate. We are here to gather the evidence and present it to the Crown Prosecution Service."

Much of the criticism levelled against his force was unfair, ignored many of the achievements of recent years and was having a detrimental effect on staff morale. "We all make mistakes, but we try to learn from our mistakes and do things better in future. My greatest fear is that my officers will become demoralised and bitter."

The problem here is that if the police decline to make value judgements about the cases they deal with, it cannot be surprising that the public, which itself was already demoralised and bitter anyway, gets the impression that they are no longer on the side of the law-abiding. And if their only response to criticism is to complain about money, it is also not surprising that people call them complacent and worse.

The lack of understanding by the police of the effect of the Martin case on the public was again in evidence in a Channel 4 News discussion in which the police representative was Superintendent Graham Hooper, of Thames Valley Police. Several times he advised viewers that if they were confronted by a burglar they should take no aggressive action; instead, they should call the police.

"The police will attend and deal with the situation," the superintendent said with smooth confidence, demonstrating that both he and the interviewer had completely missed the point at issue – that it was precisely because the police do not attend that Martin finally resorted to the gun.

The Martin case focused public concern on both the attitude and performance of the police in Norfolk and perforce, their leader. The duty of the police is to protect people and their property from criminals; if they cannot, or will not do so, there should be a strong presumption that the State is on the side of those who, confronted with violent intruders, try to protect themselves

We live in a new age when people who, like policemen, work in the protective services, now need counselling for traumas and take early retirement in large numbers for reasons of health (or the attraction of a large pension), so the Chief Constable's curious mélange of damage limitation, defence, protest and hair-shirting is regrettably what we have come to expect from people in senior positions. The truth is that for whatever reason, at the time of the Martin case policing in rural Norfolk was very poor, the residents were inadequately protected, known criminals were roaming free, looting, pillaging, and alarming country people, and at least some of the county's policemen were already demoralised and bitter. All this has to be viewed against a whacking 20 per cent hike in the police element of the Norfolk council tax the previous year. The result was that Tony Martin, and many hundreds of people like him who were not getting what they pay for, were so fed up with inefficient law-enforcement that he, and they, were prepared to take the law into their own hands. Their actions and their views were a direct consequence of what they believed was sub-standard law-enforcement in rural Norfolk.

On April 21 the Chief Constable admitted feeling sympathy for Martin. "I'm sure that Martin regrets the killing of the 16-year-old boy," he said. "I'm desperately sorry for the boy, but also for Martin. There is something rather pathetic about him now. His life is ruined too."

He warned, however, that for all the outpourings of public support for the farmer, "the morgues would be full" if all homeowners responded to burglars in the way Martin did. "Is that the sort of society we want to live in?" he asked. "That's the consequence of the gun lobby and a gung-ho attitude to violence."

This brought a caustic comment from Alex Swanson, of Milton Keynes, in a letter to the *Sunday Telegraph*: "The Chief Constable condemns the 'gung-ho attitude' of the 'gun lobby,' but I wonder what he thinks of the police in Bedfordshire who in 1998 shot dead Michael Fitzgerald whom they mistook for a burglar, but who in fact broke into his own house after forgetting his keys. No charges, of course, were brought."

Two weeks later the Chief Constable was "exclusively interviewed" on the Norfolk constabulary website. The form of the "interview" was confusing. An interview generally suggests that an interviewer is asking questions and the interviewee is answering them. In this "interview" the interviewer was not named, and the questions suggest that they may have been written in advance by someone who already anticipated the Chief Constable's replies to them. This strictly speaking is not an interview – it is, rather, a technique for putting over a public relations statement

Question No 3 asked: "Rural policing is an emotive subject at the present time. Is there any middle ground between what the public want (more high profile visible policing) and what the force can provide?"

The answer dealt at some length with the problems. "I know I need more frontline officers," the Chief Constable said. "I know I need too more support staff to ensure front-line police officers are properly skilled and supported.

"Sadly the world is not going to provide the funding that harmony requires and, given the challenges of the budget for this and next year, there is very little hope of real increase in the numbers of uniformed officers. What we have to do is maximise the numbers of staff we have and use them as effectively as possible."

The answer to the question, then, appeared to be no. The policing in Norfolk was not going to improve, despite Tony Martin, the travellers, and the rampant theft going on in the rural county. But there appeared to be no dismay at this, for "they [the Norfolk police authority] and I are in awe at the operational performance given all the constraints on each and every member of staff."

The next question came closer to home. Interviewer: "A public meeting at Emneth saw the divisional commander, a member of the police authority and an MP shouted down. Should we subject ourselves to this kind of ordeal?"

One of the problems with this kind of PR "interview" presentation is that it may seem strange that anyone who is accountable to the public should actually question whether they should subject themselves to the "ordeal" of scrutiny by ordinary people – but if it does, then it must seem strange. The Chief Constable, however, was enthusiastically on the side of public accountability:

"Local policing is designed to satisfy local needs. Whilst it might be a hard pill to swallow we must ensure our performance is coupled to need. Sometimes the demands from both sides are mutually exclusive. We have to explain and justify ourselves in the public arena. If we do not do that we do not deserve to be part of the democratic process."

The "interviewer" then asked him why he had recently sent a letter to every employee thanking them for their efforts.

The Chief Constable replied: "I was hurt by much of what the popular press have had to say, particularly in the rural policing debate and also in more focused areas and, given that I understand my staff, I know too that they would feel the pain and they are out there in the public gaze being subjected to public scrutiny much more than me."

Well, then, the "interviewer" asked finally, it could be argued that the Force has been receiving a rough ride in the media of late. Did he think their criticism was justified?

"I think the Press is unfair," replied the Chief Constable. "Some people will say, 'Well, he would say that, wouldn't he?' but my cry is for the journalists to really try to understand the complexities of policing. Why is it journalists have to go for headlines or sound bites? Frankly the public are much more discerning." [This, paradoxically, despite the public's "flood of abusive phone calls" to Norfolk Police switchboards].

And the final, hand-wringing cry: "I get disappointed when those people who should and do know better fail to seize the initiative and allow the Constabulary's name to be besmirched when sensible commentary would put our strengths and weaknesses into their real context."

The tenor of this heavily clichéd "interview" was that we must all take pains not to say anything that might harm the good name of Norfolk Police, whose performance holds their boss "in awe." Something here was radically wrong, because a polarised view was held by many rural Norfolk people, as we have seen. The police were jeered and cat-called at a packed public meeting, they regularly arrived late at the scene of crime, they were held in contempt by people who have been burgled. The Chief Constable blamed the public, then blamed the Press – anyone who criticised police inaction was blamed. The whingeing website "interview" did nothing to enhance the image of Norfolk Constabulary – some who must share in the blame for that were the Constabulary's Public Relations department for allowing it to be published.

One South Norfolk police constable who had been with the force for 30 years said that what happened with Martin could happen again. The officer did not want to be named, but admitted he was demoralised about the way parts of Norfolk were policed. "The public deserves better. I can't condone what Tony Martin did but I can understand the frustration he must have felt. A recent shake-up has left me and three colleagues covering 25 parishes."

Many senior police officers, instead of condemning Tony Martin, turned on the Government for failing to invest properly in rural bobbies. Like the Chief Constable of Norfolk, they too complained that the Home Office was refusing to provide the extra cash needed for rural policing and that they were forced to withdraw officers to towns and send them into remote areas only on demand – in other words, when a crime had already been committed.

The Chief Constable of Cumbria, Colin Phillips, sympathised with the frustration felt by Norfolk Police. He said he had asked the Government for more money for his rural force but was turned down.

"In rural areas the public do not see enough officers on the beat," he said. "Home Office research in 1999 proved beyond doubt that the so-called sparsity factor in the countryside, the increased costs of additional buildings, vehicles, staff, infrastructure, were not reflected in the formula which allocates funding to individual police forces.

"We have lobbed the Home Office Minister [Charles Clarke] to have the research included in the funding formula. Unfortunately he did not do so. We are continuing to press for this additional funding which we quite rightly say is ours." That view was certainly borne out by figures published in the *Police Service Personnel*, the statistical bulletin from the Home Office, which showed there were 50 per cent more officers per 100,000 population in metropolitan areas than non-metropolitan ones.

In April, 2000, Charles Clarke was considering a new plan: the creation of a part-time force of retired officers and volunteers to tackle rural crime. Dismissing the idea, Cumbria's Chief Constable said, "The public does not want part-time, retired or community wardens. They are demanding full-time, fully trained and equipped officers. My force would get around £2 million a year if the Home Office research was reflected in the funding we are given. This could buy me 80 more officers. The situation has been recognised, the solution has been identified, all we need is for the Government to do something."

Even so, the arithmetic here is questionable. The Chief Constable's 80 extra officers would be at a cost of around £25,000 each from a fund of £2 million. Apart from their salaries, the officers would need a considerable and costly infrastructure: cars, buildings, non-police staff, telephones, and employer costs which include funding large pensions at retirement half way through life. Policing is a people business, and in almost every business people are the biggest single cost item.

It is worth a short deviation here to take a look at the methods used to train Britain's senior police officers. To reach the highest ranks in the service, aspiring police chiefs embark on a strategic command course at Bramshill Police College in Hampshire. At least up to the time of the Martin case not a single lecture was given on that course about the practicalities of catching criminals. Candidates were taught about such matters as "managing internal and external stakeholders;" innovations in policing philosophies and strategies; developing team and leadership skills; and "involvement in human resources."

At the time of the Martin case the director of the strategic command course was Greg Wilkinson, a former assistant chief in the West Yorkshire Constabulary. He was reported as saying that although "overall crime management" is a key role for a modern police chief, catching criminals is neither the exclusive nor the primary focus of their training.

"The educational input there is very much focused on research, research skills and the wider area of criminology

– looking, for instance, at things like social exclusion, racism, that sort of thing," he said.

Recalling his six years at the top in West Yorkshire Constabulary, he said, "That is a company of 8.000 people. I was a company director. We had a top team of six. We were directors with a £360 million cash flow. That's not a small company.

"The Metropolitan Police are a phenomenally-sized company, bigger than the RAF. They are not messing about chasing criminals all day at this level. You are directing big companies and you need the ability and skills to do that and an understanding of company direction."

He was asked, upon reflection, would he not regret the phrase "messing about chasing criminals"?

He replied: "Running around catching criminals is a concept of the police 10 years ago. We are into community safety now, of which just a small part is catching criminals. We are very much into partnerships, with the community, with other agencies in the community, trying to improve the social outcomes."

As for those who said the job should be about catching criminals: "There are people who will always keep their heads in the sand," said Mr. Wilkinson.

Clearly unabashed by what all this might look like in print, Mr. Wilkinson plunged on. Jack Straw had given the police the over-arching aims and objectives. "We know what our priorities are. This year's are burglary, robbery and vehicle crime. The Government has told us that."

But that did not necessarily mean that the Home Secretary was telling them to catch more criminals. "You have to take a broader view than that. There's crime prevention. There's the fear of that [crime] happening that needs reducing. It's not only the police that can do it. There's an enormous amount that can now be done, as we have shown, with cameras in town centres.

"We are looking at the quality of life in town centres. It's far wider than catching criminals. It's taking part in the social matrix, if you like. Catching criminals is still an integral part of police work but we can't just think it's a one-tactic service."

The layman, especially if he has been a victim of a crime like burglary, might find all these statements exceedingly bizarre. So if someone was going to throw a rainbow around Bramwell College's teaching curriculum, and give support to the view that generally things were not nearly as bad as they were made out to be as regards law and order in Britain, it was most likely to be another Chief Constable. And sure enough it was. In May, 2000, addressing a conference called Strategies to Defeat Crime, Richard Childs, chief of the Lincolnshire force, rejected the notion of a "golden age" to which Britain could return "if the police did their jobs properly."

Like Norfolk's Ken Williams, Mr. Childs, 45 at the time of the Martin case, did not graduate in any discipline associated with catching criminals. His degree, from the Open University, is in Social Science, Psychology and Statistics.

Why, you may ask, so much emphasis on the educational attainment of Britain's chief constables? Because in a study published in 1991 and entitled *Chief Constables*, Robert Reiner, professor of law at the London School of Economics, and a leading authority on the police, said that the type of degrees some chief constables possess may make them more inclined to a "society causes crime – don't blame us," approach. That view was prevalent during a subsequent policing debate, when Chief Constable Childs said, "The quick and populist way today is to blame the police for getting it wrong. While sometimes we do, we are, I believe, the messengers of change and unrealistic and insatiable expectations."

Critics of the existing system of appointing chief officers believe it rewards caution and conformity and reinforces the culture that has already taken root. Most senior officers are reluctant to offend the Home Office or stray from current orthodoxies because this could threaten their promotion.

Richard Childs's speech at the Strategies to Defeat

Crime conference would have been of particular interest to Tony Martin, since Lincolnshire is Fenland and borders the Norfolk Fens. In the view of this Chief Constable, society had become disjointed, complex and multicultural in recent decades and police now had to take a joint approach with other agencies in society to tackle crime. His comments were undoubtedly inspired in part by the Martin case, and the weeks of criticism levelled at the police as a consequence of it.

"I do not deny that there is crime – always too much and disproportionate in some cases," he said. "But by claiming as some influential opinion formers do, that there was once a golden age of 'no crime, no drugs, and no violence,' and we could get back to that situation if the police did their job properly, and to say that law and order has broken down – when in this country generally it has not – those things combined together amount to scaremongering.

"This raises fears and amounts to a false impression that in those areas where people are very safe most of the time they are not. It causes worry to the elderly that they are high-risk victims when they are not.

"It leads people to think that crime is spiralling upwards everywhere, which it is not, and that recorded crime cannot be reduced, which it has been over the last six years. And for ordinary officers trying to do a decent job it gives them the impression they are undervalued and failures."

But even while this speech was being made, crime in England and Wales *was* spiralling upwards and recorded crime was not being reduced. Figures released only a few weeks after the Chief Constable's speech showed the biggest annual increase in assaults and street robberies in England and Wales for a generation, which contributed to the first overall rise in crime for seven years. Research had recently revealed that recorded crimes in the countryside had increased by about a third in the last decade. One researcher thought the true figure was double that if non-recorded crime was included – that is, crime where the victim cannot be bothered to call the police. That would mean that rural crime had risen sixfold in the decade. One of the worst areas was Mr. Childs's own county of Lincolnshire. Its clear-up rate for burglary was a meagre 12%, compared with Norfolk's pretty dismal 15%. In Lincolnshire there were 4,626 burglaries, compared with Norfolk's 3,956 – 7.8% per 1,000 population in Lincolnshire, as against 5.2% per 1,000 population in Norfolk. The clear-up rate for burglaries in adjacent Cambridgeshire was twice as high as the figure in Lincolnshire.

Asked about these poor results, a Lincolnshire police spokesman explained that its clear-up rate for burglary in the southern division, where only seven per cent of burglaries were cleared up, came at a time of several murder and serious crime investigations – a reason, or an excuse, which suggests that they were just too busy to deal with burglaries. This was scarcely likely to bring any comfort to isolated victims of burglary like Tony Martin, if they were unlucky enough to live in Lincolnshire.

The Lincolnshire police spokesman went on to insist that the emphasis was on crime reduction, and since April 1, 2000, to the three months ending in July, when these figures were released, they had seen an 18% reduction in burglary figures in the county's southern division, and a 27% reduction across Lincolnshire. This will be nothing short of an astonishing reversal of trend if it continues, and it suggests that a perusal of how crime figures are compiled might be enlightening. We shall presently see in fact that many such statistics compiled by Britain's police forces are highly suspect.

Mr. Childs thought that while community-based visible policing would remain, the fight against crime could be more successful as part of a co-ordinated partnership approach – for example, working with children excluded from school.

"But there is a price for this kind of joined-up approach for us and that is that the police can be, and are, accused of becoming 'soft on crime', and some traditionalists believe that officers working in these areas would be better employed on the streets arresting 'real criminals.'"

He added: "The changes that have taken place in social structure and schools, families and neighbourhoods over the past 30 years have significantly altered the context in which we police. Providing the kind of service that will satisfy the public appetite for nil crime or high detection, high police visibility and rapid response times, particularly in rural areas is, without almost National Health Service-scale injection of resources, virtually impossible.

"And to consistently and viciously attack the service who are the unintended messengers of that uncomfortable reality is, in my view, unfair, myopic and seriously counter-productive."

Some might say that all these generalisms had very little relationship to what was happening on the ground. At weekends in Wisbech, for instance, during April, 2000, the month of Martin's trial, the town's 19,000 people were policed by just three officers. Local people say that at times it takes 40 minutes for the station to answer the phone, by which point, as one of Martin's neighbours put it, "You may be dead." There is nothing remarkable about Wisbech. In most of the English countryside the village cop has become a distant memory as forces desperate to economise and starved of resources have retreated to more efficient stations in distant towns.

Criminals as well as law-enforcement agencies are aware that as more urban areas are covered by closed-circuit television cameras, the places to go stealing things are villages and outlying properties. The gang that burgled Martin travelled 70 miles from the East Midlands. Government response to this shift in criminal behaviour was to cut police funding, and police response was to cut policing in the very places where crimes were happening. So in March, 2000, it took detectives 25 minutes to reach a woman who was raped in front of her husband after thieves took them hostage at their home in an isolated Hertfordshire village. The nearest open police station was

20 miles away.

In that year in Britain the number of police officers per head of population was lower than in any European country except Denmark. In 1960, 80,000 police dealt with 500,000 recorded crimes a year. In the year 2000 a total of 124,400 officers – a drop of 2,500 since Labour achieved office in 1997 – faced more than five million offences a year.

A retired Cambridgeshire policeman John Chapman, 53, said: "There were times on a Sunday morning when I was the only policeman out on the street to cover a 10-mile radius. There aren't the policemen to cover these rural areas. Response times can be up to half an hour or even an hour."

In Norfolk, police promised to attend incidents within 20 minutes for country areas. The reality in the first six months of the year 2000 was 45 minutes waiting time in country areas, enough time for a burglar to be 40 or 50 miles away by the time the police arrived. Tony Martin's village of Emneth Hungate, and nearby Downham Market, which coves 120 square miles, have just 26 patrol officers and three detectives to deal with escalating crime rates.

Devon and Cornwall police force covers the biggest territorial area of any force in England, yet it has one of the lowest ratios of police officers per head of population. WPC Alison Berry, a community police officer, said, "If we get a call from someone, say, 15 miles away, by the time we get there, people are often quite upset because it has taken maybe 20 or 30 minutes. It's a long time when you're waiting on someone, when something really serious is happening, or if you think someone is in your house."

Offences like robbery and vehicle theft are rising faster in the countryside than in towns. "The problem is that we have fallen behind," said Sir John Evans, Chief Constable of Devon and Cornwall.

Alan Salisbury, of the Devon and Cornwall Police Federation, was concerned that isolated communities will turn to private security firms or even vigilantes. "If we are not there to provide the service which we want to provide to the public, alternative methods of policing will creep in.

"The last thing we want to do is to lose contact with our grass roots and find that we, the professional police service, only meet our public in confrontational roles."

John Alderson, former Chief Constable of Devon and Cornwall, thought that the Government was giving a terrifying message to rural vandals, burglars, rapists and murderers: "You can go about your business after hours in the countryside safe in the knowledge that you will not meet a policeman on the beat or be bothered by a patrol car. But even if the alarm is raised you will still have plenty of time to escape."

Plenty of time. That's what the thief who raided a Wiltshire newsagent's shop had when he wanted to get away. The newsagent, Richard Stigwood, caught the thief but had to release him because the police were too busy to respond to his call. After 24 hours a lone officer arrived to take a statement.

Anthony Bosanquet, of the Country Landowners' Association, said, "Effective policing cannot be carried out from a distant urban station. Extra resources must be given to rural areas so that people do not have to live in fear."

A "state of the countryside" survey commissioned by the Women's Institute in 1999, which covered almost 5,000 branches in England and Wales, found there was no police presence in 71 per cent of villages. In 86 per cent the nearest police station was at least two miles away. In some areas police were 40 miles away

Insufficient resources are clearly a part of the rural policing problem – Norfolk, for instance, has 176 police officers per 100,000 population, which is lower than Devon and Cornwall, the lowest ratio in Britain, in fact – but given the Bramwell College curriculum and the opinions of some Chief Constables, one might wonder if any amount of cash injection would solve the problems. We have reached the stage where one in three adults in England and Wales can expect to be a crime victim in the next 12 months. At best the criminal justice system puts an offender's name against three out of every 100 crimes we know are committed. So even if investment in policemen was doubled, most offenders would still get away with most of their crimes most of the time.

A Home Office report published in 1999 found that it took officers in rural areas three times longer to answer calls from the public than in urban areas. The recommendation was that tens of millions of pounds should be spent on an extra 1,000 officers for rural forces. There was something sadly familiar about that. When things are not going well with the National Health Service the recommendation is to chuck more public money at it. When things are going wrong in the schools the recommendation is to chuck more public money at them. When things are going wrong with the police...

On July 19 the money was forthcoming – a huge cash injection triumphantly announced by Jack Straw in the Commons. The Home Secretary had been doing some urgent behind-the-scenes sums with Chancellor Gordon Brown, it having emerged that the roll call of police officers in England and Wales was several thousands below what it was when Labour came to power in May, 1997. With only a year before the next Election, unless he could get the figure up to something respectable the Opposition would be banging the law and order drum with a vengeance.

There would now be £1 billion made available to the 43 forces in England and Wales – enough for an extra 4,000 recruits above the 5,000 already planned by chief constables. The extra money did not necessarily mean that there would be extra officers on the ground – chief constables might choose, for example, to invest it in new technology designed to relieve the burden of bureaucracy on officers. Much of the increase would be "for the service to spend as best befits local needs."

It would be imprudent to spend any of this taxpayer-funded cash until analyses have been made of the positive results of such spending – especially since recent Home Office projections suggest that even with the extra money there will be fewer officers in 2004 than there are now. Hiring 4,000 new police officers who can retire well below anyone else's normal retirement age on substantial tax-payer-funded pensions in an era where there is a probability that people will live into their nineties may not be an intelligent way of using public money to solve escalating crime.

The crime statistics for England and Wales released only the day before the announcement of the huge cash injection, show, as we have seen, the first overall rise in crime for six years, bringing the total to 5.2 million crimes, and a falling clear-up rate. In particular there was a 19 per cent rise in robberies, increases in violence against the person, and sexual offences – all crimes that are common, feared and resented by the ordinary victim. But on July 17 Channel 4 News suggested that even these figures may have been massaged – there were, as Disraeli put it, lies, damned lies and statistics. The programme demonstrated that methods of assessing crime for statistical purposes varied from county to county. In Kent, for example, 10,000 reported crimes were written off as "no crime", and never reached the statistics. In another county a compiler of crime statistics said, "I can give the Chief Constable any figure I want."

A new Home Office report published two weeks later revealed that 24 per cent of crimes alleged by the public did not get into the crime statistics. It found that many operational officers saw crime recording as a tedious administrative duty for the politicians in London rather than as vital operational intelligence.

"An additional influence is that the performance of each force is to some extent being assessed and compared on the basis of the crime figures – yet they are asked to collect the figures by which they will be judged." This led to "tension" and a reluctance on the part of forces to change their way of recording. On detection rates, the report high-lighted a tendency of forces "to trawl" the margins for detections and "generally use every means to portray their performance in a good light."

No one should misunderstand what this political-speak means. It means that the crime figures and detection rates were being fiddled. It is not impossible that had police forces across the land not adopted the culture of rivalry that led to this state of affairs, Tony Martin might have been better protected in his home and the Bleak House tragedy might never have happened.

The statistics showed that the one serious crime where the clear-up rate was consistently low across the country – an average of 15 per cent – was burglary. But this does not mean that 15 per cent of burglars are caught. In the event that a burglar is caught, he is first persuaded to confess to all the burglaries he has committed in order to give him a chance to clear his record and prevent him being charged with any of them at a later date. As a result, burglars do not confess to one burglary when they are apprehended – they confess to dozens or even scores. Each one of their crimes then goes down in statistics as one more in the clear-up rate.

Police authorities around the country have recently adopted targets to reduce different categories of crime by 25-30 per cent over the next five years. The inevitable result of targeting is that the police will have an inclination, when no informal report of a crime is made, not to encourage one. When a crime is committed on George Hoyles's Lincolnshire land he always insists on reporting it so that the police log it as a crime. But Mr. Hoyles knows the drill. So many others take the view that there is so lit-tle prospect of anything happening if they are the victim of petty theft or vandalism that it is not worth the bother of reporting it.

Recent figures showed that crime in one town centre in north Kent had dropped by 8.2 per cent over the past year. The *Kent Messenger* quoted the comments of the chairman of the local LVA: "Crime in the town has gone from bad to worse. It may well be true that reported crime is down, but there are many incidents that people do not report because they say it is not worth contacting the police."

The response of the police spokesman, who was called PC Wisdom, was that "there has been no evidence to suggest an increase in under-reporting." PC Wisdom evidently required unreported incidents to be counted by the police to whom they were not reported.

Another nasty side-effect of statistical targeting is to persuade the police to go for the soft target rather than the hard one. An example of a soft target was the case of Arthur Farrer, a solicitor who was prosecuted for revealing to his mother, who is in her eighties, where he kept the key of his shotgun cabinet. Another side-effect centres on the belief that policing is the most effective way of dealing with racism, manifested early in the year 2000 by plain-clothes officers staking out curry houses to eavesdrop on diners in order to prosecute them for any racial comments they might make. These are the stuff of the easy cop; they make successful prosecutions and put statistics in the right column. But they are also misused statistics that forfeit trust, because they make the public sceptical.

In Edenbridge in Kent, Mrs. Pamela Furno, a local housewife, organised a protest campaign against escalating crime in the town, following the closure of the police station and the withdrawal of most full-time beat officers. She gained hundreds of supporters threatening to withhold council tax payments unless Kent Police Authority took some urgent action.

She said: "All of us in this town have either been burgled or know someone who has. We have attended meeting after meeting and we didn't get anywhere. I'm sure the rest of middle England feels the way we do." A few years ago Edenbridge had six full-time police officers manning the police station. Since then the population has grown – but the police force has been reduced to two, and emergencies are dealt with from Sevenoaks, 20 miles away.

Why has crime increased on the sort of massive scale revealed by the last half century of statistics? We have heard all sorts of reasons, such as poverty, deprivation, the decline of family life, even affluence – the idea that when there are more things to steal there will be more people to steal them. These are only half truths. The principal answer is that where a community permits public disorder and low-level criminality to flourish, serious crime will soon increase too. When the lawless see that no one cares about aggressive begging, graffiti, and the like, they quickly recognise that no one is in charge and are emboldened to rob and burgle and assault. Stop crime at its root, at petty crime, or as it is sometimes called victimless crime, by arresting and incarcerating, and the big crime will stop too. Such a policy violates the most cherished beliefs of the intellectual elites; sooner rather than later, though, someone has to stand up to the intellectual elites and tell them they are wrong.

Few things have been more destructive in Britain's post-war life than the counter-culture promoted in every area of thinking by the intellectual elites – that one has a right to the state-subsidised "life-style" of one's choice, that street-sleepers are the victims of a cruel economy, that crime is society's fault, that the purpose of education is to attack discrimination. Some of this is on the wane, but the legacy lingers on.

A month after the Martin verdict the Police Federation of England and Wales, the policemen's trade union, held its annual conference in Brighton, an occasion pervaded by gloom and despondency over criticism of the police, shrinking police numbers and the failure of law and order policies. Before the conference the Federation's chairman, Fred Broughton, gave an illuminating insight into the state of policing in England and Wales.

Cases such as that of Tony Martin, he said, had served to highlight the "scandal" of rural policing. "Irrespective of whether Tony Martin was guilty or not [did this police officer apparently have some doubts about the verdict?] the problem is that communities such as his are unable to rely on the police. I think people are quite confused about policing. It is more common to see a traffic warden in a town than a police officer." Falling police numbers had also created deep problems in inner cities, with violence and disorder amounting to "anarchy" outside pubs and clubs at night in London, Leeds, Liverpool and Manchester.

Some city forces were policing "hot spots" with just half of the officers available five years ago. "There is a sense of disorder and anarchy in many of these areas. Most people avoid them altogether as there are no police officers to turn to." The service was "drowning in a demand from the public" – with 999 calls, incidents and disorder creating a 40 per cent increase in the police workload over the past six years – but the service had been given inadequate resources to pay for it.

Mr. Broughton, a constable with the Metropolitan Police, said the Federation would call for an independent royal commission to consider the state of policing. The last royal commission was in 1960, but there had been huge changes in the last 40 years and a slide downhill in the 1990s. The 1960 royal commission's report had stressed that the maintenance of law and order ranked with national defence as a primary task of government.

"Ninety police stations have closed in the last 12 months and there is centralisation of policing in most county forces," he said. "In other words, you move to targeted patrolling centrally and you close down local police stations. This centralisation has been financially driven, and I understand why, but it has been disastrous for the way we police. Centralisation has now affected vast areas of this country in terms of the partnership aspect of police – by which I mean the relations between the police and the community.

"There is a serious lack of confidence within the community because they don't know or understand what [the police] are doing for them." Rank and file police officers were reporting that "what is going on locally is breaking down and that they have not got enough support. The public is angry and frustrated about the policing service they are receiving and there is frustration on the part of officers because of that."

Chief officers, he said, were placed in "a Catch 22 situation" after they were given responsibility for police numbers by the last government but were then allocated insufficient funds "to release the number of officers required."

It was not only poor policing policy that was troubling rural Britain. Only days after the Martin verdict the Countryside Agency, a sort of rural watchdog, painted a devastating picture of crisis in the English countryside – of pretty villages and beautiful scenery masking a reality of poverty, disappearing services and the collapse of farming incomes.

With the growing sense of despair had come an erosion of the common values which have held the countryside together for generations, reported the agency, headed by Ewen Cameron, a landowner personally appointed by Prime Minister Tony Blair.

"There is an unsettling fear that villages and market towns are losing their sense of community, as well as the relative security which many have enjoyed for a long time," said the agency in its report entitled "The State of the Countryside, 2000."

The report found farm labourers face low wages and unaffordable housing – often having been priced out of the market by former city-dwellers. Unemployment was higher in the countryside, and more workers depended on part-time, seasonal or casual jobs.

Life was being made worse by the crisis in farming. The report said: "The value of our agricultural output has collapsed in the face of low world commodity prices and the high value of sterling. Coupled with other changes in agriculture, this is putting enormous pressure on farming communities."

Shops were closing in many villages and small towns –

with a devastating impact on those too old or too poor to drive. The typical village food shop was now "only marginally viable," and rural post offices were fast becoming things of the past – doomed by the electronic payment of benefits and bills, the sale of stamps in other shops, and "fear of burglary or armed robbery."

Country pubs were also closing at a rate of three per county per year.

Mr. Cameron issued a sombre warning: "Behind the rosy image of the rural idyll lie some very real problems; problems of rural isolation, a declining environment, pressurised and declining services and a vulnerable rural economy."

Commenting on the Martin trial in *The Independent*, Deborah Orr wrote: "The most significant of the extraordinary aftershocks of this terrible case is the attention that is now being focused on the contents of the [government's] white paper ... This tale of the country is very similar to our tales of the city ... the ruthless efficiency with which we are presiding over the breakdown of farming, and of traditional rural ways of life, is arrestingly similar to the manner in which industry was crushed in the final decade of the last century ... the 'tens of millions of pounds' which has been pledged by the Home Office for the policing of rural areas is something. But rural Britain needs much more than this if the rot is to be stopped."

12

...AND THE PROBLEMS OF THE POLITICIANS

As Tony Martin was being packed off to his life sentence, William Hague, leader of the Opposition Tory Party, entered the fray with a dramatic demand that householders should have stronger rights in law to defend themselves.

He told a public meeting at Alcester, Warwicks, on Thursday, April 27, 2000 that the conviction of Tony Martin had triggered "an explosion of anger and resentment among millions of law-abiding people who will no longer feel that the State is on their side."

The case, he said, highlighted defects in the legal system which no longer reflected "natural justice." Mandatory life sentences should be abolished for those convicted of committing murder in self-defence. He promised that a future Tory government would re-balance the justice system "with a strong presumption that the State will be on the side of the people who protect their homes and their families against criminals."

He went on, "Politicians aren't doing their job if they don't listen and respond to the unprecedented public outcry which has greeted this murder conviction. What is the point of having a police service and prisons when three criminals, with 114 convictions between them, are allowed to wander free to terrorise rural communities?

"Most of the time these three men were fined paltry sums or given community service. Occasionally they got short prison sentences, and even then they were released after just a few months behind bars. Their histories of repeated crimes and repeatedly lenient sentences is sadly familiar in today's courts.

"No wonder the public despair and the police ask what the point is of catching criminals when they just get released back on to the street. Part of the blames lies with a liberal legal establishment that too often appears to put the concerns for the rights of criminals before the rights of millions of vulnerable people."

In speaking out about the conviction of Tony Martin, the Tory leader took the case from the media spotlight and thrust it into the arena of political debate.

His political opponents joined with the police and judiciary to attack him, despite a Teletext poll in which 98 per cent of viewers thought he was right to press for an overhaul of the law. Of 4,935 votes, 4,825 backed him, with 110 against.

Referring to the fury his remarks had engendered in his opponents, he said, "I wanted this to happen. It is the only way to get people to connect with what is happening."

In his speech Mr. Hague revealed a series of proposals which he claimed would ensure "natural justice" for those who protect their homes and their families against criminals. He thought the current "objective" test of reasonable force should be made "subjective," switching the balance from an intruder back in favour of the homeowner who uses a weapon in self-defence. If all this sounded exciting and new it wasn't – this change was actually recommended by the Criminal Law Revision Committee in 1980. The government then in office which did not take it up was a Tory one.

Mr. Hague also believed that the police and Crown Prosecution Service should be allowed to exercise greater restraint in charging people in cases of self-defence. He declared that he was examining possible changes in the law so that where excessive force is used by a homeowner and a death occurs, the reduced charge of manslaughter should apply. The maximum penalty for manslaughter, like murder, is life, although judges have discretion to impose a lesser sentence.

But in his proposals the Tory leader neatly side-stepped the views of a vast number of Britons who thought and still think that it was disgraceful that Martin was in jail at all. These were the people who would ask why Martin was charged with any crime if he were acting in defence of his property, and thought he was acting in defence of his life. Under the Hague proposals Martin might have gone to prison for a long time, as people found guilty of manslaughter frequently do. It would be unrealistic for any politician to imagine that jailing someone for a long time for defending their property and probably their lives would not provoke a public outcry – whether the charge was murder or manslaughter. Even so, it was a reflection of the strength of public feeling that the murder trial had generated that now a senior politician had rallied – in empathy, if not defence – to Martin.

Mr. Hague's ideas, which many people would say were not nearly sufficiently far-reaching, were greeted with cries of 'opportunism' by Labour MPs who, remember, were elected on a "Tough on crime, tough on the causes of crime" slogan. Mr. Hague replied, "The charge implicitly accepts that any politician talking about the issues I raise is tapping into a deep vein of public support. It suggests that there is something dishonourable about doing so. I do not accept this.

"I believe that the public's instinct that our law and order system is not providing us with the level of protection that we want is right. I believe that the public instinct that criminals should not be allowed to commit crime repeatedly without paying a proper penalty is right.

"I believe that the public instinct that, for all that extra tax we are paying, police numbers should not be falling is right. Seeing these instincts become public policy is the proper job for a politician."

To charges that he was inciting violence by encouraging people to take the law into their own hands, and fostering a 'lynch mob' mentality, he said, "Criminals are the people who have taken the law into their own hands, the people who ignore police, the people who have contempt for the victim. With more police, tougher sentencing and clearer law, the law-abiding citizen will be able to follow the law and protect himself at the same time."

The Martin case was again reduced to a political punch-bag in the Commons on May 3, when the Tory leader clashed with Tony Blair during Prime Minister's Questions. The following day the issue was raised again by Martin's MP, Dr. George Turner (Labour, Norfolk NW), in an observation that did nothing for his constituent. "The nature of the reporting and the media commentary surrounding the trial of my constituent has done much to raise the fear of crime in rural areas," he said. "The comments we've had from local Conservatives in their eagerness to attack the Government have, in my view, undermined the police." This seemed curiously out of step with the comment on future action made by his fellow area MP, Gillian Shephard, at the angry public meeting at Emneth on September 8, 1999. (See Chapter 3).

But Margaret Beckett, the Leader of the House, admitted that Mr. Hague had made a "legitimate point" in calling for a review of the law which demands a mandatory life sentence for those who commit murder in self-defence. This sensible comment had to be tempered, however, by another silly piece of political snidery. She told Dr. Turner: "I share your concern, and I thought it was a good and classic example during the exchanges between Mr. Blair and the Opposition, of the short-sightedness and folly of Mr. Hague in the way that he raises these issues."

Like a rag doll torn between two snarling dogs, the issue of law and order was thus reduced to political in-fighting while Tony Martin, the cause of it all, languished in prison. Inevitably Prime Minister Blair had to respond, but he too had nothing new to say.

"I remind the Conservatives that when in power crime doubled, and in all their 18 years in office they never once introduced the vague measures they are now proposing." he said.

The newspaper columnist Auberon Waugh, who rarely agrees with Mr. Blair, was also sceptical. Describing Martin's life sentence as "monstrous," he said, "I think we must assume that they [the Tories] have no intention of altering the present arrangement whereby ordinary private citizens who might be prepared to look after themselves are prevented from doing so by the police."

A couple of weeks later, in the first appearance by a leader of the principal opposition party at an annual conference of the Police Federation, Mr. Hague again attacked the "liberal establishment" which he said had failed to tackle crime. In a warmly applauded speech he rejected "the defeatist nonsense that says crime is just a function of economic and social trends."

He said, "This liberal thinking on crime, which has pervaded our criminal justice system for 40 years, has failed this country. Criminals are not moral zombies sliding down a trend line on a graph. They make choices and we should make them pay for those choices.

"I want criminals to be fearful of getting caught and of punishment, so they will choose not to commit crimes. I want to make convicted criminals unwilling to commit more crimes or at least to keep them under lock and key so that they can't. We need to give you the political support by defeating the liberal nonsense that says the war against crime can't be won. We need more police officers and less political correctness – more PCs and less PC."

From prison Tony Martin himself commented on this fiery Tory approach, "What Mr. Hague says, that people who defend their homes against intruders will have the law stacked in their favour under the Tories, is admirable. But this huge increase in rural crime hasn't just happened during the Labour Government. It was increasing while the Tories were in power, too."

Earlier, Tory MP Ann Widdicombe, Shadow Home Secretary, had joined in the fray. On April 23 she said she thought householders should be free to injure intruders without fear of prosecution. Police had to act after Barras was killed, because "where there is a dead body, there would have to be a trial."

She went on, "But if people hit a burglar over the head, as is far more common, it is unacceptable that they risk prosecution. There needs to be much greater presumption by the Crown Prosecution Service that force is reasonable."

Although this lukewarm view appeared to add nothing to the debate, Labour MPs still protested that she was advocating "a cosher's charter." But Norman Brennan, of the Victims of Crime Trust, said, "Your rationality with dealing with an intruder is very different at 2 a.m. than in the cold light of day."

The former Tory chairman Lord Tebbit, who survived the Brighton bombing of 1984 and who keeps a licensed shotgun at his Devon home for sporting purposes, weighed in with a more interesting comment. He said that shortly after the IRA murdered the MP Ian Gow in 1990, he was disturbed late at night by a noise outside his house.

He looked out of the window and saw two men, one of whom was underneath his car. Only when he approached them with his shotgun under his arm did he recognise one of them as a local policeman. He later heard that they had parked their own vehicle up the drive to avoid waking him.

Lord Tebbit said that had they been terrorists planting a bomb under the car he would have been justified in shooting them. Fortunately he didn't because he went forward to identify them first. He said, "A good sportsman always identifies the game before shooting it, and I'm not in the habit of shooting owls or budgies when I mean to fire at pheasants or partridges." Nonetheless, he supported

William Hague's call for new laws so that homeowners can protect themselves against intruders.

Despite a dash of liberal bravado put out by some Labour MPs and Party supporters, the shooting of Fred Barras had the Government squirming over accusations that it has concentrated on urban policing to the cost of rural communities. Jack Straw got ready to set off a growing Commons revolt by beginning to entertain demands that people should be given more protection if they are obliged to take the law into their own hands.

Ministers were now considering "giving judges the right to downgrade murder charges to manslaughter for people who kill in self-defence, and to give householders the right to defend their homes without being automatically prosecuted." This does not augur well for the future, since both these proposals are already in place – we have already seen that the judge in the Martin case told the jury they could return a manslaughter verdict if they wanted – so what's new?

A "Labour source" explained the Government's dilemma: "The difficulty in legislating in the wake of the Martin case is that he used an illegally-held gun to shoot someone in the back. But we are aware of the strong public concern that the law needs amending and we will meet that concern."

There are two points here. First, the issue that the gun was illegally held and that Barras was shot in the back are separate matters which are marginal notes to the central issue in the Martin case. Second, when will the public concern be met? "The Government will make no formal response until the Martin case appeal in June, when it is set to give new guidance on what is 'reasonable' use of force," the same source said. But the Martin appeal was not held in June – it was not then due in the Appeal Court until October, and in fact the whole of the year 2000 came and went and the appeal was still not listed for hearing.

More far-reaching proposals about defending one's home against intruders would not be forthcoming immediately. "Labour was likely to address the issue in its manifesto for the General Election, which is expected next spring."

That legislation, then, might be put into effect any time between the next two to six years, if it does not go the way of many another election promise and never be put into effect at all.

Interestingly, the further away a politician was from the epicentre of the storm, the more bland the comments became. The Conservative MEP for the East Midlands, Roger Helmer, who of course operates mainly in Brussels, said, "I do have sympathy with the fact Mr. Martin had suffered repeated burglaries. Rural areas do need to be properly policed so that another tragedy like this does not happen again."

Which was very profound.

Tony Martin received the same sentence as Kenneth Noye, a man with a violent past who knifed a man to death in a road rage incident, and the same sentence as Dr. Harold Shipman, who was jailed for life for killing 15 of his patients and may have killed hundreds more. The reason he got the same sentence is that the law of the land decrees it. When capital punishment was finally abolished in 1969, Parliament, against the advice of the judiciary, insisted that it must be replaced by mandatory life sentences. Politicians could see no difference between one murder and the other – just as hanging was the only answer to murder in the pre-execution era, so a life sentence must be the only answer to murder in the post-execution era.

The Right wing of the Tory Party fought over the years against any reform to this stringent provision, despite a wave of official reports showing that the situation was flawed and could not be sustained. The Butler Report, from a committee chaired by R. A. Butler in 1975, was uncompromising in its criticism of mandatory sentencing. So, three years later, was a report by the Advisory Council on the Penal System. Two years after that, the Criminal Law Revision Committee also declared that mandatory sentencing was wrong. The same conclusion was reached by the all-party Penal Reform Committee in 1986 as it also was by the House of Lords Select Committee in 1988.

None of these advisory bodies were consumer pressure groups, the sort of active lobby to which the Government has all too quickly capitulated today. They were all advisory bodies to Government, experts paid by government to sit down and consider what was necessary to reform the law, it being understood that law must always be reformed. Yet not in any single instance did government take any notice of them. Thus for more than 25 years Parliament has echoed the rigid, uncompromising attitude of Home Office Minister Paul Boateng, who on Channel 4 News a few days after the Martin verdict, made it clear that the Labour Government would not change the law in order to introduce degrees of murder.

He was adamant about that and appeared to be vexed that it should even be suggested. "Murder is a very serious thing," he told viewers with suitable gravitas. He blamed Mr. Hague for fomenting trouble – earlier in the same week the Tory leader had been blamed for playing the race card when he asked for firmer asylum-seeking laws and now it seemed he was playing the crime card. A Tory spokesman then had a go at Labour's record on crime, and it must have seemed to viewers that all this sort of political face-scratching revealed was that we did not have statesmen capable of raising the issues of Tony Martin and what is reasonable self-defence to the human level they deserved.

But even as Mr. Boateng was speaking, behind the scenes in Downing Street something was stirring. The Prime Minister himself sat down and wrote a confidential memo to his senior Government colleagues, a memo famously leaked eleven weeks later, on "touchstone issues" which were giving him cause for concern. The issues, he wrote, added up to a sense that the Government – "and this even applies to me" – were somehow out of touch with gut British instincts. He went on:

"The Martin case – and the lack of any response from us that appeared to empathise with public concern and then channel it into the correct course – has only heightened this problem. We need a thoroughly worked-out strategy stretching over several months to regain the initiative in this area."

After summarising action needed on the issues, the Prime Minister wrote:

"My thoughts are:

"Possibly on the Martin case, asking a senior judge to look at changing the sentencing law, i.e. to allow lesser sentences than life. We also need a far tougher rebuttal or alternatively action, re the allegations that jurors were intimidated."

One of the recipients of this memo was Home Secretary Jack Straw, who after reading it let it be known that he was prepared to change the law of self-defence to incorporate new guidelines, which would be drawn up by the Court of Appeal considering the Martin case. Mr. Straw, we learned, was reluctant to speak out on the specific issue because he would have a judicial role to play in approving Martin's tariff on his life sentence. A Home Office spokesman said, "The Home Secretary cannot ask or tell the Court of Appeal to issue guidelines, but it is something we expect them to do. We will have to wait until then to see if new legislation is necessary."

Notice how throughout all this there is a gentle buck-passing action going on. Why, for instance, must the Court of Appeal frame guidelines on self-defence – the issue of what steps a man may take to protect his property and his life? Is it not the job of government to produce these guidelines, thereby allowing the people to throw out the government if it disapproves of them? What is an elected legislative for if it cannot itself initiate, debate and legislate?

Again, if ministers, prompted by the Prime Minister, were having second thoughts about the whole thing – a sudden awareness that the common law of self-defence needed clarification – why was Martin, whose self-defence was considered at the time to be excessive but upon review might now be considered to be something less than excessive, still languishing in prison? The question needs to be addressed because it now seemed that he had been sent there on what appeared to be admitted as unclear law or even bad law – law that might be so bad that "we will have to see if new legislation is necessary."

Time and again after the Martin verdict ordinary members of the public protested about this bad law. A *Daily Telegraph* reader, P. R. Belchamber, of Battle, East Sussex, wrote to his newspaper on April 27: "Tony Martin was not the victim of just a succession of crimes by persons who should have been behind bars. He was also the victim of the present law-and-order policy, with its politically driven requirements, which result in the police concerning themselves more with political correctness than with catching criminals, and the courts handing down 'soft' sentences rather than punishments to deter re-offending.

"If the shameful treatment of Mr. Martin proves to be the catalyst for the long-overdue changes in the law and its application, we shall all owe this sad man a great debt of gratitude."

In the same newspaper next day, Professor Christie Davies, of the University of Reading, said that despite Labour's promise to get tough on crime and its causes, the British people were now experiencing a rising incidence of both violent and property crime. The government had done very little to ameliorate the situation, "and that much of what it has done has been concerned with appeasing lobbies such as the race relations industry or the feminists." Prison did at least take burglars, car thieves and muggers out of circulation.

"Why can a government hysterically punitive on drugs, racial and sexual offences not take these everyday inflictions on the ordinary victim as seriously as they deserve?" Professor Davies asked.

Today anyone unwise enough to take the law into his own hands would be punished far more severely than those responsible for the attacks or invasion of dwellings.

"The State is far more concerned to preserve its own monopoly of law enforcement than to protect its citizens. Yet it is inevitable that people will in time turn to vigilante justice if the State fails to protect them. Labour has done next to nothing to protect the person and property of the citizen, and is likely to end up undermining not merely its own standing but the very authority of government and the criminal justice system."

Despite the Prime Minister's concern about the lack of Government response to the wave of public anger which followed Martin's conviction, despite the continuing anger of householders across Britain, the Government was in no hurry to right this wrong. In mid-summer, 2000, Martin was suddenly removed from Bullingdon to Gartree Prison in Leicester. This is a category B prison which is home to prisoners serving life sentences.

A Prison Service spokesman said, "When prisoners serving life sentences have served several months at one prison, during which time they are under constant assessment, it is standard procedure to move them. It is nothing to do with who the individual prisoner is." Martin, he said, was likely to stay at Gartree at least until his appeal was heard.

Days after this move another memo was leaked. This concerned Martin's "tariff" – the actual time he should serve in prison. When a prisoner gets life no one in the court apart from the judge knows how long the sentence will be. After the verdict the judge recommends a tariff, which is approved by the Lord Chief Justice and then approved and monitored by the Home Secretary. This form of secret sentencing, passing as it does from the jurisdiction of the court to the jurisdiction of a politician, is the norm in Britain.

We learned through the leak that the trial judge, Mr. Justice Owen, had first recommended a tariff of eight years, then changed it to nine. However, the Lord Chief Justice, Lord Woolf, believed there were "mitigating circumstances," which were not explained, and that Martin should be considered for release in eight years. The final tariff would be set by the Home Secretary.

Mr. Justice Owen's report on the case in which he recommended the tariff, said that much of the public sympathy for Martin was "based on very inadequate accounts of the evidence" and concluded: "He is never likely to re-offend but he deserves punishment." This would have surprised most criminologists, since the actual evidence in the Martin case was much less complex than in many other celebrated murder trials. What public sympathy was about in this case was not based on inadequate accounts of the evidence, it was based on the principle involved – and that was something the public seemed to understand far better than anyone in the judiciary, the legislature or the executive.

Even more surprising is that if this leaked memo was genuine, the judge was actually recommending a shorter sentence for the murder of Barras than the sentence of 10 years he passed on Martin for wounding Fearon. (See Chapter 4). Since as far as the two burglars were concerned, all the facts in the case were identical, this seems to indicate that the wounding of Fearon was considered more serious than the murder of Barras.

On same day that the Tony Martin tariff memo was leaked, more than 80 of Northern Ireland's most feared and reviled terrorists – murderers and those involved in murder – were released under the terms of the Good Friday Agreement. Most of them had served a fraction of their sentences for murder, bombing, conspiracy to murder and attempted murder – that fraction being measured in months rather than years.

In the three-act comic opera entitled, "Tough on crime, tough on the causes of crime," this was the grand finale.

13

A BURGLAR BECOMES A JUDGE

When the celebrated humorist J. B. Morton, who wrote under the pseudonym of Beachcomber, retired from his literary career, he explained that the world had become so bizarre that events he once dreamed up as comic were actually now happening regularly in real life, and that therefore whatever he wrote no longer appeared to anyone to be funny. Morton, then, would have loved the revelation in April, 2001, that burglar Brendan Fearon was being consulted about the length of time he thought Tony Martin should stay in prison because he – Fearon that is – was a victim of crime. This was to be Fearon's right under the Victim Support Charter.

The burglar wrote a typewritten letter from his cell in Stocken Prison, Leicestershire, to "Dear Tony." It read:

"I have been visited by the Victim Support Group in relation to my feelings about you gaining parole in the future.

"I was therefore forced to think about how remorseful you may be. Judging from the cold words of your distorted truth in the paper reviews, my thoughts are not overly optimistic."

Fearon's letter suggested that Martin would only be at peace with himself once he had admitted his crimes, and added that he himself had done just that.

"I feel you will gain your sense of truth in time, as you and I know what happened that fateful night," he wrote. "Reconciliation will not occur until you face up to your doings as I myself have done so."

And like the true penitent he was, facing up to his doings and gaining his sense of truth, this man who had now been elevated to the judicial bench to help decide the fate of the farmer he had terrorised and robbed, added: "We was not there to take your belongings merely to escape your dogs and didn't mean to be intruders."

The burglar's pathetic lecture to his victim, sanctioned by a legal group set up by the Home Office, went rambling on remorselessly: "Whatever the reason may have been for us being there, that shouldn't have led to a little boy dying as there is no making amends for that little boy.

"What is so sad is that you haven't even stressed your sorrows for taking a human life and given the little boy's family a second thought as they have received a life sentence which there is no going back from (so sad). I hope you feel remorse as it's the only way forward."

Martin was understandably upset by this piece of legally-inspired torture and did not reply. However, Tory MP Ann Widdecombe, the shadow home secretary, described it as "madness," and went on: "Whatever the rights and wrongs about the degree of force Tony Martin used, it's turning common sense upside down to consult a burglar about the liberty of his victim."

Gerald Howarth, a member of the Commons home affairs select committee, agreed. It was, he said, a farce, and utter lunacy, and he would write to the Home Secretary to make sure that on no account should Fearon's views be taken into consideration.

To be fair to Jack Straw, it is possible that he may himself have been just a little concerned when he was confronted with this grotesque inversion of morality emanating from his own department. Perhaps he might not have been told about it. At any rate, hard on the heels of the disclosure we learned that the Home Secretary had ordered a review of the Victim's Support Charter. "The Martin-Fearon case is very unusual and I can understand concerns about consultation with Fearon," Mr. Straw said, a quote that possibly even J. B. Morton couldn't have improved upon.

But until the review happens – if it ever does, for Mr. Straw was never the fastest mover in politics, and he was replaced as Home Secretary a few months later – Fearon was entitled to have his view considered should Martin seek early release in 2009, that is, ten years after he was jailed. The fact that Martin was facing the possibility of being in jail until 2009 not just for something he had done to Fearon, but for something he had also done to Barras, seemed to have escaped Home Office vigilance. One has to assume that the burglar was being assigned to act as a judge on behalf of his dead companion as well. The law was evidently determined to go on headlong making an ass of itself.

While all this was going on Fearon himself was half-way through his three-year sentence for burgling Bleak House. He was seeking early release – although apparently Tony Martin, the victim of his crime, was not to be consulted by the Home Office on whether that should happen. Fearon asked to be released under curfew and to be electronically tagged, so that he could be near his father, who had developed bone cancer.

Mr. Joseph Fearon, whose behaviour throughout the Martin case was a model of dignity, restraint, and plain common sense, had other problems in his life, for another son, Neil, had been jailed for five years in 2000 for cheating elderly women out of £40,000. He did not think that his son Brendan's parole plan was a good idea. Calling on him to abandon it, he said, "I say to Brendan, leave it alone. Your friend was killed and you were shot and you are lucky to be alive. Mr. Martin should not be in prison but you should. Shut your mouth and finish your time. You make an idiot of yourself by carrying on like this."

He felt he did not need his son's help until the burglar

was released at the end of his sentence. "I am not well and I am just trying to get better. I need to put this behind me. My son needs to do the same and move on with his life but he must serve his time. He has done very wrong but he is still my son and I love him."

Someone else who was about to arrive in jail was Fred Barras senior, the father of Fred Barras. Only six weeks after seeing Martin jailed for the Bleak House murder, 45-year-old Barras took a leading role in a £400,000 raid on a clothing warehouse in which a woman security guard was tied up and had a gun held to her head. The Barras gang stole three lorries and their contents belonging to the clothing firm Next.

Two of the lorries were found in a hangar at a disused airfield near Goole, East Yorkshire, where Barras had a caravan. Two of his relatives also lived there. In June, 2001, Barras was convicted of conspiracy to rob and sentenced to 14 years. Leeds Crown Court heard that his lengthy list of previous convictions stretching back over 32 years included cases of assaulting police and theft, and numerous motoring offences.

Martin, meanwhile, had other things to think about. In August, 2000, his friends had announced that he had decided to drop his defence team – solicitor Nick Makin and barrister Anthony Scrivener, QC.

Malcolm Starr, who was handling the announcements, said Martin was led to believe from the outset there would be no case to answer and that he would not go to prison. "In view of that he has come to the conclusion that he cannot keep faith with the same defence team. The appeal grounds are very strong and a new team will only add strength to this."

Max Clifford said: "This is entirely Tony's decision, but I'm not surprised. He has been rather unhappy with the defence team since the outcome of the trial. He has had a lot of time to think about it and has been growing increasingly dissatisfied."

At that precise moment no new team had been

appointed for the appeal but within days the new solicitors were named as Saunders and Co, a London firm, with James Saunders acting for Martin and Michael Wolkind, QC, as leading counsel.

Then a most unsatisfactory row broke out. Nick Makin's firm, M and S Solicitors, refused to release the defence papers to the new team until they were paid £37,000, an amount which they claimed was outstanding as a result of work done on the case after the verdict. The obvious source of payment was the Tony Martin Support Fund. But, insisted Saunders and Co, M and S were granted a full legal aid certificate for the trial to include counsel's fees. Not so, replied M and S. So, on September 25, 2000, Saunders and Co asked the High Court to compel M and S to release the papers. The judge adjourned the application until the end of October, when it was granted, on condition that the disputed £37,000 was paid into a bank to be argued over in a later civil action. The money was put up partly by the Support Fund and partly by Martin's mother.

In another application in the same court, however, the judge refused legal aid for the appeal, the grounds being that under new regulations enacted by the present government, any assets outside the family home must be used to finance the defence.

The delays caused by these actions were unfortunate, because without the defence papers the new solicitors could not prepare a case for the Appeal Court. Something of what was going on behind the scenes can be gauged from the fact that Saunders and Co then lodged "a comprehensive letter of complaint" about Mr. Makin to the Office for the Supervision of Solicitors. Newsletter No. 2 from the Tony Martin Support Group declared: "These are very serious allegations which have serious repercussions for the case." But Mr. Makin's claim was subsequently upheld by an enquiry.

And so, as Christmas, 2000 arrived, Tony Martin was still in jail and still had no idea when his appeal might be heard. He told a journalist that he feared he would be left to rot. Malcolm Starr, who visited him, described him as being "up and down." But he was hardly forgotten. He received more than 4,500 cards and letters from well-wishers, giving him, he said, enormous encouragement to face his uncertain future. In reply, he sent out a hand-written message to all of them: "I would like to thank all my friends and well wishers for the support you have given me during the darkest moments of my life. We still have a long way to go during the year 2001. I would like to wish you all a peaceful Christmas and New Year."

Half way through that year Martin had been in prison for 15 months – time enough for law enforcement authorities to deal with burgeoning crimes and lower than ever detection rates. In fact, despite all the political rhetoric, matters were getting steadily worse. Britain's crime statistics made it the most violent country in the industrialised world, a shameful reflection on a country that once set the pattern for international behaviour standards. Figures published in July, 2001, showed crime detection rates at their lowest level ever, with fewer than one in five offences being cleared up. The record was even worse for burglaries and car thefts, with only one in ten cases being solved. Twelve years previously the overall detection rates stood at more than one in three. In the year 2000 the number of crimes solved by police fell by nearly 73,000.

These figures are scarcely extraordinary given the fact that more than 600 police stations closed in the 1990s – nearly 200 of them closed during the Labour Government's first term of office. In the run-up to the 2001 General Election the Government was conceding that it would go to the electorate with fewer police than when it took office.

Fred Broughton, Chairman of the Police Federation, said about this: "The whole centralisation of policing is counter-productive to real community policing. The closure of rural and suburban stations is making the police more remote. Not only are people not seeing a uniform presence on the street but they haven't even got local police stations to have a link with."

Almost exactly the same words were being used two years previously, when the outcry began about the shooting of Fred Barras.

The Home Office itself had revealed at the beginning of 2001 that the cost of crime in England and Wales was a staggering £60 billion a year – 6.7 per cent of the entire Gross Domestic Product of the UK. And this, it added, was a conservative figure. The total cost of burglaries in terms of law enforcement time was £2.7 billion; the average bill for a burglary was £2,300.

As far as law and order was concerned, the Government didn't seem able to get anything right. The political paranoia following the 1997 Dunblane shootings was revealed for what it was – paranoia. After Dunblane, when handgun ownership was proscribed, more than 160,000 handguns were surrendered to the police. But in the two years following the ban the number of crimes in which a handgun was reported to have been used increased from 2,648 to 3,685 – up 40 per cent. Their use was at its highest level since 1993. This reinforced what many handgun owners said at the time of Dunblane – that there is no direct link between the unlawful use of handguns and their lawful ownership.

Some belated moves were afoot after the 2001 General Election to tackle police pension feather-bedding, which is at the nub of failed police recruitment campaigns. The Home Office appeared to be understanding that it could not put off reform of the lucrative police pension scheme. As there is no dedicated pension fund for the police, payments to retired officers come from the same pot of money as daily policing. Because more officers retired early and lived longer, the sum spent on pensions doubled during the 1990s. Fifteen per cent of police spending – up from £820 million in 1998 to £1 billion in 2001 – goes on pensions, and 49 per cent of police officers take early retirement on medical grounds. The other 51 per cent can retire at 49 after 30 years service. The pension scheme allows constables earning £26,000 a year to retire with a guaranteed index-linked income of £17,000 and launch a new career – an inducement for officers to leave the force faster than any government can maintain numbers by recruitment. And as average police numbers continued to fall during the incarceration of Tony Martin, 20,000 convicted criminals benefited from early release from prison under the Government's tagging scheme.

In the spring of 2001 Martin's new defence team was considering asking the Appeal Court to reduce his conviction to manslaughter on the grounds of diminished responsibility.

Did this mean that he was, after all, mad? Not at all. It meant simply that his state of mind was so stressed at the time of the shootings, as a result of the previous burglaries, that he was not completely responsible for his actions. As evidence that he could be affected by stress, a trawl through his medical health history had revealed that in the 1970s he had suffered a breakdown. He had attempted to walk 90 miles in deep snow from his home – he was then living in March, in Cambridgeshire – to London.

He was found 20 miles away at Haddenham and taken to a psychiatric hospital. Unable to identify himself, he was kept there for several days before being released.

For a plea of diminished responsibility to succeed, the defence would have to show that he was not just under strain (as was claimed at his trial) but actually suffering from a severe mental condition at the time. In fact, the jury were guided by the trial judge to consider the duress that he was under as a repeated victim of burglary, but evidently this did not weigh heavily on their decision making.

Diminished responsibility is obviously not a complete defence, because if it was accepted the charge would be reduced to manslaughter. But it would leave Martin, who by this time had served 10 months of his sentence, with the possibility of being released within a year.

With this new plea in mind, psychiatrists set to work at

Gartree Prison to determine whether he was suffering from a long-term illness. He reportedly found the interviews disturbing and asked that they submit further questions to him in writing.

Other strategies were also under consideration. James Saunders said: "We intend to show that the jury were not given a full and accurate picture of the evidence, and it is our case that if they had known the truth he would have been acquitted. The Appeal Court may send the case back to the Crown Court for retrial in these circumstances."

New evidence under discussion included a defence ballistics expert's report that contradicted police testimony. The report held that Martin fired the lethal shot from the stairs, not from the lounge, and that evidence of spent shotgun powder was found on the wall of the stairway. Martin, it will be remembered, pleaded all along that he shot only from the stairs. He pleaded too, that continuous attacks on his farm had left him feeling vulnerable and stressed. Both these views were turned aside by the prosecution. An observer at this stage could be forgiven for pointing out that the new defence team was uncovering matters that must have been already known, matters which were casting Tony Martin in an entirely different light. Once again the spectre of a prosecution case that was deeply flawed began to present itself.

By early May, 2001, the new legal team had secured an Appeal Court hearing date. The case would be held before Lord Chief Justice Woolf and was expected to last for three days, beginning on Monday, July 16. Another date that was not publicised was July 2 – the date when Martin would apply to the court for bail ahead of the appeal hearing.

In the event, neither of these two things happened. There was no appeal hearing in July, and no application for bail earlier that month.

Instead, out of range of press or public, lawyers had agreed on new dates. Those representing the prosecution made it clear to those representing the defence that they

intended to fight the Martin appeal with the same vigour
with which they had fought the case and won in April,
2000. To achieve this end, they needed more time for
preparations and they also required a ten-day hearing. Ten-
day slots in the legal calendar are not easily obtainable with
only three months notice, so two alternate dates were pen-
cilled in for the autumn. The defence case now focused on
submissions for a re-trial which, if granted, would need to
be performed expediently. This could not have been of
much cheer to Martin who, like Hamlet 400 years earlier,
had had his fill of "the law's delay."

For the moment, then, there can be no satisfactory ending to Tony Martin and the Bleak House Tragedy, because
the ending has not yet been written. We are left to hope
that when this tattered remnant of British justice is finally
sewn up, the sum of all its parts will bear better scrutiny
than the parts reported in this book.